AFRICAN THEOLOGY

AFRICAN THEOLOGY

Inculturation and Liberation

Emmanuel Martey

ORBIS BOOKS

Maryknoll, New York 10545

Third Printing, September 1995

Library of Congress Cataloging-in-Publication Data

Martey, Emmanuel.
    African theology : inculturation and liberation / Emmanuel Martey.
      p. cm.
    Revision of author's thesis (doctoral).
    Includes bibliographical references.
    ISBN 0-88344-861-0 (pbk.)
    1. Black theology. 2. Liberation theology—South Africa.
  3. Theology, Doctrinal—Africa, Sub-Saharan. I. Title.
    230'.0967—dc20—   93-16262
                                                 CIP

In Memory of My Dear Mother
Okaikai Okai
(Alias Naaba Kai)

For My Dear Father
Nii Martey Krobo

Contents

Acronyms

AACC	All Africa Conference of Churches
ABRECSA	Alliance of Black Reformed Christians in Southern Africa
ACP	Africa, the Caribbean and the Pacific
AICA	African Independent Churches Association
AICs	African Independent Churches
ANC	African National Congress
ATR	African Traditional Religion
AZAPO	Azanian People's Organization
AZASO	Azanian Students' Organization
BCM	Black Consciousness Movement
BCP	Black Community Program
BPC	Black People's Convention
BTP	Black Theology Project
CEAO	Communauté Économique de l'Afrique Occidentale
CEEAC	Economic Community of Central African States
CODESA	Convention for a Democratic South Africa
COSAS	Congress of South African Students
COSATU	Congress of South African Trade Unions
EAAT	Ecumenical Association of African Theologians
EAC	East African Community
EATWOT	Ecumenical Association of Third World Theologians
ECOWAS	Economic Community of West African States
EEC	European Economic Community
ERP	Economic Recovery Program
ICT	Institute for Contextual Theology
IDAMASA	Interdenominational African Ministers Association of South Africa
IMF	International Monetary Fund
LPA	Lagos Plan of Action
NCBC	National Committee of Black Churchmen (USA)
NF	National Forum
NUSAS	National Union of South African Students
OAU	Organization of African Unity
PAC	Pan African Congress
PTA	Preferential Trade Authority
SACC	South African Council of Churches

SACP	South African Communist Party
SADCC	Southern Africa Development Coordination Conference
SAP	Structural Adjustment Program
SASO	South African Students' Organization
SECAM	Symposium of Episcopal Conferences of Africa and Madagascar
SSBR	Society for the Study of Black Religion (USA)
UCM	University Christian Movement
UDF	United Democratic Front
WARC	World Alliance of Reformed Churches
WCC	World Council of Churches
WOSA	Workers Organization for Socialist Action
ZANU	Zimbabwe African National Union

Preface

The African search for authentic and prophetic theology has at once been a *rejection* of the dominant Western theological paradigms and an *acceptance* of African realities and worldview in theological hermeneutics. Consequently in Black Africa, African theology and South African Black theology have come to represent two different schools of theological hermeneutics. They are therefore not synonymous. Expressed respectively in terms of "inculturation" (or "Africanization" or "indigenization") and "liberation," there has thus been a tension or polarity between these two theological traditions since the early 1970s.

The main emphasis of this study is that such a tension is not necessary, since in the African theological reality, the two foci are not contradictory but complement each other. In fact, they represent two sides of the same process. Consequently, theological hermeneutics in Africa must necessarily have a unitary perception of inculturation and liberation. The African theologian in neocolonial Africa, like the black theologian in racist South Africa, must grapple with sociopolitical and economic as well as with religiocultural issues. The need for such an integral vision is called for not only by the fact that the gospel of Jesus Christ is a gospel of political and cultural liberation, but also that the African theological reality itself calls for cultural and political emancipation.

My interest in theological unity in Africa has been motivated by two factors: my understanding of contemporary theology and my perception of the continent of Africa.

Doubtlessly whatever definition would be given to contemporary theology, among the communities of the oppressed, it has become part and parcel of the liberation struggle of the poor people of God for full humanity or for the meaningfully abundant life which Jesus the Christ talked about (John 10:10).

Furthermore, although the continent of Africa is made up of heterogeneous elements and there are observable differences between the histories of neocolonial Africa and South Africa, nevertheless there is more that brings all black Africans together than there is that separates them.

This study was originally a dissertation which has been updated with a few changes and revisions for publication. Since the 1960s the political landscape of the African continent has continued to change. This is even more so with southern Africa in the 1990s. Certainly the end of apartheid

xi

and the movement toward nonracial democracy and majority rule evidence that South Africa is not separated from the rest of the continent. No doubt, these changes also have theological consequences. While these changes justify the main thesis of this work and provide much support for the conclusions I have drawn, they also render certain expressions ambiguous. For instance, more than anyone else, I am aware of the ambiguities and inadequacies which have been left without satisfactory explanation. For example, such expressions as "independent Africa," used here to denote Black Africa outside South Africa, becomes equivocal with majority rule in South Africa. Furthermore, such terms as "African theologian," used to characterize theologians outside South Africa, and "black theologian," used for those in South Africa, are ambiguous since "black theologians" are *Africans* and "African theologians" are also *black*. However, these expressions and others like them have been used for the sake of convenience. It is hoped that the comprehensive bibliography at the end of this book may also assist the reader to search for answers to some of the questions raised but to which adequate answers may not have been provided.

This study on the unitary vision of the African theological reality would not have come to fruition without the guidance of and encouragement from Professor James H. Cone, my academic advisor and chairman of my dissertation committee, whose inestimable suggestions, invaluable support and creative insights have been a delight and an inspiration. Dr. Cone's inspiring influence also came through his former students, especially Gwinyai Muzorewa, Josiah Young, Dennis Wiley, Alonzo Johnson, Kelly Brown, George Cummings, Dwight Hopkins, Chung Hyun Kyung and Augustine Musopole.

Professors Kosuke Koyama and Christopher Morse were on my dissertation committee, and they offered invaluable theological insights. Dr. Bonganjalo Goba, who also sat on my dissertation committee, not only offered invaluable theological insights but also gave very strong support to my work. Theological discussions with Dr. Goba — at his office at 475 Riverside Drive in New York City, where he served as the Regional Secretary for Africa of the United Church Board for World Ministries, United Church of Christ — were tremendously encouraging.

I am greatly indebted to Susan Perry, who took time to read through the manuscript, offering invaluable suggestions and calling my attention to useful sources.

Finally, my gratitude goes to my wonderful family — my dear wife, Nana Ofosua and our two sons, Emmanuel (Nii) and Christus (Fiifi) — for their unwavering support and patience.

EMMANUEL MARTEY

AFRICAN THEOLOGY

Introduction

The characteristic features of both African theology and South African Black theology and how each relates to the other evidently demonstrate how *doing theology in Africa* can be an onerously complex task to undertake.

A student of theology in Africa realizes that although African theology and South African Black theology have both come out of the womb of Africa, they are not identical. Another factor which adds to the complexity is the underlying fact that even though the two theological traditions are different in terms of their histories, emphases and functions, nonetheless, their methodologies can be seen as alternatives among black theologians in South Africa and among African theologians in independent Africa.

Furthermore, the way Africa itself is fragmented by ethnicity and by European colonization exacerbates this intricacy. For instance, the colonial legacy has divided sub-Saharan Africa into at least six fragments: anglophone Africa, francophone Africa, Portuguese Africa, Belgian Africa, Spanish Africa and apartheid South Africa. Of these, anglophone and francophone Africa and South Africa form the three major zones where theological activity has been the most intense.

Each of these three major "theological zones" has had its own distinctive cultural-political movement which has influenced religious thought and has been the source of theological motivation.

Therefore, while in independent Africa the *Negritude movement* in francophone Africa and *African personality* in anglophone Africa contributed significantly to the emergence of African theology of indigenization (or inculturation),[1] in apartheid South Africa, the *Black consciousness movement* contributed immensely to the emergence of Black theology of liberation.

Even though the content of these cultural-political movements has been the same — namely, the struggle of the black African for emancipation from the forces of domination, oppression and social injustice — the differences in the political and socioeconomic structures, as well as the ideological and cultural diversity between neocolonial Africa and South Africa, have apparently created a theological-hermeneutical tension between theologians on both sizes of the Zambezi River, the natural division between South Africa and the rest of sub-Saharan Africa.

Consequently, in their efforts to wrestle with Africa's plethora of problems, African and South African Black theologies have each employed a

1

distinctive theological hermeneutic which it felt would be the most effective weapon to fight against hypocrisy, heresy and forces of death.

Thus, while African theologians pinpointed the religiocultural sphere as the main domain of Africa's dehumanization and exploitation and therefore employ inculturation hermeneutics and see African culture and religion as the dominant sources for the theological enterprise, black theologians also see the sociopolitical and economic structures as the major determining factor for oppression and domination and therefore in their theological struggle emphasize liberation hermeneutics, which will bring about radical transformation of evil and oppressive structures.

So, instead of envisioning both religiocultural and politico-socioeconomic factors as mutually interpenetrating elements which must shape African societal life and experience, both African and black theologians have used much energy fighting a battle over a false dilemma—a battle which, doubtlessly, has obstructed rather than facilitated more effective development in theological and transformative praxis.

Indisputably, the dialogical encounter between African theology and South African Black theology especially, within the contexts of the Ecumenical Association of Third World Theologians (EATWOT) and the Ecumenical Association of African Theologians (EAAT), as well as within the All Africa Conference of Churches (AACC)—although indirect—has contributed tremendously in reducing the tension and polarity between the two theological systems. However, recent publications of some theologians from both sides of the Zambezi, such as Jean-Marc Ela[2] and Gabriel Setiloane,[3] evidence that this polarity is not completely over.

The purpose of this study, then, is threefold. First, it seeks to examine critically the tension between "inculturation" and "liberation" as given expression in African theology and South African Black theology respectively.

Secondly, it is to delineate the reasons for the differences between the two theological traditions and to bring to theological consciousness observable weaknesses or pitfalls which have so far made it seem difficult, if not impossible, to reach for a dynamic definition of inclusive theology in Africa.

Finally, since my analytical investigation has demonstrated that, in the African theological reality, the two foci—inculturation and liberation—are not contradictory but complement each other, I have here emphasized that black African theological hermeneutics must necessarily have a unitary perception of inculturation and liberation.

Although there is now a substantial body of writings on both African and South African Black theologies, the student interested in these traditions realizes that much effort has not been made toward an integral synthesis. Even though a few black African theologians endeavor in their writings to emphasize such a need, there has not been a major study undertaken on the synthesis of inculturation and liberation in Africa.

Therefore, theological study of the connection between religiocultural and sociopolitical and economic realities of the African continent is still in its infancy. The present position is a frustrating one, since it has been demonstrated in this study that not only does the gospel of Jesus Christ contain nuances of both political and cultural theological liberation, but also the African theological reality itself calls for an integral vision of cultural and political liberation.

Of the works which have emphasized both political and cultural liberation in Black/African theology, some deserve to be mentioned. Although Gwinyai Muzorewa's *The Origins and Development of African Theology* (1985)[4] is not a comparative study but—as the title implies—traces the origins and development of the major theological trends in Africa, by challenging African theology not to ignore "the African political world" but "articulate the concepts of freedom, human equality and liberation" (55) and Black theology to "call for political as well as cultural liberation . . ." (113), the author has carried into the efforts at synthesis perspectives which concern both African and Black theologies. This position is further strengthened in his later book, *An African Theology of Mission* (1991).[5]

With his *Black and African Theologies: Siblings or Distant Cousins?* (1986),[6] Josiah Young not only initiates a very significant conversation for people of African descent on both sides of the Atlantic concerned about what it means to be black and Christian in a world dominated by whites, but also, in his emphasis that even among black African theologians the themes of liberation and indigenization converge, he has brought much to the task of synthesis (cf. 106ff.).

Bonganjalo Goba's *An Agenda for Black Theology: Hermeneutics for Social Change* (1988)[7] also deserves to be mentioned. Even though the author's main interest is to challenge "the black Christian community to evolve a biblical hermeneutic arising out of our historical consciousness under the oppressive structures of Apartheid" (8), he made an essential contribution toward integral synthesis when he emphasized not just politics, but also the role culture plays, both as the context within which the Christian faith manifests itself and as the medium for theological reflection.

The significance of Dwight Hopkins's *Black Theology USA and South Africa: Politics, Culture and Liberation* (1989)[8] for our present study is its identification of both the political theological trend and the cultural theological approach in black theological reflection in South Africa. This emphasis on the existence of the two theological directions in South African Black theology—and also in African theology, as Josiah Young has observed—shows the dialectic of the African theological paradigm.

In this study, my main focus is on theological reflection in "Black Africa" or sub-Saharan Africa and therefore does not include North Africa or Africa north of the Sahara. Even within the area south of the Sahara, I will concentrate primarily on the three main theological zones: francophone Africa, anglophone Africa and apartheid South Africa.

Although it is appropriate to describe any theology emerging from sub-

Saharan Africa as "African theology," or "Black theology," for that matter, strictly speaking, the two theological systems under our investigation are "Black African" theologies, since they do not include contemporary Coptic and Ethiopian Orthodox theologies or theologies of North African theological giants of the patristic period.

My analysis of Black/African theology therefore places some restrictions on this study. To a certain extent, this omission is regrettable because, for example, a study of the theology of the Coptic church in Egypt that emerged as Egyptian nationalism against Byzantine imperialist domination would provide a remarkable opportunity for black African theological struggle.[9]

Most quotations from theological and other writers in this study have been altered from sexist exclusive language to nonsexist inclusive language. However, in certain cases and within certain contexts they are not altered, because I do not want to conceal the biases especially of African male theologians.

In this study, I have emphasized what I called the dialectics of the African theological paradigm. Inasmuch as African and Black theologies have been operating from within different horizons, evidences of a running tension between the two traditions will persist. Veritably, dialectically opposed horizons can generate opposed theologies and methods to justify, defend and legitimize those different horizons.

Essentially, a dialectic deals with oppositions or conflicts—conflicts that may arise as a result of contrary histories, contrary interpretations or contrary assessments and therefore contrary methods and contrary theologies. The task of a dialectic is to uncover these conflicts and point to a direction that will objectify the subjective differences of the two contending hermeneutics in order to promote new theological insights.

Such an enterprise, I believe, will foster a new movement toward a synthetic interpretation in which each hermeneutic overcomes its own conflicts so as to be able to ascertain the ambivalence at work in the other and the manner in which to resolve the conflict.

Since all theologies come out of a particular sociohistorical context, it is necessary to provide the historical backgrounds of both African and Black theologies if the tension between inculturation and liberation is to be understood. Accordingly, chapter 1 provides the different historical backdrops of the two theological traditions. These differences are granted within the frame of the struggles which Africans in both independent and South Africa have carried out against foreign domination at the political and cultural levels.

But do differences in historical backgrounds necessarily mean differences in the African theological reality? Wrestling with this crucial question, chapter 2 attempts a working definition of the African reality. It identifies two inseparable dimensions and discovers that the pluralistic character of the African reality has made it difficult for both African and black theologians to agree on a theological interpretation that truly defines or reflects African reality. Chapter 2 therefore argues that these pluralistic traits of the African reality do not warrant an exclusively one-dimensional analysis. It also stresses an overriding common denominator of African theological reality which brings the whole continent together. The implication this has for African theological hermeneutics is also discussed.

Chapters 3 and 4 examine African theology and Black theology respectively and each in relation to the other, so as to review the theological tension between inculturation and liberation. This is done by selecting two theological categories as case studies for each chapter. In each of these case studies, I seek to demonstrate that the inculturation-liberation difference cannot be defined simply between African and black theologians; it is also among African theologians and among black theologians in South Africa.

Chapter 5 therefore discusses the dialectic character of the theological enterprise as seen in African and Black theology—a dialectic that is best represented in Jesus Christ, who is confessed as both human and divine. Having posed a critical assessment of the two theological systems, the chapter attempts a synthetic interpretation and emphasizes a unitary perception of the two foci. Instead of the one-dimensional analysis, the chapter therefore advocates a multidimensional analysis of African society to embrace race, gender, class and culture. In conclusion, the implications which this theological analysis has for the future of theology in Africa are discussed.

It is my hope that this study will make some contribution to the theological enterprise, especially to the inculturation-liberation debate and the ongoing search for a synthetic interpretation. As members of EATWOT, most African and black theologians are aware of the association's acknowledgment of the need for a synthesis. EATWOT has already identified the two main categories—the religiocultural and the socioeconomic and political—as vital for integral liberation.

As a study on synthetic interpretation, this work also seeks to address the need for a more holistic understanding of the African theological reality as well as the struggle for liberation in the various aspects of African existence.

Furthermore, this study has discovered the common theological agenda for both inculturation and liberation hermeneutics and therefore has been able to pinpoint where both African theology and South African Black theology find a common ground. It is therefore hoped that this will not only activate a *direct* dialogue between African and South African Black theologies but will also initiate a solidarity movement toward a liberative theological praxis on the continent.

NOTES

1. In this study, the terms *Africanization, indigenization* and *inculturation* will invariably be used interchangeably to refer to African theological hermeneutics,

which lays much emphasis on African culture and worldview as vital for theologizing.

2. See Jean-Marc Ela, *African Cry* (Maryknoll, N.Y.: Orbis Books, 1986); cf. his *My Faith as an African* (Maryknoll, N.Y.: Orbis Books, 1988).

3. Gabriel Setiloane, *African Theology: An Introduction* (Johannesburg: Skotaville Publishers, 1986). More on this issue is discussed in chapters 3 and 4.

4. Gwinyai H. Muzorewa, *The Origins and Development of African Theology* (Maryknoll, N.Y.: Orbis Books, 1985).

5. Gwinyai Muzorewa, *An African Theology of Mission* (Lewiston, N.Y.: Edwin Mellen Press, 1991).

6. Josiah U. Young, *Black and African Theologies: Siblings or Distant Cousins?* (Maryknoll, N.Y.: Orbis Books, 1986).

7. Bonganjalo Goba, *An Agenda for Black Theology: Hermeneutics for Social Change* (Johannesburg: Skotaville Publishers, 1988).

8. Dwight N. Hopkins, *Black Theology USA and South Africa: Politics, Culture and Liberation* (Maryknoll, N.Y.: Orbis Books, 1989).

9. Cf. Deane William Ferm, ed., *Third World Liberation Theologies: An Introductory Survey* (Maryknoll, N.Y.: Orbis Books, 1986), p. 59.

1 | Historical Background of African and Black Theologies

In one sense the spiritual dynamic of the African Revolution arises out of the impact of the Gospel and Christian education, and the Church has the duty to give a sense of direction to the human aspirations it has helped to awaken. This revolution is primarily concerned with [humanity] and [human] dignity in society. Since the Church is primarily concerned with [the human being] in his [or her] relations to God and neighbor it cannot be indifferent to the African search for a fuller human life in new societies.
—All Africa Conference of Churches[1]

But beneath the surface there is a spirit of defiance. The people of South Africa have never been a docile lot, least of all the African people. We have a long tradition of struggle for our national rights, reaching back to the very beginnings of white settlement and conquest 300 years ago. Our history is one of opposition to domination, of protest and refusal to submit to tyranny.
—Chief Albert Luthuli[2]

THE IMPACT OF THE AFRICAN REVOLUTION ON AFRICAN THEOLOGY

For those coming from the underside of history, theology has always been a *struggle*, a struggle against all enslaving and dehumanizing forces. In Africa, it has been part and parcel of the revolutionary struggle to be fully human in a world that denigrates black humanity. The impact of the African revolution on the emergence and development of contextual theology in Africa has been tremendous as it impressed upon the African church and its leaders the need to respond and relate their gospel faith "to the African search for a fuller human life in new societies."

The roots of this revolution, which began in the political arena, could be traced to the end of the nineteenth century and, especially, the first decade of the twentieth, when a more organized black resistance to colonial oppression and racism started with the rise of pan-Africanism and gained

7

more momentum with African nationalism after World War II. The African revolution has undergone many phases and has had important interim goals. But its ultimate objective has always been to bring total liberation to the African in all areas of human existence—political, social, economic, cultural and religious. Differently put, it is to bring full humanity to the African. This was how the African church understood and interpreted it. For instance, at its 1965 Enugu Consultation, the All Africa Conference of Churches (AACC) defined the African revolution as "a movement of liberation of African peoples from colonial domination and from the enslaving aspects of traditional societies."[3]

From the writings of both Africans and blacks of the diaspora, African Christians have learned how colonialism drained African societies of their very essence, trampled African culture underfoot, undermined African institutions, confiscated its lands, smashed its religions, destroyed its magnificent artistic creations and wiped out extraordinary possibilities.[4] Furthermore, these same Africans have become aware of the irrelevancy of North Atlantic theology to the African situation; for example, they have read European theologians and know how some of them opposed the violence of the two world wars. But none of these theologians, not even Karl Barth, despite his stance against the naked aggression and violence of Nazi Germany, addressed the issue of colonial violence and military oppression against African people.

Therefore, as "a movement of liberation" struggling against oppressive and exploitative forces from both outside and within the African continent, the African revolution placed a "theological compulsion" upon African Christians and especially the church, which, in the eyes of the mission-trained nationalists, was an instrument of imperialist oppression. In response, African Christians and church leaders began a thoughtful survey of this "movement of liberation" that was throbbing throughout the life of the continent and, in the process, brought the African revolution under the focus of Christian thought and theological interpretation.

It soon became clear, however, that this theme of liberation, which became the language of the African church in the mid-1960s, was not to be found in the theological lexicon of the early African theologians who began writing in the late sixties. Rather, their response to the revolutionary struggle gave rise to a theological current called "African theology," which focused narrowly on the cultural-religious dimension of the African revolution but refused an engagement in dialogue with the critical issues raised by political and economic factors of the continent. Whenever one recalls today that the revolution, which in fact radicalized African church leaders, began as a *political movement of liberation*, one wonders why the theological perspectives that emerged did not develop with a similar focus—taking liberation seriously.[5]

However, one only begins to understand if one comes to know that the very concept of adapting the gospel message to suit the African situation had come from Western missionaries whose interests "the seed of perpetual Western superiority and domination" would continue to protect.[6] Certainly, evidence such as this provides much support for the South African black theological critique that "When the Africans seem to be encouraged to produce indigenous theology, they are just being used — as they have always been — to solve the psychological problems of the missionaries."[7]

There is, of course, a sense in which one can say that the critics — both whites and blacks — who found the espousal of sociopolitical liberation within Christian theology so abominable were, in fact, the beneficiaries who represent the ideological interests of the oppressive status quo.

Historically, there have been three areas of resistance in the revolution against foreign domination: political, cultural and religious. It is these factors, in my opinion, that have contributed to the emergence of African theology. However, I will focus on the first two, since culture and politics were the key factors that gave rise to tension between African theology and Black theology.

THE POLITICS OF EMANCIPATION

Politically, the objectives and philosophy of the African revolution are defined by the three closely related components of the African liberation movement, namely, pan-Africanism, nationalism and socialism. According to Kwame Nkrumah, the first president of Ghana, these political components are so interrelated that "one cannot be achieved fully without the other," and no authentic liberation can be gained by any territory if one of these is missing.[8] While pan-Africanism and African nationalism provided the framework within which African theology was to emerge,[9] some African Christians also found within socialist principles a means of expressing revolutionary sociopolitical and economic aspirations that could create new modes of interaction and form a model for the future. All three components, pan-Africanism, African nationalism and socialism, evidence suggests, have a single underlying purpose: the liberation of the black race. But since African theology, unlike Black theology, especially in its second phase, which began in the early 1980s, has not taken socialism (including Marxism) seriously in its methodology, I reluctantly omit the socialist aspect of the struggle and concentrate on the two components — pan-Africanism and African nationalism — that have played a key role in developing African theology.[10]

PAN-AFRICANISM

Pan-Africanism is a system of ideas and, as such, it does not lend itself to a simple definition. What makes the task of definition even more onerous is the fact that these ideas have not come from an individual person or a single group at one particular moment in history, but rather are an assembly of related ideas expressed over the years by people of African descent from both the continent and the diaspora who were addressing the African question.

These ideas expressed their worldview, their goals and prescribed (sometimes contending) strategies for the achievement of these goals. For instance, the view of pan-Africanism advanced by blacks of the diaspora such as W. E. B. DuBois, Marcus Garvey, George Padmore and others differed from that espoused by later African nationalists, which gave birth to the Organization of African Unity (OAU).[11] Even among Africans themselves there are observable differences.[12] For example, Kwame Nkrumah's view of pan-Africanism differed from Julius Nyerere's, and both from Nnamdi Azikiwe's.[13] However, for all the seeming differences and contending strategies, the fundamental objective of the Pan-African movement has always been the oneness of all people of African descent and the commitment to black liberation.

This significant objective has not only provided the relevant context within which African theology has emerged; more importantly, it offers enormous opportunities for more creative theological work in the future among blacks on both sides of the Atlantic. It is encouraging indeed that black theologians have already begun talking seriously about "Pan-African Theology."[14]

The pan-African spirit may be traced to the last decades of the nineteenth century and is seen in the liberating ideas and political philosophy of Edward Wilmot Blyden, whose "Pan-Negro" ideology has been described as "the most important progenitor of Pan-Africanism."[15] It is this same spirit of black solidarity that led to the 1900 Pan-African Conference in London, which declared with W. E. B. DuBois at this gathering that "the problem of the twentieth century is the problem of the color line."[16] The full dimension of pan-Africanism seemed to have been reached when DuBois began his series of pan-African congresses from 1919 to 1945.[17]

A careful study of these conferences provides a view of the intellectual world of the Pan-African movement. The programmatic activities of the various pan-African organizations reveal a collective consciousness of certain particular goals and prescribed strategies for achieving such goals. From these congresses, three main concerns emerge, from which we can agree on the meaning of pan-Africanism. These include: *unification* of all black people, commitment to the *empowerment* of black people and the *liberation* of all black people.[18] From this threefold goal, pan-Africanism can be described as a body of ideas behind the Pan-African movement which aims at bringing all people of African descent together to empower them to be instruments of their own liberation. To achieve this goal, pan-Africanism, especially the transatlantic version, has developed different strategies—from that of protest and the assimilation view of integration to that of the Garveyist "Back to Africa" movement.

Since Nkrumah planted pan-Africanism in Africa after the fifth congress, it has manifested itself in two distinct forms, especially after the formation of the OAU in 1963. Now, at the trans-Saharan level, distinction has been made between pan-Africanism as a *movement of liberation* and pan-Africanism as a *movement of integration*. As a liberation movement, pan-Africanism concerned itself with the struggle for decolonization of all African countries and for the isolation of white minority regimes in Southern Africa. The integration movement concerned itself more with greater political and economic integration beginning at the regional level, as evidenced in the formation of the Economic Community of West African States (ECOWAS) and the defunct East African Community (EAC). The liberation movement has had much more success than the integration movement, as the record shows on Zimbabwe, Guinea-Bissau, Angola, Mozambique and Namibia. Now all eyes are on South Africa, as persistent resistance has forced the nationalist government to "close the book on apartheid" and move toward a nonracial democracy.

Today, while trans-Saharan pan-Africanism finds institutionalization in the OAU, the older transatlantic version still continues at a more cultural level. These ideas of black unity without an institutional framework could be seen in the Sixth Pan-African Congress held in 1974 in Dar-es-Salaam. It is obvious that the purpose of pan-Africanism — to give all people of African descent a sense of identity, self-determination and emancipation — has provided the relevant context for African theologians "to formulate theological constructs on Africanization" and liberation.[19] As a movement which not only reaffirms African identity and sovereignty but also takes a definite stand against colonialism, racism and neocolonialism, pan-Africanism, despite all its limitations, can be an effective instrument of African liberation and thus offers great opportunity for authentic theological enterprise.

AFRICAN NATIONALISM

Of the three political components of the African liberation movement, African nationalism has had the greatest impact on the African church. The movement constrained Christians to translate reality into dialogue with the God of their faith and thus to confront the issues in terms of their theology. It is not surprising therefore that at its inaugural assembly in Kampala in 1963, AACC included in the topics discussed what it called the "Theology of Nationalism."[20]

African nationalism emerged when the contradictions between Western-claimed democratic values and colonial autocratic oppression became apparent to Africans. Although a Western philosophy, it became an effective weapon in the hands of Africans in their struggle against imperialism. Nationalism then became "the chosen philosophy of the colonial independence movement."[21]

Strictly speaking, it was the Pan-African movement, especially its fifth congress in Manchester, which "provided the outlet for African nationalism and brought about the awakening of African political consciousness."[22] However, like the ideology of pan-Africanism itself, the spirit of African nationalism can also be traced back to the nineteenth century, particularly to Edward W. Blyden, whose views on colonialism expressed "both racial and nationalistic positions aimed at achieving a particular type of social revolution."[23] Blyden considered the European as an intruder whose colonial activities in Africa were as dehumanizing and degrading as the slave trade. He then echoed the truth of the situation: "The eighteenth century stole the black man from his country; the nineteenth century steals his country from the black man."[24] Blyden's political and cultural ideas greatly influenced the nineteenth-century African church and its leaders.

The challenge that came from nineteenth-century pioneers and, especially, post-World War II nationalists to Christianity and the African church was remarkably significant, for the religious nationalism of African church leaders was to give rise to a new theological thinking and awareness in which black Africans sought to interpret their Christian faith into African categories.

The reaction of the African church to the changes brought by African nationalism "has been one of gratitude and appreciation," as it saw the preaching of the gospel as "one of the most dynamic 'prime movers' of social change in Africa."[25] Perceiving the nationalist attitude as both a fruit of and a reaction against Western colonialism, the church called on the West to "recognize that as a result of its rule African people have been brought . . . to the point where they are critically assessing what colonialism has done to them."[26]

The church then made a sharp distinction between African nationalism and Western nationalism, and entreated the West to refrain from prejudging the African connotation of nationalism, which differed from its occidental manifestation. In the latter, nationalism had meant divisiveness and colonialism. On the other hand, the dominant motif of African nationalism, explained the African church, had a twofold thrust: toward *liberation* from European colonial domination and toward *consolidation* of national unity. The church declared: "The two dominant motifs of African nationalism — liberation and consolidation — are the exact opposite of those of Western nationalism — colonialism and divisiveness."[27] However, this "liberation motif," it must be reiterated, was absent in the theological interpretation of early African theologians. Even though the church recognized the limitations of African nationalism, it nevertheless underscored the fact that it "is at the moment an indispensable source of spiritual dynamics for the African people" and implored Western Christians "to help the Western nations to reorientate their relationships to African peoples and nations."[28]

African nationalism also preoccupied the 1963 inaugural assembly of the AACC. In its statement on "The Church and Nationalism," the assembly did not merely see nationalism as "opposition to foreign domination" but, more importantly, as "the common desire of a people to work together for their emancipation from any form of bondage, whether colonial, economic, social or racial."[29]

THE "ACT OF CULTURE"

The African, wrote Edward Blyden in the nineteenth century, "will not fade away or become extinct before the Europeans as the American and Australian aborigines."[30] And in the twentieth century, Amilcar Cabral wrote: "One of the most serious mistakes, if not the most serious mistake, made by the colonial powers in Africa, may have been to ignore or underestimate the cultural strength of African people."[31]

Indeed, gone are the days when it was imperative for African Christians and theologians not only to defend the religiosity of African people, but also to prove their cultural maturity. Today, the irrationality of a racist theory of a Lévy-Bruhl interests no one but the racist. Evidence shows how strongly Africans resisted the attempts of both the colonial administrator and the missionary to dehumanize and obliterate their cultural identity. Black African writers and poets have expressed the cultural nationalism of black people in their works. The First Congress of Black Writers and Artists, held in Paris in 1956, was described as the "most important cultural event in the history of the Pan-African movement."[32] This was followed by a second congress in Rome three years later. The first congress, with its theme "The Crisis of Black Culture," struggled against three evils that it called the "shameful practices of this twentieth century," namely, "colonialism; the oppression of the weaker peoples; and racialism."[33] This cultural assembly then called on theologians and other professionals to "participate in the historic task of unearthing, rehabilitating and developing [black] cultures so as to facilitate their being integrated into the general body of world culture." They were also urged "to struggle to create the practical conditions for the revival of and the growth of Negro cultures."[34]

Cultural resistance has always been an integral and determining part of Africa's struggle for liberation. Perhaps the postindependence African theorist who more than anyone else stressed culture as a factor of resistance to foreign domination is Amilcar Cabral. For Cabral, the domination of a people "can be maintained only by the permanent and organized repression of the cultural life of the people concerned." He then explained: "In fact, to take up arms to dominate a people is, above all, to take up arms to destroy . . . their cultural life. For as long as part of that people can have cultural life, foreign domination cannot be sure of its perpetuation."[35]

Cabral saw the foundation of a people's liberation lying in their inalienable rights to have their own history whose continuity lies in culture. The aim of national liberation, according to Cabral, is to regain this right that had been usurped by imperialist domination. He stressed liberation as an act of culture: "If imperialist domination has the vital need to practise cultural oppression," argues Cabral, then, "national liberation is necessarily an *act of culture*." He thus sees the liberation movement as "the organized political expression of the struggling people's culture."[36]

With this discussion on the role of culture in the liberation movement, Cabral made a significant contribution to the development of political thought as well as to theological hermeneutics: Political liberation cannot be achieved apart from cultural liberation and vice versa. With this stress on the reciprocity of political and cultural liberation, Cabral has indeed left much to posterity. For those searching for a theology of political and cultural liberation, his praxis serves as an invaluable source. From Cabral's analysis, it becomes clear that "culture, which in the hands of academics tends to become the monopoly of an elite, or becomes the object of dispassionate academic analysis, is now put in the service of liberation."[37] So, like Frantz Fanon, Cabral has taught us that during the struggle of God's people for liberation, "Culture is not put into cold storage."[38]

This concept of culture as an effective weapon in the liberation struggle, or the notion of liberation as "an act of culture," is becoming prominent in the new wave of African theology and among young African theologians. For example, in their report of EATWOT VII meeting at Oaxtepec, African theologians declare:

> A careful analysis of contemporary African history and society shows that culture has been and still remains the only efficient weapon for the liberation struggle in Africa. The true African Revolution has been cultural. It is African culture which has saved the black American identity. It is also this same culture which has radically called the whole colonial system into question.[39]

But Africa's cultural struggle against Western cultural imperialism, to which Cabral and other contemporary writers refer, also has its historical roots in the nineteenth and early twentieth centuries. Of particular interest are the most prominent reactions against European cultural domination as expressed in the two cultural-political concepts—negritude and African personality. I will discuss and assess the impact which these cultural movements have had on African Christian thought and action.

THE IMPACT OF NEGRITUDE AND AFRICAN PERSONALITY

Africa's struggle against Western cultural imperialism was first given conceptual formulation by Edward W. Blyden, when he articulated the nineteenth-century theory of *blackness*. In his efforts to combat racist mythologies, Blyden "focused on 'the virtues of black civilization' and promoted the concepts of 'blackness' and 'Negro Personality,' thus inventing positive new myths about race and the black personality."[40] This concept of blackness was to be followed later by twentieth-century African ideologues such as Léopold Senghor and others. Senghor himself has celebrated Blyden as the "foremost precursor both of Negritude and African Personality."[41]

In his teachings, Blyden urged "black authenticity" and found the basis for inspiration in African traditional life. He wrote,

> Now if we are to make an independent nation – a strong nation – we must listen to the songs of our unsophisticated brethren as they sing in their history, as they tell of their tradition, of the wonderful and mysterious events of their tribal or national life, of the achievement of what we call their superstitions.[42]

Blyden also saw African Personality as "the sum of values of African civilization, the body of qualities which make up the distinctiveness of the people of Africa."[43] These two concepts – African (black) personality and blackness (Negritude) – were later to be "instrumental in sustaining the struggle for African independence by opposing colonization as a process of falsification and depersonalization of Africans and by criticizing imperialism as a means of exploitation."[44]

Among African nationalists, the Negritude movement became "a cultural phenomenon with a political facet."[45] Therefore, like African Personality among English-speaking Africans, Negritude as a cultural-political concept among French-speaking Africans was a revolt against Western imperialism, particularly against French policy toward African cultures. "The French forced us to seek the essence of Negritude," writes Senghor, "when they enforced their policy of assimilation and thus deepened our despair."[46] Repudiating certain intrinsic values of Westernism, Negritude aimed at extolling African values by arousing the consciousness and pride in the cultural and physical aspects of the black heritage. In anglophone Africa, African Personality also became a driving force behind the African revolution, and was aimed at reviving "the cultural and spiritual unity of the African people, and to promote research into every aspect of [African] heritage."[47] According to Nkrumah, the spirit of a people can only flourish in freedom, and he underscores the fact that African Personality can find full expression and be meaningfully projected in the world society only when "the liberation and unification of Africa is completed."[48]

The challenge that these cultural movements posed from the 1930s onwards, and the concomitant criticisms from the mission-trained African nationalists against the Christian churches, impressed upon African church leaders the need to respond and to relate their Christian faith to the raging wind of change that was then blowing across the continent.[49] The church took the cultural revolution seriously, and in response to the nationalists' appeal to come to grips "with traditional practices and with the worldview that these beliefs and practices imply," African theologians began to "favor the search for Christianity's essential message, one which would penetrate

African ways of thinking and living."[50] Thus, a new orientation for the indigenization of the church, as well as its theology, began to emerge from the 1950s onwards in both francophone and anglophone Africa. Best examples of this new current can be seen in such collective works as *Des Prêtres noirs s'interrogent* (1956)[51] and *Biblical Revelation and African Beliefs* (1969),[52] and in individual publications of African theologians such as Vincent Mulago's *Un Visage africain du Christianisme* (Paris, 1965), E. Bolaji Idowu's *Towards an Indigenous Church* (Oxford, 1965), J. C. Bahoken's *Clairières métaphysiques africaines* (Paris, 1967), John Mbiti's *New Testament Eschatology in an African Background* (Oxford, 1971) and others.

In francophone Africa, although the theological debate began with the publication of Placide Tempels' *La Philosophie Bantoue* in 1948,[53] it was the publication of *Des Prêtres noirs s'interrogent* that was "considered as the starting point of the modern African Theology Movement."[54] Historically, therefore, *Des Prêtres noires s'interrogent* — a collection of writings by black priests studying in Europe — was the "first explicit manifestation of a new radical current" that represented "a solidly nationalist reflection on Christianity."[55] If Tempels' *La Philosophie Bantoue* was greeted with suspicion, *Des Prêtres noirs s'interrogent* was received with annoyance, especially from missionaries and European theologians; notable among them was Professor (Canon) A. Vanneste of the Catholic Institute of Lovanium, who later became the dean of the Faculty of Catholic Theology in Kinshasa, Zaire.[56] However, among Africans the publication was "welcome as the first manifesto of modern Black African Theology"[57]; and for African theologian Tharcisse Tshibangu, Vanneste's pupil, this evidenced an affirmation of "a 'theology with an African color' based on the specific thought pattern of African culture."[58]

These cultural movements, however, have all had their critics, from both secular writers[59] and African theologians. Notable among these theologians is Jean-Marc Ela, who not only sees Negritude as an ideology of the ruling class with scarcely any real hold on the masses, but also as an outmoded ideology that "constitutes an obstacle to the liberation of Africa."[60] He writes:

> One cannot help but notice that the traits by which African identity is defined belong to a Western conceptual heritage. In a sense, the sources of Blackness are European. The Senghorian portrait of the Negro is permeated with the Western thought of the eighteenth and nineteenth centuries.

Ela then concludes,

> Blackness is not a theory welling up from the base, where the masses live in misery and injustice. It is an ideology developed by a bourgeois elite. The masses refuse it. Only superficially is Blackness an antidote

for foreign ideologies that know nothing of the black world. It is a
system belonging to ivory-tower intellectuals.[61]

Certainly, it is Ela's theological project that compels him to reject both
Negritude and the "indigenization" theology to which it gave birth. As a
liberation oriented theologian whose concern is especially for the liberation
of the African peasants, Ela finds it difficult to accept an "abstract theory"
that has no liberation praxis: "For all its vaunting of sociocultural specificity,
Blackness only promotes the values of the past, thus espousing a dead view
of society, creating a mystique of vain expectation, and doing its best to
check the revolt of the hungering masses by feeding them soporifics."[62] Thus
for Ela, Negritude is an ideology of "alienation" rather than of "authenticity."

But not all African theologians concerned with liberation share Ela's
opinion. For instance, the "African Report" of EATWOT VII (Oaxtepec)
takes to task the "many superficial critics [who] have not understood very
well the deeper meaning of a movement such as Negritude." It is Negritude,
the report argues, "which has driven the colonizer out."[63]

A study of the AACC report of the Kampala inaugural assembly[64] and
subsequent assemblies shows how the African church seriously took up the
challenge posed by both the political and cultural factors of the African
revolution. Like the AACC among Protestants, the Symposium of Episcopal
Conferences of Africa and Madagascar (SECAM) has also been responsible, with a post-Vatican II spirit, for bringing authenticity to African
Christianity among Roman Catholics.[65]

Thus, by the second half of the 1960s, the stage was set for African
Christians in both Catholic and Protestant churches and in francophone
and anglophone areas to pursue their respective perspectives on *Africanization*. The initiative now became African, and the theses of the new models
of conversion and theologizing were integrated, with emphasis on the new
premises of the doctrine of African independence—Negritude and African
Personality.[66] Explaining one of these new models, V. Y. Mudimbe has
shown how a theology of incarnation, for instance, emphasized "negritude
and black personality as expressions of an African civilization, African history with its own symbols as a preparation for Christianity, and ... the
experience of slavery, exploitation and colonization as signs of the suffering
of God's chosen ones. The most striking feature of these intellectual positions," continues Mudimbe, "resides in the theoretical distinction between
the program of political liberation which should permit a transformation
of the traditional civilization and that of rethinking Christianity as an integral part of the local culture."[67] Mudimbe then proposes three major trends
that contributed to the development of a theology of incarnation. These
are:

(a) A strong interest in the Africanization of Christianity insofar as
it would permit a divorce between Christianity and Western history

and culture and would introduce African features into the church.

(b) A search for an African element in the field of theology and religious activities, which might keep pace with the ideological objectives for political and cultural autonomy. This trend mainly characterizes Roman Catholic African theologians.

(c) A vigorous interest in traditional religions, leading to the supposition that in general anthropologists' and missionaries' works are neither dependable nor acceptable. This encourages new programs and projects which will be the responsibility of African scholars.[68]

Having analyzed the roles that pan-Africanism and African nationalism played in the political sphere and Negritude and African Personality played in the cultural realm to combat racism, exploitation and colonialism and to promote African theology, I will now examine the impact that political and cultural factors in the black struggle for liberation have had on the emergence of Black theology in South Africa.

THE BLACK STRUGGLE AGAINST WHITE DOMINATION AND APARTHEID IN SOUTH AFRICA

Black theology in South Africa, like African theology in the northern part of the continent, has been tremendously influenced by the black African struggle against white supremacist domination. As in the rest of Africa, the struggle has been fought on all fronts—political, cultural and religious. But since it is the political and cultural factors that have played the key role in the controversy between African theology and Black theology, investigation of the historical background of South African Black theology will also be limited to these two areas.

THE POLITICS OF RESISTANCE

Since the beginning of continuous interaction between the racial groups in South Africa in the seventeenth century, the entire political history of the country has evidenced a progressive trend toward complete monopolization of power in the hands of the white minority. It is this differential power which has shaped group positions between dominant whites and subordinate blacks. First under Dutch colonialism and then under British imperialism, South Africa became a colony, and white domination in the territory was firmly established. Gradual expansion from the Cape culminated in the formation of the Union in 1910. With the achievement of the so-called Republic (1961) under the Afrikaner Nationalist government, the end of the road to Afrikanerdom was accomplished by the Boer.

With the support of and justification from the White Dutch Reformed churches, the Afrikaner experience of God gave rise to a theology that sought to provide sustenance for their resistance against British imperialist oppression and to help Afrikaners build a "nationhood." It also became "a creed by which a European people cut off from their original homeland, found themselves an elect people in a new place."[69] The alacrity of Afrikaners to deify their history on an alien continent is succinctly and forcefully expressed in the often quoted statement of Afrikaner former Prime Minister D. F. Malan. He said:

> Our history is the greatest masterpiece of the centuries. We hold this nationhood as our due for it was given us by the Architect of the Universe [sic!]. [God's] aim was the formation of a new nation among the nations of the world. . . . The last hundred years have witnessed a miracle behind which lie a divine plan [sic!]. Indeed, the history of the Afrikaner reveals a will and determination which makes one feel that Afrikanerdom is not the work of men but the creation of God.[70]

After the republic was established, the National Party government was no longer threatened and challenged by the British imperialist; now the challenge came from the black African. The weapon the Afrikaner chose for meeting this black challenge was *apartheid* — a policy with the task of preserving and safeguarding the racial identity and supremacy of the white minority racial grouping in South Africa. Thus the context and the historical condition within which Black theology is to be placed is a situation in which the ruling authorities, far from defending citizens' civil rights, have rather taken the lead in increasingly restricting black freedom. Both informal and formal norms (the State Constitution and apartheid legislation) consistently "uphold the principles of *Herrenvolk democracy*, i.e., a democracy only for the dominant racial caste."[71] In this unjust system, the government's policy of apartheid was supported, protected and justified by the Afrikaner churches.

It is important to remind ourselves from the very outset that the South African history of conflicts and resistance has a longer history than apartheid itself, since this sinful and heretical ideology was built on rules and practices that can be traced back to the arrival of the Dutch and the *free-burghers*. Besides, since Afrikaner civil-theological interpretation of history was based on the past,[72] it behooves me to give a very brief historical survey of the earliest period of frontier violence that dominated so much of the life of the Boer, and the resistance that came from the Africans — first from the various African tribes and then from the African nationalist movement. Then we can understand how today's liberation struggle against apartheid was, as Chief Luthuli said, but the latest in a long history of resistance against encroaching white imperialism that began more than three hundred years ago.

AFRICAN TRIBAL RESISTANCE

Since the first sign of a permanent European settlement became apparent when the *Verenigde Oost-Indische Compagnie* set up a refuelling station for Dutch vessels on the Cape in 1652, conflicts between the indigenous people and the European intruders have never ceased. The first South African blacks to deal with this inauspicious confrontation were the Khoisan.[73] The main reason the Khoisan fought the European intruders on military lines, even though they did not meet the latter's superior weapons on equal terms, was to defend their land, water and pasture—the resources that represented "the capital upon which tribal life had been based."[74] William Wilson has summed up the Khoisan-Boer encounter in this early period. He writes,

> As first contacts were made with small wandering bands of Bushmen hunters and Hottentot pastoralists, the Boer cattle raids and encroachment on land previously solely occupied by Africans produced an "endless series of frontier wars and counterraids by the aborigines." The Boers, with superior resources (guns, wagons, and horses), virtually exterminated the Bushmen who fought to retain their hunting grounds and eventually reduced the Hottentot tribes to the status of serfs after capturing their land and cattle.[75]

With their military superiority, the Boer expanded the colonial boundary, coerced the now-impoverished Khoisan to work on white farms and assimilated them into their legal system. By the second half of the eighteenth century, the Boer had reached the Great Fish River, to confront yet another African tribe—the Bantu.

The Bantu tribes, among whom were the Zulu, the Xhosa, the Sotho and the Ndebele, were, like their southern Khoikhoi neighbors, pastoralists on the move; but they were also cultivators of the land, like the *trekboers*. They were large and highly cohesive nations with complex political and military organization. The first Bantu-Boer skirmish took place as early as 1702 on the eastern frontier.[76] By this time, as a result of scarcity of pastureland, the nature of the warfare had changed "from quasi-recreational pastime to a serious struggle for survival, necessitating the institution of a much more rigorously controlled politico-military system."[77] Both the Bantu and the Boer sought land for ample grazing grounds, but the latter, with their technical advancement, were able to defeat and dispossess the Bantu of their land and livestock. It was between these two groups that the "Kaffir Wars"—a series of wars also referred to as the Hundred Years War from 1779 to 1879—were fought.[78]

But Dutch colonial rule was to be jeopardized by the Napoleonic wars in Europe, and the British, whose occupation of the Cape began in 1795, took control of the colony eleven years later. To escape from British domination, the Boer embarked upon their "Great Trek," on which their subsequent history—as interpreted by Afrikaner civil religion—is centered. This trek became for a European people "formal proof of God's election ... and [God's] special destiny for them."[79] In this civil-theological interpretation, it was "the Christian faith [which] seemed to provide the rationale necessary to justify the situation," and it was Christianity which "was used to justify and explain what happened."[80] Thus, by the turn of the twentieth century, all the African tribes had been incorporated into the political, economic and legal system of European settlers. Deprived of their ownership, Africans still remained on the land, but as tenants, laborers and aliens. Although they herded cattle and planted corn as before, now the cattle belonged to the master, the corn was pledged against taxes, and their labor became the property of others.[81] But this African tribal resistance has significance for later generations in that it provided "a potent ideological element in legitimating [the] armed resistance"[82] embarked upon by the black African nationalists against apartheid and the white minority regime between 1960 and 1990.

BLACK AFRICAN NATIONALIST RESISTANCE

In a sense, Christianity contributed both positively and negatively toward the rise of African nationalism in South Africa. On the one hand, it was the educated black Christians who became the "carriers" of the movement; they initiated it and gave it its ideological shape. For some of these black Christians, the new faith became a cohesive force in a society of ethnic diversity, and they saw its value as "a source of political ideas." Christianity on the whole "functioned as a guide for cultural, political and social judgments" that also provided blacks with "a language of protest."[83] It should therefore be understood why Ethiopianism became one of the earliest expressions of African nationalism.[84]

But, on the other hand, some Africans also saw European Christianity as an instrument of divisiveness among blacks and therefore sought unity elsewhere — in politics. This led to the birth of the *Imbumba Yama Afrika* (Union of Africans) whose aim was to promote African unity and articulate black interests in a white-dominated society. For example, in his speech in 1883 on the purpose of the *Imbumba*, S. N. Mvambo saw as "a great mistake," the many church denominations that had been brought to black people by whites. He lamented,

For the Black man makes the fatal mistake of thinking that if he is an Anglican, he has nothing to do with anything suggested by a Wesleyan, and the Wesleyan also thinks so, and so does the Presbyterian. [We] must make sure that all these three are represented ... [and] we must be united on political matters. In fighting for national rights, we must fight together. Although they look as if they belong to various churches, the white people are solidly united when it comes to matters of this nature. We blacks think that these churches are hostile to one another, and in that way we lose our political right.[85]

By the end of the nineteenth century and the beginning of the twentieth, two main approaches to politics had become evident. Blacks with a more integrationist/accommodationist view, prepared to work together with sympathetic whites toward a nonracial representative government, were represented by the *Imbumba*.[86] Blacks with a radical Africanist view, convinced that black self-preservation and progress could best be achieved through exclusively black organizations and prepared to challenge white supremacy and power, were represented by Ethiopianism. These differences were to become more pronounced in later nationalism, as is seen between the African National Congress (ANC) and the Pan Africanist Congress (PAC), with the former accommodating non-Africans and the latter excluding them. It was the second, radical approach that was responsible for the isolated armed resistance against white power after the Kaffir Wars, such as the Bambata Rebellion in 1906.[87]

The formation of the Union in 1910 demonstrated that all African protests prior to that time were unsuccessful. The formation of the ANC in 1912, formally the South African Native National Congress, was a direct response of African elites to the establishment, two years before, of the all-white Union government. All along, the ANC has had the central aim of attaining national liberation for the black African majority. This objective is believed to be the cornerstone of a free and democratic South Africa, albeit, the means and tactics for achieving this goal have changed through the years as conditions changed. For example, the ANC moved from a reformist conciliatory position to a more militant stand when the Afrikaner National Party introduced apartheid in the late 1940s. In 1949, it adopted the Program of Action which, among other things, led to the Defiance Campaign in 1952. The ANC multiracial stance allowed it to enter into a Congress of Alliance with left-wing groups in South Africa that adopted the Freedom Charter in 1955. The adoption of the charter had serious consequences for African nationalism. It was followed by both the Treason Trial (1956-1961) and the breakaway in 1959 of the PAC.[88]

Sharpeville 1960 was a turning point in the black nationalist struggle. Under a new law which, ironically, followed the massacre of blacks by whites, both the ANC and the PAC were banned and a state of emergency was declared. This forced the more militant activists of the two organizations, after an apparent failure of nonviolent strategies, to examine the violence option left for them. Consequently, *Umkonto we Sizwe* (Spear of the Nation) and *UmAfrika Poqo* (Africans Alone), the armed wings of the ANC and the PAC respectively, were launched.[89] When the ban was lifted in 1990 and some political prisoners, including Nelson Mandela, were released, the nationalist struggle entered a new phase altogether, namely, a negotiation phase.

The negotiation process revealed important differences not only between black nationalists and the white regime but also among black nationalists themselves. On the one hand, the government of F. W. de Klerk preferred a transitional government based on an amended constitution which, for the first time, would include a blacks' chamber in parliament. Such a power sharing, the government argued, would ensure strong protection for the white minority. Thus, instead of an interim government or a constituent assembly, the regime favored a multiparty conference to agree on terms for a constitution and transitional government arrangements. It was therefore not surprising that the Convention for a Democratic South Africa (CODESA)—the name given to such a multiparty conference—excluded organizations that refused to negotiate a settlement.[90]

On the other hand, black nationalists objected to any special privileges for whites and called rather for a *new* constitution which, based on democratic principles, would extend political rights to all races in South Africa. However, there were disagreements among nationalists as to how this could be achieved. For instance, while the ANC suggested the establishment of an interim government composed of representatives of the entire South African population, which would oversee the promulgation of a new constitution and sponsor elections in which every South African would participate,[91] militant black organizations such as the PAC, AZAPO and the Workers Organization for Socialist Action (WOSA) preferred a democratically elected constituent assembly to decide on a new constitution.

The PAC, for example, demanded that *elected* representatives of all political parties to a constituent assembly draw up a new constitution, under which a democratic government would be elected. This representation, PAC contended, must be proportionate to the percentage of votes acquired by each political party nationally.[92] Black militant nationalism condemned ANC's advocacy of a representative interim government as a government not democratically elected but based on power sharing and therefore defending the oppressive status quo. Thus, while the ANC advocated an interim government to supervise a constituent assembly and then be replaced by an elected government under a new constitution, the PAC, like AZAPO and WOSA, saw an elected constituent assembly as the only acceptable means of arriving at a new constitution.[93]

THE BLACK CONSCIOUSNESS MOVEMENT
AND BLACK LIBERATION

In the aftermath of Sharpeville, when black political activities had seemingly died down following the banning of both ANC and PAC, the inextinguishable spirit of the African before the European was once again demonstrated. The espousal of African cultural values and black political aspiration gave birth to a new movement and a philosophy that was to be the driving force behind the black struggle. This movement came to change the face of black politics and the life of the Christian church. As a cultural-political movement, this force was to permeate every aspect of the oppressed black community life. With the view to rediscovering black people's cultural roots, the Black Consciousness Movement (BCM) engaged in cultural activities and embarked on the reinterpretation of black history.

Like Negritude and African Personality, the BCM in South Africa also aimed at the liberation of blacks; but unlike the two philosophical concepts, black consciousness conceived of liberation in more holistic terms, affecting every dimension of black existence. BCM was also a more inclusive concept, in that it was able to draw adherents from both intellectuals and the masses of the people and was not limited to a small group of politicized leaders. Black Consciousness provided a bridge that joined together all the ethnic groups within the black community; it also brought together students from African as well as Colored and Indian constituencies.

Black Consciousness interpreted the South African situation using the Hegelian theory of dialectic materialism. From the *thesis* of white racism and the *antithesis* of black solidarity, a new *synthesis* of true humanity was envisaged—a true humanity without regard to color or race and in which there was no place for power politics.[94] The South African Students' Organization (SASO), led by Steve Biko, affectionately called the "father of Black Consciousness," defined the concept as "an attitude of mind and a way of life."[95] First, as *an attitude of mind*, Black Consciousness made black people see themselves as independent and complete in themselves, making them free to express and affirm their full humanity. Black people became aware that "their humanity is constituted by their blackness."[96] It also made them aware that the strongest tool in the hands of the oppressor was the mentality of the oppressed, for "If one is free at heart, no man-made chains can bind one to servitude, but if one's mind is so manipulated and controlled by the oppressor as to make the oppressed believe that he is a liability to the white man, then there would be nothing the oppressed can do to scare his powerful masters."[97]

Second, as *a way of life*, Black Consciousness examined critically the oppressive status quo of the apartheid system by using black values. It addressed itself to the authenticity of black history, culture and religion. It rejected white supremacy and affirmed black humanity. Black Consciousness sought to liberate blacks from both psychological alienation and physical oppression. It insisted that liberation should begin with liberation from the psychological oppression of an inferiority complex and from physical oppression "accruing out of living in a white racist society."[98]

The means the BCM chose to achieve its objective was that of "conscientization." The Black Theology Project (BTP) was one of the many projects launched by the BCM to conscientize the oppressed black community in its struggle for freedom and full humanity. This conscientization was concerned about the nature and praxis of the struggle whose goal was to bring "total authentic liberation."[99] Thus with the launching of the project, the BCM proved to contain within its essence the theological seed of resistance to apartheid and of liberation.

BLACK THEOLOGY AND THE BLACK CONSCIOUSNESS MOVEMENT

As African cultural nationalism in the form of Negritude and African Personality challenged Christians in francophone and anglophone Africa, so did the BCM challenge Christians in South Africa to question the common faith they shared with their white oppressors. Put differently, the BCM impressed upon black Christians the need to reflect the Christian faith as they engaged meaningfully in the struggle of their people: It is a "way of thinking and acting by black Christians as they attempt to discover the political implications of the faith in a given situation."[100]

The development of Black theology can be divided into two phases in which the BCM has taken on different roles. The first phase began in the early 1970s as a theological expression of the BCM. Until it was banned in 1977, the BCM was the sole uniting force that brought black theologians together.

If the task of the pre-1977 phase of the BCM was to "conscientize" black people to the situation in which they were and the situation in which they ought to be, in the post-1977 phase, its task became one of translating the cultural revolution in the minds of oppressed blacks into political action, arousing them to become vehicles of their own liberation and to repossess the land taken by their white oppressors. As a strategy for achieving this, there began to emerge an explicit analysis of the political economy of the country. Much attention was now given to the *black worker* who, it was believed, could exert great pressure on the capitalist system and therefore on the political system. The emphasis thus shifted from *race* to *class* struggle. It is not surprising, therefore, that the Azanian People's Organization (AZAPO), with its National Forum (NF), targeted "racial capitalism" and developed a "worker struggle" strategy. Black theologians belonging to this new phase of Black Consciousness used Marxist and neo-Marxist analyses to uncover the dynamics of racial capitalism in South Africa. This is exemplified in the use of historical materialism by Itumeleng Mosala.[101]

The second phase of South African Black theology began in the early 1980s with conferences organized by the Black Theology Task Force of the Institute for Contextual Theology (ICT). Whereas the publication of *Essays on Black Theology* formally inaugurated the first phase in 1972,[102] the second phase was ushered in by *The Unquestionable Right to be Free* (1986).[103] If the Black Theology Project of the University Christian Movement was the organizational framework within which the former operated, in the latter, it was within the Black Theology Task Force of the ICT.

A comparison between the two phases evidences a shift that has taken place in Black theology which makes it rather more complex. This has come about because of a shift in political praxis that has caused ideological divisions among black theologians. With the banning of the BCM in 1977, the early 1980s witnessed the emergence of various organizations whose ideological stance differed considerably from that of the BCM. These groups adopted the principle of *nonracialism*, including people of all races. These developments had a great impact on Black theology, whose agenda had always been set by the struggle against apartheid and white domination. For instance, the emergence of the United Democratic Front (UDF) in 1983 and the Congress of South African Trade Unions (COSATU) in 1985, as well as student organizations such as the Congress of South African Students (COSAS) and Azanian Students Organization (AZASO), which adopted the progressive nonracial position by subscribing to the Freedom Charter, posed tremendous ideological challenges to organizations that still upheld the Black Consciousness philosophy, such as AZAPO. That these ideological divisions existed among black theologians was evidenced when the 1983 Conference at Wilgespruit Fellowship Centre became "a combustion chamber."[104]

Although the first phase of South African Black theology had ignored Marxist analysis, the second phase began to take Marxist analysis of South African society very seriously. Consequently, apparent divisions emerged among black theologians between the advocates of the Race-Analyst approach and the Class-Analyst approach. In addition, there were others who wanted to hold both race and class together in creative tension as the best way to understand the South African situation. Frank Chikane explained the complexity of the situation:

> Although the division on the surface seemed to be between the Black Consciousness Movement and the progressive democrats, a division based on a play between the class and race models or the combination of these models in trying to understand the South African society, it seems that the real divisive matter was the attitudes of these groupings to the historical liberation movements, the African National Congress (ANC) and the Pan-African Congress (PAC).[105]

Other observable factors distinguish the second phase from the first, and perhaps the most significant of these is the inclusion of women's issues, which was conspicuously missing in nascent Black theology. The editors of *The Unquestionable Right to be Free* (1986) rightly described the inclusion of a feminist perspective in the volume as "the single most important feature of this publication on Black Theology and the black struggle in South Africa."[106]

Again, whereas Black theology in its early stage was rather polemic, definitional, more compositional and less academic as most of its advocates were not professional theologians, the second phase, which went beyond the prolegomena, took a more academic approach and "dwelt upon its content ... engaging fully in the actual reflection and interpretation of the Word of God in the South African situation."[107] The key theologians during the early phase included Manas Buthelezi, Bonganjalo Goba, Mokgethi Motlhabi, Desmond Tutu, Allan Boesak and Simon Maimela. In the second phase, the list was extended to include Itumeleng Mosala, Buti Tlhagale, Takatso Mofokeng and Frank Chikane. The BTP now publishes the *Journal of Black Theology in South Africa* as a "forum for the exchange of theological ideas and a contribution to the development of Black theology in South Africa."

Finally, whereas in the first phase Black theology was the only prophetic theological voice that black Christians used to combat apartheid, in the second it seemed to have become but one of the so-called contextual theologies that were being advocated mainly by white liberals whose main purpose was to change the black theological agenda which, in the early phase, had excluded them.[108]

CONCLUSION

African theology and South African Black theology are not synonymous. The former developed in independent, or more precisely, neocolonial Africa, and the latter, in apartheid South Africa. Investigation of the key factors in their respective histories suggests strongly that these two theological systems are not the same. They are different not only in terms of their histories, but also in terms of their emphases. Insofar as Africanization or indigenization is identified as the theme of the first, with an emphasis on culture, and liberation is identified as the theme of the second, with an emphasis on politics, the two remain dissimilar although not contradictory.

Therefore, finally, the following two conclusions, which are to be seen as dialectically related, could be drawn. 1) The polarity between African theology and Black theology may, in a sense, be attributable to the differences in the historical backgrounds and emphases of the two theologies. 2) Analyses of the key historical moments reveal a single (common) underlying motif in the political and cultural struggles in both independent and South Africa. Thus, while the differences in the historical backdrops may seem to justify a tension polarity, the common underlying motif in the two struggles — cultural and political — suggests the need to come to a dialectic understanding of these factors as two sides of the same liberation process.

NOTES

1. See Report of the Commission on "The Christian Basis for Participation in the African Revolution" of the All Africa Conference of Churches' Consultation held at Enugu, Nigeria, in 1965 under the theme: "The Christian Response to the African Revolution" in AACC, *Consultation Digest: A Summary of Reports and Addresses* (Geneva: WCC, 1965), p. 92.

2. Albert J. Luthuli, "Apartheid: This Terrible Dream," Nobel Peace Prize Address delivered in Oslo, December 11, 1961, in David Mermelstein, ed., *The Anti-Apartheid Reader: South Africa and the Struggle Against White Racist Rule* (New York: Grove Press, 1987), p. 18.

3. AACC, *Consultation Digest*, p. 92.

4. Aimé Césaire, *Discourse On Colonialism* (New York: Monthly Review Press, 1972), p. 21. Cf. Kwame Nkrumah, *Towards Colonial Freedom: Africa in the Struggle Against World Imperialism* (London: Panaf Books, 1973).

5. See James H. Cone, "Reflections from the Perspective of U.S. Blacks: Black Theology and Third World Theology," in Virginia Fabella and Sergio Torres, eds., *Irruption of the Third World: Challenge to Theology* (Maryknoll, N.Y.: Orbis Books, 1983), p. 235f.

6. See Aylward Shorter, *African Christian Theology: Adaptation or Incarnation?* (Maryknoll, N.Y., Orbis Books, 1977), p. 150.

7. Manas Buthelezi, "Toward Indigenous Theology in South Africa," in Sergio Torres and Virginia Fabella, eds., *The Emergent Gospel: Theology from the Developing World* (Maryknoll, N.Y.: Orbis Books, 1978), p. 63.

8. Kwame Nkrumah, *Revolutionary Path* (New York: International Publishers, 1973), p. 463; cf. also his *Handbook of Revolutionary Warfare* (London: Panaf Books, 1968), p. 24.

9. See Gwinyai H. Muzorewa, *The Origins and Development of African Theology* (Maryknoll, N.Y.: Orbis Books, 1985), esp. Ch. 4, pp. 46–56.

10. Perhaps an exception ought to be made for C. S. Banana and the few Africans who are interested in Julius Nyerere's *Ujamaa* philosophy based on the traditional concept of "familyhood." See, e.g., C. S. Banana, *Theology of Promise: The Dynamics of Self-Reliance* (Harare, Zimbabwe: College Press, 1982).

11. See for instance, W. E. B. DuBois, *The Souls of Black Folk* (New York: Bantam Books, 1903, 1989); Amy Jacques Garvey, ed., *The Philosophy and Opinions of Marcus Garvey, or, Africa for the Africans,* vols. 1 and 2 (Dover, Mass.: Majority Press, 1986); and George Padmore, *Pan-Africanism or Communism?* (London: Dobson, 1956).

12. See, e.g., J. Ayo Langley, *Ideologies of Liberation in Black Africa 1856–1970: Documents on Modern African Political Thought from Colonial Times to the Present* (London: Rex Collings, 1979). Because of these diversities, it may be helpful to distinguish between (i) the older *transatlantic pan-Africanism* which seeks the solidarity between all people of African descent on the main continent and in the diaspora with such founding fathers as DuBois, H. Sylvester-Williams, Garvey and Padmore; (ii) the narrowly defined *sub-Saharan pan-Africanism* which seeks solidarity among black Africans within the continent south of the Sahara as advocated by the more conservative African nationalists such as Hastings Kamuzu Banda of Malawi and Felix Houphouët-Boigny of Cote d'Ivoire (the Ivory Coast); and (iii) the *trans-Saharan pan-Africanism* which embraces both black Africa south of the Sahara and Arab Africa north of the Sahara. This solidarity is what is expressed in the Organization of African Unity (OAU). It must, however, be pointed out that there are some Africans who embrace more than one of the different versions of pan-Africanism; an example is Nkrumah, whose support for both transatlantic and trans-Saharan pan-Africanism is unequivocal. Cf. Ali A. Mazrui and Michael Tidy, *Nationalism and New States in Africa: From about 1935 to the Present* (London: Heinemann, 1984), pp. xiiif.

13. See Kwame Nkrumah, *Africa Must Unite* (New York: International Publishers, 1963), pp. 132ff., also his *Revolutionary Path*, pp. 465f.; Julius Nyerere, "The Dilemma of the Pan-Africanist," in J. Ayo Langley, ed., *Ideologies of Liberation in Black Africa, 1856–1970*, pp. 342–53; cf. Nnamdi Azikiwe, "The Future of Pan-

Africanism," in J. Ayo Langley, ed., *Ideologies of Liberation in Black Africa*, pp. 302–27.

14. See Josiah Young, *Black and African Theologies: Siblings or Distant Cousins?* (Maryknoll, N.Y.: Orbis Books, 1986), esp. Ch. 5, pp. 106–16.

15. Hollis R. Lynch, *Edward Wilmot Blyden: Pan-Negro Patriot, 1832–1912* (London: Oxford University Press, 1967), pp. 249f. Edward Blyden was born in the West Indies but emigrated to Liberia in 1851 at the age of nineteen. His scholarly attainment and brilliance made him become actively involved in education, church and politics. Earlier in 1862, in a sermon to a black (colored) congregation in the United States, Blyden had urged black people not to content themselves with living among other races, but to build up Negro states: "An African nationality," he said, "is our great need, and God tells us by [God's] providence that [God] has set the land before us, and bids us go up and possess it." See Blyden, *Liberia Offering* (New York: 1862), pp. 75f. Cited in V. Y. Mudimbe, *The Invention of Africa: Gnosis, Philosophy, and the Order of Knowledge* (Bloomington, Ind.: Indiana University Press, 1988), p. 106.

16. W. E. B. DuBois was the chairman of the committee on the address from this conference. For the full text of this address, see "Address to the Nations of the World by the Pan-African Conference in London, 1900" in Langley, *Ideologies of Liberation in Black Africa*, pp. 738–39. This conference was organized by the African Association formed in 1897 under the leadership of Henry Sylvester-Williams, a West Indian barrister.

17. The 1919 conference, which was held in Paris, is generally regarded as the First Congress of the Pan-African Movement, which has led DuBois to be regarded as the "Father of Pan-Africanism." The second congress was in 1921, and was held successively in London (August 28), Brussels (August 29–September 2) and Paris (September 3 and 5). The third took place in 1923 in London and Lisbon; and the fourth in New York in 1927, sponsored by the organizations of black women in the United States. The fifth congress, in which more Africans participated, took place in Manchester in 1945.

18. See W. Ofoatey-Kodjoe, "Pan-Africanism, A Contemporary Restatement: Fundamental Goals and Changing Strategies," in James E. Turner, ed., *The Next Decade: Theoretical and Research Issues in Africana Studies* (Ithaca, N.Y.: Cornell University Press, 1984), pp. 109ff.

19. Cf. Muzorewa, *The Origins and Development of African Theology,* p. 47.

20. AACC, *Drumbeats From Kampala* (London: Lutterworth, 1963), p. 11.

21. Martin Minogue and Judith Molloy, eds., *African Aims and Attitudes: Selected Documents* (New York: Cambridge University Press, 1974), p. 2; cf. Eliewaha E. Mshana, "Nationalism in Africa as a Challenge and Problem to the Christian Church," *African Theological Journal*, no. 1, February 1968, p. 21. Mshana explains African nationalism this way: "In Africa, nationalism is the expression of the desire of the African peoples to end their subordinate status and to enter the world community. . . . [It is] the common desire of a people to work together for their emancipation from any form of bondage, whether colonial, economic, social or racial." See also Muzorewa, *The Origins and Development of African Theology*, p. 48, where he describes African nationalism as "the struggle against domination by overseas imperialists."

22. Kwame Nkrumah, *Ghana: The Autobiography of Kwame Nkrumah* (New York: International Publishers, 1957), p. 54. Cf. Alexandre Mboukou, "The Pan-

African Movement, 1900–1945: A Study in Leadership Conflicts Among the Disciples of Pan-Africanism," *Journal of Black Studies*, vol. 13, no. 3, March 1983, pp. 280f. For instance, Mboukou writes: "At the Manchester Congress, the Pan-African Movement abandoned its emphasis on race per se and acquired mostly nationalistic overtones. The Black Africans were now talking of the decolonization of Black Africa through their own efforts, thus dealing a solid blow to the reformist program of the early Pan-African Conference and Congresses. The leadership of the movement was now in the hands of Black Africans." See also Ali Mazrui, *Toward a Pan Africana* (Chicago: University of Chicago Press, 1967).

23. Mudimbe, *The Invention of Africa*, p. 99. Hollis Lynch has also described Blyden as "the ideological father of the idea of West African unity" who influenced ideologues such as Nkrumah, Senghor and Azikiwe, and "inspired nationalism in the individual territories." Lynch, *Edward Wilmot Blyden: Pan-Negro*, pp. 249f.

24. Edward W. Blyden, *Christianity, Islam and the Negro Race*, New Edition (London: Edinburgh University Press, 1967), p. 337; cited in Mudimbe, *The Invention of Africa*, p. 129.

25. All Africa Churches Conference, *Africa in Transition: The Challenge and the Christian Response* (Geneva: WCC, 1962), p. 12. In 1963, the name All Africa Churches Conference was changed to All Africa Conference of Churches.

26. Ibid., p. 16.

27. Ibid., p. 66.

28. Ibid., pp. 66–67.

29. AACC, *Drumbeats From Kampala*, p. 60. Following this definition, the AACC distinguished four forms of nationalism, namely: (i) nationalism toward freedom and political independence; (ii) nationalism toward the creation of national unity; (iii) nationalism to conserve the traditional way of life, mainly for older nations; and (iv) nationalism which develops into an ideology of totalitarianism, such as national socialism.

30. Edward W. Blyden, *Christianity, Islam and the Negro Race*, p. 263; cited in Mudimbe, *The Invention of Africa*, p. 124.

31. Amilcar Cabral, *Unity and Struggle: Speeches and Writings* (New York: Monthly Review Press, 1979), p. 147.

32. Immanuel Wallerstein, *Africa, The Politics of Unity* (New York: Random House, 1967), p. 15.

33. See "The First Congress of Negro Writers and Artists, Paris, 1956" resolution in Minogue and Molloy, *African Aims and Attitudes*, p. 226.

34. Ibid., pp. 225–26.

35. Cabral, *Unity and Struggle*, pp. 139–40.

36. Ibid., p. 143.

37. Langley, *Ideologies of Liberation in Black Africa*, p. 57.

38. Frantz Fanon, *The Wretched of the Earth* (New York: Grove Weidenfeld, 1963), p. 245.

39. See the "African Report" presented at the Second General Assembly of EATWOT held at Oaxtepec, Mexico, in 1986, in K. C. Abraham, ed., *Third World Theologies: Commonalities and Divergences* (Maryknoll, N.Y.: Orbis Books, 1990), p. 36.

40. Mudimbe, *The Invention of Africa*, p. 131.

41. See Senghor's "Foreword" to Hollis R. Lynch's collection, *Letters of Edward Wilmot Blyden* (New York: KTO Press, 1978), pp. xv–xxii.

42. Blyden, *Christianity, Islam and the Negro Race*, p. 91; cited in Mudimbe, *The Invention of Africa*, p. 114. On African Personality, Blyden elsewhere wrote: "It is sad to think that there are some Africans, especially among those who enjoyed the advantages of foreign training, who are blind to the radical facts of humanity as to say, 'Let us do away with the sentiment of Race. Let us do away with our African Personality and be lost, if possible, in another Race'. . . . When you have done away with your personality, you have done away with yourselves. . . . Therefore honor and love your Race. Be yourselves, as God intended you to be or [God] would not make you thus. . . . If you are not yourself, if you surrender your personality, you have nothing left to give the world." See Edward W. Blyden, "Study and Race," a lecture he delivered on May 19, 1893, before the Young Men's Literary Association; in Henry S. Wilson, ed., *Origins of West African Nationalism* (London: Macmillan, 1969), pp. 249–50.

43. Mudimbe, *The Invention of Africa*, p. 133.

44. Ibid.

45. James Ngugi, "National Culture," an extract of his essay "Toward a National Culture," in Minogue and Molloy, eds., *African Aims and Attitudes*, p. 242.

46. Léopold Senghor, "Negritude and African Socialism," extracts in Minogue and Molloy, *African Aims and Attitudes*, p. 230. The term *Negritude*, meaning "Blackness," was invented in the early 1930s by the colored Martinican poet-politician Aimé Césaire, but its ideology has been defined by Léopold Senghor. See Senghor, *Liberté I: Négritude et Humanisme* (Paris, 1964).

According to Senghor, Negritude is "the whole complex of civilized values—cultural, economic, social and political—which characterize the black peoples, or, more precisely, the Black-African world." See Minogue and Molloy, eds., *African Aims and Attitudes*, p. 231; cf. Rupert Emerson, "Pan-Africanism," in Irving L. Markovitz, ed., *African Politics and Society: Basic Issues and Problems of Government and Development* (New York: The Free Press, 1970), p. 451. For the different shades of meaning given to Negritude, its achievements and critics, see Janheinz Jahn, *Neo-African Literature: A History of Black Writing* (New York: Grove Press, 1968), pp. 239–76. The journal *Présence Africaine*, which was founded by Alioune Diop, became the focal point of the Negritude Movement.

47. Kwame Nkrumah, *Revolutionary Path*, p. 205.

48. Ibid., p. 206; cf. William E. Abraham, *The Mind of Africa* (Chicago: University of Chicago Press, 1962), p. 32, where he defines African Personality as, "the complex of ideas and attitudes which is both identical and significant in otherwise different African cultures."

49. See, for instance, Adeolu Adegbola, "A Christian Interpretation of the African Revolution," in AACC, *Consultation Digest*, pp. 17–24, also in G. F. Vicedom, ed., *Christ and the Younger Churches* (London: SPCK, 1972), pp. 32–41; E. W. Fashole-Luke, "The Quest for African Christian Theologies," *Scottish Journal of Theology*, vol. 29, 1976, p. 159; cf. All Africa Churches Conference/World Council of Churches, *African in Transition: The Challenge and the Christian Response* (Geneva: WCC, 1962).

50. Mudimbe, *The Invention of Africa*, p. 56; cf. Adrian Hastings, *A History of African Christianity* (Cambridge: Cambridge University Press, 1979), p. 119.

51. A. Abble et al., *Des Prêtres noirs s'interrogent* (Paris, 1956). For Jean-Marc Ela, "Everything that was said in *Des Prêtres noirs s'interrogent* years ago bears the

mark of the Negritude movement." See Jean-Marc Ela, *African Cry* (Maryknoll, N.Y.: Orbis Books, 1986), p. 122.

52. Kwesi Dickson and Paul Ellingworth, eds., *Biblical Revelation and African Beliefs* (London: Oxford, 1969). Cf. C. G. Baëta, ed., *Christianity in Tropical Africa* (London: Oxford, 1968).

53. Placide Tempels, *La Philosophie Bantoue* (Paris: Présence Africaine, 1948).

54. Engelbert Mveng, "African Liberation Theology," in Leonardo Boff and Virgil Elizondo, eds., *Concilium 199—Theologies of the Third World: Convergences and Differences* (Edinburgh: T&T Clark, 1988), p. 22. For the African response to Tempels' *La Philosophie Bantoue*, see Alexis Kagame, *La Philosophie bantu-rwandaise de l'être* (Brussels, 1956); cf. Mudimbe, *The Invention of Africa*, pp. 50ff., and John Mbiti, *African Religions and Philosophy* (London: Heinemann, 1969), pp. 10f.

55. Mudimbe, *The Invention of Africa*, p. 56.

56. For Professor A. Vanneste's opposition to "African Theology," see Mveng, "African Liberation Theology," p. 22; also Patrick A. Kalilombe, "Black Theology," in David F. Ford, ed., *The Modern Theologians: An Introduction to Christian Theology in the Twentieth Century*, vol. II (New York/Oxford: Basil Blackwell, 1989), p. 202. Cf. T. Tshibangu, *Le propos d'une théologie africaine* (Kinshasa: Presses Universitaires Zaire, 1974), pp. 14ff.

57. Mveng, "African Liberation Theology," p. 22; see also p. 34, n. 8, for the names of the eleven black priests who contributed to the volume.

58. See Kalilombe, "Black Theology," p. 202.

59. See for example, Wole Soyinka, *Myth, Literature and the African World* (Cambridge: Cambridge University Press, 1976), where he accused the Negritude movement for "having laid its cornerstone on a European intellectual tradition" (p. 134); and also his jejune remark that "a tiger does not proclaim its tigritude." Cf. Ezekiel Mphahlele's critique in his *The African Image* (London: Faber and Faber, 1962).

60. Ela, *African Cry*, p. 122; cf. pp. 123, 125.

61. Ibid., pp. 123, 125, respectively.

62. Ibid., p. 125. See also his *My Faith as an African* (Maryknoll, N.Y.: Orbis Books, 1988).

63. In Abraham, *Third World Theologies*, p. 36.

64. See AACC, *Drumbeats From Kampala*.

65. See the detailed discussion on the contributions of African Catholicism and Protestantism in this regard in Chapter 3.

66. Cf. Josiah Young, "African Theology: From 'Independence' Toward Liberation," *Voices from the Third World*, vol. X, no. 4, December 1987, pp. 41-48; also Mudimbe, *The Invention of Africa*, p. 58.

67. V. Y. Mudimbe, *The Invention of Africa*, pp. 58–59.

68. Ibid., p. 59.

69. Karl Hertz, "Tutu and Boesak: Liberation Theology as Praxis," *Mid-stream*, vol. 26, no. 1, January 1987, p. 81.

70. S. W. Pienaar, ed., *Glo in U Volk: D.F. Malan as Redenaar, 1908–1954* (Cape Town: Tafelberg, 1964), pp. 235–36. Cited in T. Dunbar Moodie, *The Rise of Afrikanerdom: Power, Apartheid, and the Afrikaner Civil Religion* (Berkeley: University of California Press, 1975), p. 1. For more detailed information about the sacred saga of Afrikanerdom, see pp. 1–21.

71. William J. Wilson, *Power, Racism and Privilege: Race Relations in Theoretical*

and Sociohistorical Perspective (New York: Free Press, 1973), p. 198.

72. Moodie, *The Rise of Afrikanerdom*, p. 11.

73. The term *Khoisan* here refers to two early groups in South Africa, the *Khoikhoi* (or *Khoi*), whom the white settlers contemptuously called "Hottentots," and the *San*, who were also called *Bushmen* by the white colonists. While the former constituted a pastoral society, the latter were hunter-gatherers.

74. C. W. de Kiewiet, *A History of South Africa: Social and Economic* (London: Oxford University Press, 1957), p. 82.

75. Wilson, *Power, Racism and Privilege*, p. 23.

76. Lebamang Sebidi, "The Dynamics of the Black Struggle and Its Implication for Black Theology," in I. J. Mosala and B. Tlhagale, eds., *The Unquestionable Right to be Free* (Maryknoll, N.Y.: Orbis Books, 1986), p. 4.

77. Robert W. July, *A History of the African People* (New York: Charles Scribner's Sons, 1970), p. 234.

78. See Pierre Van den Berghe, *South Africa: A Study in Conflict* (Berkeley: University of California Press, 1965), pp. 23, 25f.; Sebidi, in *The Unquestionable Right to be Free*, p. 75; and July, *A History of the African People*, p. 263.

79. Moodie, *The Rise of Afrikanerdom*, p. 3.

80. John de Gruchy, *The Church Struggle in South Africa* (Grand Rapids, Mich.: Eerdmans, 1979), p. 177; cf. van den Berghe, *South Africa*, p. 28.

81. July, *A History of the African People*, p. 264.

82. Richard Gibson, *African Liberation Movements: Contemporary Struggles Against White Minority Rule* (New York: Oxford University Press, 1972), p. 32.

83. Marjorie Hope and James Young, *The South African Churches in a Revolutionary Situation* (Maryknoll, N.Y.: Orbis Books, 1981), p. 36.

84. For instance, with their interpretation of Psalm 68:31 to mean "the evangelization of Africa under African leaders," the Ethiopian churches resisted white racism and domination. See ibid., p. 37.

85. Statement made by S. N. Mvambo in December 1883 on the Purpose of *Imbumba Yama Afrika*, cited in Thomas Karis and Gwendolen M. Carter, eds., *From Protest to Challenge: A Documentary History of African Politics in South Africa 1882–1964*, vol. 1 (Stanford: Hoover Institution Press, 1972), p. 12.

86. This integrationist view was also held by John T. Jabavu's *Imvo Zabantundu* (Native Opinion) — the first black newspaper which played an important role in the black protests against native disfranchisement, pass regulations and other discriminatory measures.

87. See William J. Pomeroy, *Apartheid, Imperialism and African Freedom* (New York: International Publishers, 1986), p. 157; cf. Karis and Carter, *From Protest to Challenge*, pp. 9f.

88. It was the opening clause of the preamble of the Freedom Charter — "That South Africa belongs to all who live in it, black and white . . ." — which unveiled the ideological differences in African nationalism. The PAC strongly opposed the opening clause and argued that the charter conceded in advance that the land did not belong to Africans when it proposed to share it with "all who live in [South Africa]." Thus, the fundamental difference between PAC Africanists and ANC Charterists is seen in the conflicting answers that each group gives to the question: "Who owns the land in South Africa?" While the Charterists argue that it belongs to all — black and white — the Africanists say the land belongs to indigenous Africans. See James

Leatt et al., eds., *Contending Ideologies in South Africa* (Grand Rapids, Mich.: Eerdmans, 1986), pp. 97f.

89. With the *Umkonto*, the ANC developed a strategy to sabotage installations without taking human lives. The *Poqo* also had its own strategies.

90. Both right-wing white extremist groups and militant black organizations which would object to any (compromising) agreements reached did not take part in CODESA negotiations. Thus, white extremist groups such as the Afrikaner Resistance Movement and the Conservative Party, as well as black militant groups such as the PAC and the Azanian People's Organization (AZAPO), were excluded.

91. Cf. Nelson Mandela, "De Klerk's Referendum Gives Veto Power to Whites," *Los Angeles Times*, February 26, 1992.

92. "Declaration of the Consultative Congress of the Pan Africanist Congress of Azania, December 16, 1991, Cape Town," issued by Barney Desai, Secretary for Publicity and Information of the PAC.

93. Workers Organization for Socialist Action, "The Politics of Negotiations," *Workers Voice*, no. 2, November, 1991, p. 15; cf. p. 9.

94. Steve Biko, *I Write What I Like* (San Francisco: Harper & Row, 1986), p. 90; cf. his article, "Black Consciousness and the Quest for a True Humanity," in Basil Moore, ed., *The Challenge of Black Theology in South Africa* (London: C. Hurst & Co., 1973), pp. 36–47. For other definitions that have been given to the concept, see Motsoko Pheko, *Apartheid: The Story of a Dispossessed People* (London: Marram Books, 1984), p. 170.

95. Ibid., p. 91.

96. Allan Boesak, *Farewell to Innocence: A Socio-Ethical Study of Black Theology and Power* (Maryknoll, N.Y.: Orbis Books, 1977), p. 1.

97. Biko, *I Write What I Like*, p. 92.

98. Pheko, *Apartheid*, p. 170.

99. Bonganjalo Goba, "The Black Consciousness Movement: Its Impact on Black Theology," in Mosala and Tlhagale, eds., *The Unquestionable Right to be Free*, p. 66.

100. Ibid., p. 60.

101. See Itumeleng J. Mosala, ed., *Biblical Hermeneutics and Black Theology in South Africa* (Grand Rapids, Mich.: Eerdmans, 1989).

102. See Mokgethi Motlhabi, *Essays on Black Theology* (Johannesburg: University Christian Movement, 1972). But this was soon banned by the South African government, and the British edition, Basil Moore, ed., *Black Theology: The South African Voice* (London: Hurst, 1973) and the American edition, Basil Moore, ed., *The Challenge of Black Theology in South Africa* (Atlanta: John Knox Press, 1974) were published.

103. See Mosala and Tlhagale, eds., *The Unquestionable Right to be Free*. This was the publication of essays from the two conferences organized by ICT in 1983 and 1984.

104. Ibid., p. xv.

105. Ibid.

106. Ibid., p. vi. Cf. pp. 129–33 and pp. 169–74 for the essays of Bernadette I. Mosala and Bonita Bennet respectively.

107. Ibid., p. viii.

108. E.g., John de Gruchy identifies several trends in contextual theology which include: confessing theology; Black theology; African theology; prophetic theology;

and people's theology. See John de Gruchy, "South African Theology Comes of Age," *Religious Studies Review*, vol. 17, no. 3, July 1991, p. 218; also his "The Challenge of South African Theology—The Making of South African Theology: From Colonial Theology to the Kairos Document," a paper presented at the Hoff Lectures, n.d., p. 14. Cf. the list given by the ICT's "What Is Contextual Theology," Part I, *AACC Magazine*, vol. 2, no. 3, December 1984, pp. 14–15.

2 | African Reality and Theological Hermeneutics

The Living Word of the Lord has led us to consider the realities of Africa today. . . . We realize that African unity is the unity of spirit and soul, an individual historical unity that may even transcend geographical differences. Our unity contributes to the total community of God without being blown away in the wind of unspecified universalism. We deplore anything that seeks to shake the solidness of our deep-rooted unity, whether economic isolation, power manipulation, or even styles of life.
— Pan African Conference of Third World Theologians.[1]

DEFINING THE AFRICAN REALITY

Analysis of the African context must begin with African reality—reality which is to be located in time and space. Thus, the locus of African reality is African history. The value of history for a dispossessed people or those who have been deprived of their past cannot be overemphasized. For such a people, history is an enabler that controls their lives; it prepares them to live more humanely in the present and to meet rather than to forecast the future. Rediscovery of their history deepens the sympathies, fortifies the will and liberates the mind.

It should therefore be understood why, at the Second General Assembly of the Ecumenical Association of Third World Theologians (EATWOT), Africans emphasized history as the first methodological approach to African contextual analysis and to African theological interpretation. African theologians explained the importance of such an emphasis: "For Africans, there is no liberation without their historical presence, since they have been expelled from the field of history by their oppressors. Liberation, if true, must be historical liberation; if not, there is no liberation."[2] Furthermore, they acknowledge the fact that Africa's present condition has come about as a result of five centuries of African history that has largely been caused by contact with Western capitalist imperialism. Therefore, whenever the question of African people's liberation is raised, there is always the need to begin with "historical rehabilitation."[3]

In this rehabilitation effort, African historical reality must be viewed as a unity, a combined presence of traditional Africa and the influences of

Euro-Christian and Arabic-Islamic elements. Besides, as a historical reality, African reality is never a "closed" reality; it is always open. The different dimensions of this coherent reality open themselves to the theological investigator who approaches them with the right questions concerning human existence, its relation to the Supreme Being and to the rest of the world.

The coherence of Africa's historical reality is distorted and its totality falsified if this reality is reduced exclusively to a single dimension, say, the *cultural dimension*, or to only its *political dimension*. The African historical reality is not a unidimensional reality but consists of different aspects, each of which may also, in turn, have different faces. For instance, the reality of apartheid, which has largely shaped and nurtured present South African society, can be observed and interpreted from the standpoint of political history and economic history as well as from church history. Even its cultural undertones can no longer be ignored. The same is true of colonialism, which can also be interpreted from different perspectives. Each of these perspectives has a specific way of raising questions as well as finding answers to them.

Because of this pluralistically dimensional character of the African reality, it has become extremely difficult for theologians both north and south of the Zambezi River to unanimously agree on a theological interpretation that truly defines African reality. Here the differences between the proponents of African theology and the exponents of Black theology may be attributable to divergent interpretations of what each camp considers to be the defining characteristic of African reality. In both theological movements, these interpretations are seldom made explicit. In this sense, the debate between African theology and Black theology, which has come to be expressed theologically in terms of Africanization (or inculturation) versus liberation is, in fact, a *hermeneutic debate* between two different schools of theological interpretation in Africa.

Certainly, there is not a single universally accepted manner of interpreting reality, and one should not expect African theologians from both north and south to embrace or agree easily on a theology supposedly defined by a single coherent African reality, though we can ascertain certain common features in what Africans, as a people, are revolting against and are struggling to achieve. To be sure, there are differences in the social, economic and political structures and ideological presuppositions between independent Africa and South Africa. These differences could even be extended to include cultural, linguistic and ethnic diversity. However, for all these divergences, there is an overriding common denominator that binds the whole continent together. It is from this unyielding commonality that a common theological perspective or a synthetic theological interpretation may become possible. In their efforts to come to terms with this common reality in their different environments, both African theologians and Black theologians have already adopted in their theologies two different hermeneutic procedures: "Africanization" and "liberation."

In light of what has been said above, a profound question emerges: What is this African theological reality in which both Africanization and liberation find a common ground? In the "African Report" presented at EATWOT's Second General Assembly at Oaxtepec—a report presented jointly by theologians from both independent and South Africa—this reality was expressed as a theological challenge to all who seek to interpret the gospel of Jesus Christ within the African social context:

> The social underdevelopment of Africa represents a fundamental aspect of the anthropological pauperization of the African person. If we define pauperization as the fact of becoming or making poor, namely being deprived of all that we have acquired, all that we are and all that we can do, we shall recognize that Africa is subjugated to structures which result in complete pauperization: political, economic, and social. When it is not a matter of being deprived of all that we own, but rather of all that we are—our human identity, our social roots, our history, our culture, our dignity, our rights, our hopes, and our plans—then pauperization becomes anthropological. It then affects religious and cultural life at its very roots.[4]

The "anthropological pauperization of the African person" occurs at two different levels—the politico-socioeconomic level and the anthropologico-religiocultural level—with liberation and Africanization as the two respective responses. This kind of pauperization of the African is what has been expressed in theological circles as *anthropological poverty*, referring not only to "what we have" (affected at the sociopolitical and economic level), but also "who we are" (affected at the religiocultural level).[5]

The struggle against this anthropological pauperization of the African person is what gives Africa its theological agenda. It is indeed the pivot on which all relevant African theological interpretations and methodological considerations must rotate. Contextually, any attempt at giving theological interpretation to this agenda must wrestle with the two interpenetrating dimensions of African reality, and any God-talk in sub-Saharan Africa must be done in the light of these unyielding dimensions of African theological reality.

Unfortunately, the emergence of South African Black theology in the early 1970s brought a "hermeneutic division" between theologians in independent Africa and in South Africa. While the former located the African theological problem in the religiocultural dimension and therefore sought a *cultural* solution, the latter saw the problem mainly in the sociopolitical and economic structures and thus sought a *political* solution. Consequently, theology in Africa was deeply affected by the tension between the two contending hermeneutic approaches. Each of these approaches concentrated exclusively on one dimension of African reality at the expense of the other and failed to take into consideration the interwoven and interpenetrating nature of their inseparability.

At this point, it is worth attempting a first approximation to answer the question as to what features demarcate the boundaries of the religiocultural dimension and the sociopolitical and economic dimension of African reality which have respectively engaged the theological attention of Africans in independent Africa and in South Africa.

THE RELIGIOCULTURAL DIMENSION

As already noted, it is to the religiocultural dimension of African reality that early African theology appealed for a solution of the African problem. It is now time to take a closer look at this important aspect of African theological reality and try to assess whether or not African theology's neglect of the political dimension, which resulted in the tension with black theologians, had any theological validity. The African religiocultural existence is characterized by *cultural pluralism*, and in sub-Saharan Africa, the three major types of cultural pluralism are based on diversities in religion, ethnicity and language.

Religious Pluralism

Religion in Africa is a cultural reality; for centuries, it has been an integral expression of the African cultural background. Today, religion is still powerful in determining the thoughts and actions of the educated lawyer in modern cities and towns, as well as of the African peasant in the villages. Religion permeates every aspect of African life and, therefore, there is no dichotomy between the religious and the sociopolitical. Even the drum that accompanies the traditional ruler to the *durbar* grounds speaks a religious language.[6] Such a unitary perception of life in the African context doubtlessly has theological implications.

Contemporary Africa is a continent of mixed religion with three major religious traditions: the *host* religion — African traditional religion (ATR) — and the two guest religions — Christianity and Islam. Although these guest religions — the religion of the cross and the religion of the crescent — have gained much ground at the expense of the host religion, nonetheless the underlying philosophy and worldview of traditional African religions have by no means declined. In addition, ATR has been the foundation upon which many of the new religious sects of both Christianity and Islam have been based.[7]

Africa's religious pluralism presents the continent with a triple religious heritage for any authentic conversation about both the human experience of reality and of the Ultimate Reality. The theologian must therefore listen to all the perspectives on reality in the continent before proclaiming this by word and action. Differently put, the theologian in a religious pluralistic society must respect the "otherness" of other interpreters of God and draw insights from them through a genuine dialogue. It is to this end that African theologians are to be commended for stressing ATR as a source of African theology; there is indeed a theological treasure residing in traditional African religious culture that African and black theologians must unearth and bring to theological consciousness. However, when the focal lens is shifted to Islam in Africa, the picture becomes grim indeed. Although evidence suggests that Islam is the majority religion in the African continent today, most contemporary African theologians are either reluctant or make no effort to include Islamic religious culture in their theological expressions and interpretation of African social reality.[8]

With less than 30 percent of the African population Christian, the majority of Africans who have their humanity pauperized or denied are non-Christian. Consequently, any theology that calls itself *African* but neither considers how the majority of Africans—most of whom are Muslim—perceive "their ultimate concern and symbolize their struggle for liberation in the idiom of non-Christian religions and cultures," nor addresses itself to their daily experiences is indeed "an esoteric luxury of a Christian minority" which the struggle for full humanity cannot afford to entertain.[9] The theologian, like the sociologist, must seek to analyze the effects of religiocultural systems on human behavior, as religious beliefs and ideas have a profound influence on praxis. In the case of Africa, Islam must no longer be excluded in theological discourse, for its continued exclusion is an impoverishment of the African theological reality.

Perhaps it is here that we might take an invaluable insight from African thinkers whose works in the nineteenth and the twentieth centuries stressed the importance of Africa's triple religious heritage and therefore provide enormous opportunities for authentic African theological reflections. The first of such great thinkers is Edward W. Blyden who, in his *Christianity, Islam and the Negro Race* (1888) distinguished three religious systems in Africa which influenced the lives of the people: traditional religions (which he described with the then-prevalent but derogatory term "paganism"); Islam; and Christianity.[10] For Blyden, who was an ordained Christian minister as well as a statesman, "paganism" had a superior morality; he rejected missionary Christianity by insisting that only black Christians could successfully evangelize Africa. But he also saw Islam as superior to "paganism."

Because of Blyden's admiration and sympathy for Islam, he has been said to be "spiritually and politically a Muslim."[11] Islam, for Blyden, was not only dynamic, well-organized and independent, but it also had more influence in Africa. As far as Africa was concerned, Islam had "practical superiority" over Christianity. Blyden also saw Christianity as a religion of the oppressor and as racist. He wrote, "Mohammedanism, in Africa, has left the native master of himself and of his home; but whenever Christianity has been able to establish itself . . . foreigners have taken possession of the country, and, in some places, rule the natives with oppressive rigor."[12] For certain reasons, Blyden saw Arabic, the language of Islam, as a good preparation for Christianity in Africa.[13] But Blyden is by no means the only African thinker who has defined the African reality in terms of the combination of the three religious influences. Perhaps no postindependent African theorist has emphasized so forcefully the need to combine the presence of traditional Africa, Islamic Africa and Euro-Christian Africa as Kwame Nkrumah in his ideological statement, *Philosophical Consciencism*.[14]

Like other African analysts, Nkrumah does not deny the traditional African egalitarian concepts of humanity and society. However, he also believes that such an old egalitarian society no longer exists; rather, we now live in a different society *because* of the influences of Islam and Euro-Christianity. Therefore, if there is to be genuine growth and development of contemporary African society, Nkrumah insists, there is the need to forge a new harmony "that will allow the combined presence of traditional Africa, Islamic Africa and Euro-Christian Africa, so that this presence is in tune with the original humanist principles underlying African society."[15] But unlike Blyden, Nkrumah's bias rather leans toward traditional Africa, for "in the new African renaissance, we place great emphasis on the presentation of history." He adds that African history must be written as the history of African society and any other outside contact "must find its place in this history *only as an African experience, even if as a crucial one.*"[16]

Certainly, both Islam and traditional religion have made invaluable contributions to the African theological reality, and the church in Africa is aware of that. For example, at its Second General Assembly in Abidjan in 1969, AACC gave special attention to Islam in Africa and the contribution that it could make toward African theological expression. Giving reasons why Islam is attractive to most Africans and enjoys incontestable prestige, AACC resolved to intensify its "Islam in Africa Project," which, among other things, should pay special attention "to the promotion of a true dialogue and a movement towards African theological expression."[17]

Ethnic Pluralism

The issue of ethnicity in Africa is a complex one. It is not easy to define an ethnic group. Ethnic groups may be organized around a common history, beliefs and tradition, and may share common social, economic and political activities, as well as a conviction that the membership of the group has common interests and a common destiny. As a sociocultural group, members of an ethnic unit may also propound a cultural symbolism that expresses their cohesiveness. It is primarily this symbolism that distinguishes one ethnic group from another. Explaining the characteristics of such a symbolism, R. H. Bates writes:

The symbolism is characterized by one or more of the following: collective myths of origin; the assertion ties of kinship or blood, be they real or putative; a mythology expressive of the cultural uniqueness or superiority of the group; and a conscious elaboration of language and heritage. In addition, ethnic groups differ from other groups in their composition; they include persons from every stage of life and every socio-economic level.[18]

What is not all that clear among analysts is the relation between "ethnic group" and "tribe." It is not precisely clear where one ends and the other begins. For instance, while some analysts insist that "ethnic groups should be distinguished from tribal groups,"[19] others seem to use both terms interchangeably.[20]

Whatever term one uses, it is clear that in Africa today "ethnicity" is looked upon with disfavor, especially in politics, since ethnic pluralism "has been seen as a major source of social and political conflict in the black African nations."[21] In some countries, conflicts between the state and ethnic or subnational groupings are overtly expressed, which may even lead to a breakdown of the political system. Ethnic group differences have presented obstacles to national unity in many countries, including Burundi, Nigeria, Kenya, Gambia and others.

In South Africa, the situation seemed different in the sense that, unlike the rest of Africa, where governments' efforts were to promote state-ethnic relations, South Africa was a society where the state deliberately promotes ethnic antagonism and racial division. With the policy of apartheid, the white minority regime deliberately promoted ethnic conflicts to ensure the control over all racial and ethnic groups through the tactics of divide and rule. The creation of the so-called homelands was seen as a furtherance of ethno-nationalism which, unfortunately, some blacks accepted. With the acceptance of this ethno-nationalistic ideology, black capitalists have emerged, whose exploitation in the black townships today presents a new challenge to both black workers and black theologians. As if this ethno-nationalistic division of blacks were not enough, the Afrikaner oppressor government tried to buttress its oppression and domination by playing off rival oppressed black groups against one another. Thousands of blacks lost their lives in the early 1990s as a result of different waves of increasingly random killings among black rival groups. Such rivalry among oppressed groups benefited no one but the oppressor, as it tended to paralyze every effort to forge a united political front against apartheid.

Therefore, to entrench white domination, the South African government developed a strategy that insisted on the ethnic distinctiveness of Zulus, Xhosas and other African tribal groupings and claimed that they could not be a single political constituency. This strategy by the racist government to systematically *denationalize* and to *retribalize* the African population had been described as "a core feature of 'grand apartheid'."[22] But this definitional criterion changed when it came to whites, who were treated as a single group, whether they were of Dutch, French, English, German, Portuguese, or Polish national origins or whether they spoke different languages or were from different religious and confessional backgrounds.

As far as the politics of Africa is concerned, ethnicity has not been given a very positive connotation. On the one hand, states have been pulled apart by the dual claims of state coherence and ethnic autonomy; on the other hand, the state itself has promoted ethnicity to entrench the ethnic domination of the Afrikaner. No doubt ethnic conflicts and "tribalism" pose a great challenge to both church and theology in Africa, as they participate in the struggle of God's people for full humanity. For instance, as a multiethnic institution, what role has the church to play in situations such as these? In its analysis of the African reality, how has African theology responded to the problem of ethnic conflicts? And if, as Pieris reminds us, tribalism is often "exploited ideologically by the enemies of social change [and] the strategy of 'divide and rule' can thwart liberation movements,"[23] then how are black theologians in South Africa responding to the ethnic conflicts in that country? How are hostilities among tribal factions in the black townships to be defused?

Certainly, the issue of ethnic pluralism as an *African* reality cannot be ignored by African and Black theology. The different manifestations—both positive and negative—in the phenomenon of ethnicity must be explored and distinctions made between those aspects that make positive contributions to the development of humankind and those that project negative results. For example, all the positive elements in ethnicity that provide a feeling of identification, cultural anchorage and a mold for shaping and nurturing African humanity must be identified and promoted. On the other hand, negative manifestations of ethnicity, such as tribalism and all that goes with it (nepotism, corruption, divisiveness and so forth) must be exposed and denounced.[24] Evidence suggests that ethnic conflicts promoted the slave trade and helped advance colonial oppression.[25]

How theology in Africa responds to the issue of ethnic diversity will determine whether this phenomenon will be a catalyst for enrichment in a pluralistic society where identities can be acquired, borrowed and exchanged for empowerment or an impoverishing factor that can generate only conflicts, inter-ethnic intra-racial violence and divisiveness.

But also in Africa, when the concept of ethnicity and theology are brought together, another kind of "conflict" emerges. In fact, the way in which the concept of ethnicity is acted out in theology in Africa is another illustration of theological tension. The inculturationists, for instance, prefer to use an "ethnic or ethnographical approach," claiming cultural specificity to illustrate what to them constitutes a *difference* in African theological reflection. This is illustrated in John Mbiti's *New Testament Eschatology in an African Background* (1971), which uses the ethnocultural worldview of the Akamba of Kenya, and in John Pobee's *Toward an African Theology* (1979), which also uses the worldview of the Akan of Ghana.

The liberationists take a different approach. There is, on the one hand, a rejection of the ethnographical approach, as shown in Manas Buthelezi's article, "Toward Indigenous Theology in South Africa."[26] For Buthelezi, Africa's problem in theology is seen not so much in its content or what he calls the "ethnographical approach" as in the "anthropological approach," not so much in the focus on the African worldview as on the creator of that worldview, namely, the African person.[27] On the other hand, liberation-oriented theologians also show a tendency to replace the concept of ethnicity with clear class consciousness. For Burgess Carr, for example, tribalism in Africa should be seen as class struggle.[28]

Language Pluralism

Africa is classified into at least four major language families. There is, first of all, the *Congo-Kordofanian*, which embraces the Niger-Congo and the Kordofan languages and includes the Sudanic languages of West Africa extending eastward to the Bantu of Central, East and Southern Africa. The *Afro-Asiatic* group belongs to the Semito-Hamitic family. It consists of the Berber languages of North Africa, the Ancient Egyptian, Semitic, Cushitic and the Chadic languages. The *Nilo-Saharan* groups languages in the Sudanic belt, such as Songhai and Kanuri, together with the many Nilotic northeastern languages. Finally, there is the *Khoisan*, which combines the Khoikhoi and the San languages, which are characterized by click sounds.[29]

As an expression of the African cultural heritage, language has certain implications for theological reflections in Africa. It is important to remember that when I talk of language, I not only mean *spoken* language, but also Black African poetry and Black African literature, which are expressions of African cultural nationalism. Also included is Black African art, which, according to Engelbert Mveng, is "essentially a *cosmic liturgy* and a *religious language*" that "is anthropological, cosmological, and liturgical."[30] If linguistics, the science of language, is said to have attained such "a degree of accuracy sufficient for it to be used for diagnosing the past,"[31] then the study of African languages will equip the theologian with an invaluable means of exploring the history of African societies. Undeniably, the riches of African culture lie hidden in African languages, waiting to be uncovered. Language can be said to represent a key that offers African theologians enormous opportunities for discovering the culture of African people:

> Language is like a bank or a museum in which, over the centuries, each ethnic group has deposited all it has built up and accumulated in the way of mental and material tools, memories and resources of the imagination. By means of an in-depth and wide-ranging study of the language (both infra- and supra-linguistic), through religious documents, fable and legal customs, medical and educational prescriptions, instruction in craft and technical skills, it is possible to uncover the entire grid pattern underlying a culture or civilization: how people

think, how they behave . . . their conceptions of . . . love, the hereafter, human destiny, and so on.[32]

The student who delves into the study of toponyms, anthroponyms and hydronyms in Africa will no doubt be exposed to pools of African religiosity and spirituality revealing not just African concepts of the Supreme Being, but also those of humankind and the rest of creation. Pieris shows this significant aspect of language pluralism when he points out that "each language is a *distinctly new way* of 'experiencing' the truth, implying that linguistic pluralism is an index of religion, culture and sociopolitical diversity."[33] For Pieris, the theological implication of language pluralism is contained in the very understanding of "language." Prepared to go beyond the nominalist view of language as the outward expression of truth, Pieris explains:

> I think it is only partially true to say that religion is an "experience" of Reality and language is its "expression"; the converse is closer to the truth: *language is the "experience" of Reality and religion is its "expression."* Religion begins with language. Would it be wrong to say that language is a *theologia incohativa* — an incipient theology?[34]

Of course, one cannot help agreeing with Pieris that language is very significant in the discussion of theological reality and that it is with language that the theologian must begin, for language is the experience of reality, as "the concepts of language are formed by the immediate connection with reality."[35]

In the African context, language has not only been the medium through which "truth" and "reality" become established; it is as well a medium through which "order" has also been established. It may be recalled that one of the main features of imperial oppression was the control over language, which was also the medium to perpetuate the hierarchical structure of power.[36] Even decades after the colonizer has "left" the scene, there has been no cultural-linguistic independence. Most African governments see the vernaculars as both divisive and a hindrance to rapid modernization. It is only in East Africa that the Swahili language has served as a uniting force in Tanzania, Kenya and Uganda.[37] Evidence suggests that lack of linguistic unity within the countries in Africa has often created political problems as one political unit (the country) consists of several ethnic units and, therefore, linguistic diversity.

In Africa, lack of linguistic unity has created more than just political problems. Language poses a problem for theologians who continue doing theology in the language of the oppressor. It poses a problem also for the African church, which uses French or English as a common language for inter-ethnic, intra-racial dialogue. If language, as we have established, is at the very heart of culture, and if it is impossible for an authentic African cultural revolution to take place using a foreign language, then African writers, including theologians, must take African languages seriously.

But in their report to the Second General Assembly of EATWOT at Oaxtepec, African theologians, though aware of this problem, explained why it is necessary for African writers to use exoglossic languages such as English and French. For them, using the language of the oppressor is part of the cultural struggle for liberation from anthropological pauperization:

> That is why the cultural struggle for liberation cannot content itself with being defensive. It must be offensive and even aggressive. We must push the opponent into a corner. Such is the task for modern African artists and writers. We are wrong to ask them to write in African languages, because their task requires the use of Western languages for the moment. Meanwhile they have to struggle for the birth of a literature in national languages. Two cultural events of recent years illustrate that glorious fight ... Léopold Senghor's election at the French Academy and the choice of Wole Soyinka as Nobel Prize winner for literature.[38]

Thus, unlike Audre Lorde, who might be wondering whether the master's tools could indeed be used to dismantle the master's house,[39] African theologians are fully convinced that the gun, in efficient hands, could well kill its owner.

THE SOCIOPOLITICAL AND ECONOMIC DIMENSION

African Theologians of EATWOT have pointed out:

> Among the Third World continents, Africa appears essentially as a land of domination and exploitation, quartered, torn apart, divided, atomized, trampled under foot. It is the continent where frequently the people have no dignity, no rights, and no hope. These challenges are becoming more intolerable considering that natural catastrophes—which are desperately repeated—are added to evils caused by human mischief and injustice.[40]

Adrian Hastings makes a similar observation:

> The white conquest of most of today's Republic of South Africa in the 19th century was simply part of the wider scramble for Africa. The Zulus and the Xhosa, like the Ashanti and Benin, were conquered by British arms. The subsequent transference of power over black natives to white settlers was achieved by Act of Parliament in Westminster. Neither the past nor the present South Africa can be

seen apart from the history of imperialism and anti-imperialism in the wider continent.[41]

With the plethora of problems facing the black African on the African continent, only the superficial observer would separate the theological realities of South Africa from the rest of the continent. Arguably, the political and economic structures of South Africa are certainly different from those of the countries of independent Africa, but so are Nigeria's from Zimbabwe's or from Uganda's. The pluralism that characterizes Africa's existence is not unique to the continent's religiocultural life. For instance, the forms of government of the fifty-five countries in the continent cannot easily be grouped into identifiable categories. Moreover, their level of political maturity, defined in terms of duration of independent existence, covers a wide range—from Liberia in 1847 to Namibia in 1990.

South Africa, unlike most countries south of the Sahara, is a modern industrial state with the most advanced economy. However, such diversity should not blind us to the real African collective identity. There is more that unites Africans on both sides of the Zambezi than that which separates them. Like any other African state (perhaps with the exception of Liberia and Ethiopia), South Africa had been a colonial state; the only difference now is that, unlike the rest, it is still not completely governed by Africans. We must not also forget that the oppressive and dehumanizing conditions which blacks on both sides of the Zambezi are facing today—be it the most hideous racism or classism or neocolonialism—are but different ramifications of the same Western capitalist imperialism. In Africa, the gospel of Jesus Christ doubtlessly confronts us in our varying situations of political crisis, yet the basic problem of anthropological poverty is the same: "The oppressed majority in South Africa is but one wing of the great black population of Africa as a whole."[42]

Since Africa's political and economic patterns were both inherited from colonialism and the continent's socioeconomic plight "is historically rooted in the exploitation that resulted from the expansion of the world capitalist system,"[43] it is our theological task to examine the various ramifications of Western capitalist expansion in both independent and South Africa that have retarded and continue to retard the growth and development of black Africa. Is it possible to identify those factors that differentiate South Africa from the rest of black Africa? Do these factors have any hermeneutical consequence for theological reflection in both areas?

The Political Factor

In different parts of Africa today, the concrete political realities have been dominated by the ramifications of capitalist imperialism, which in the history of African people has been associated with slavery and the slave trade, colonialism, racism and neocolonialism. In decolonized Africa this domination has taken on the form of neocolonialism, while in South Africa it has been a combination of racism and colonialism of a special type.[44] "Imperialism," writes Kwame Nkrumah, "which is the highest stage of capitalism, will flourish *in different forms* as long as conditions permit it."[45]

In South Africa, the racial syndrome is the preeminent system that divides the population and permeates practically every dimension of human life. More than any other single factor, it regulates the sociopolitical structure of the country. Racial identity, Allan Boesak tells us, "determines with an overwhelming intensity, everything in a person's life."[46] The evils of apartheid and how it robbed black people of their humanity has been dealt with by many writers—Africans and non-Africans, theologians and non-theologians. African and black theologians have demonstrated how cancerous this system of apartheid is in the body politic of the world, what a "harsh and bitter reality" it is,[47] and how it is "one of the greatest scandals in the history of humanity, ranking with the blindest Nazism or anti-Semitism."[48]

Even though apartheid as a term seems to have been replaced in the official lexicon of the South African government, the basic principle remains. For instance, the constitutional "reforms" announced by the racist regime in the mid-1980s just scratched at the surface, relaxing "petty apartheid" while "grand apartheid," the actual pillars of this evil system, remained intact. Far from being a means of preserving ethnic integrity and eliminating racial conflicts, as the white South African government would have us believe, apartheid, with its numerous repressive laws and inhuman policies such as the Group Areas Act or the "homelands" policy, was clear evidence of a plan to divide and rule. Furthermore, the way the March 1992 all-white referendum was conducted without even consulting any of the negotiating parties of CODESA (most of whom were black) and the government's reluctance to accept an elected constituent assembly or an interim government to prepare and supervise democratic elections—in spite of the referendum—evidenced that, for the majority of black South Africans, the book of apartheid was not completely closed.

If the methods which the perpetrators of apartheid have adopted to oppress and dehumanize blacks in South Africa are overt and crude, the methods employed by the perpetrators of neocolonialism to exploit and depersonalize the African are covert and subtle. Kwame Nkrumah identified neocolonialism as a more serious form of imperialism because, "for those who practise it, it means power without responsibility and for those who suffer from it, it means exploitation without redress."[49]

The parallels that can be drawn between the effects of apartheid on black South Africa and the effects of neocolonialism on independent Africa are remarkably striking.

Apartheid purports to give political freedom to blacks with the homelands policy, but the white government "still acts as guardian" for these "Black nations."[50] Similarly, neocolonialism concedes "flag-independence" to African states with all the outward manifestations of international sovereignty, but, in reality, their economic systems and thus their political policies are "directed from outside."[51] The struggle against apartheid has brought ideological divisions among its black victims. The differences between ANC and PAC seem irreconcilable and disagreements still prevail between "race analysts" and "class analysts" as to the most effective analytical weapon to use to dismantle that evil system—an ideological debate that has entered and affected black theological reflection.[52] So also the struggle against neocolonialism has created among independent African states socialists and procapitalists; liberationists and integrationists; as well as "Unificationists," "Pluralists" and "Functionalists" within the Organization of African Unity (OAU).[53] Consequently, the concepts that should shape and guide African and black struggles lack clarity about the best means to fight the common enemy.

In South Africa, apartheid has employed different mechanisms to deliberately perpetuate ethnic tension among blacks in the interest of more effective control. In independent Africa, neocolonialism has also played rival tribal groups against one another, which, in the short political history of African states, had resulted in rampant coups d'état, civil wars, rebellions, or irredentism, in which an ethnic group sought to change its political allegiance from one political system to another, as was the case with the Ewe in Ghana and Togo and the Somali in Kenya and Ethiopia.

Again, if apartheid has been so cruel as to cause its victims to revolt against the system, as we saw in the Sharpeville and Soweto uprisings, neocolonialism has also caused untold hardships that invited uprisings, revolts and even revolutions. For example, both the 1979 uprising and the 1981 revolution in Ghana led by Jerry John Rawlings, like the 1983 Burkina Faso revolution led by Thomas Sankara, were desperate protests against imperialist domination which took the form of uprisings against the local elite and businessmen and women who collaborated with powerful external forces to plunder the nation's wealth.

In the apartheid state, whites are oppressing blacks, and whites have among black people collaborators who assist in perpetuating the acts of oppression. In the neocolonial states of Africa, blacks are also oppressing blacks and Africans collaborate with external forces to extract their nations' wealth. Again, in both areas, many have ended up in jail without trial for their political beliefs. Oppression is oppression, no matter who perpetuates it.

The parallels could go on and on. In the end, apartheid and neocolonialism, which have respectively dominated the realities of South Africa and independent Africa, are, in fact, two sides of the same "capitalist coin." Of course, the methods each adopts may differ, but to the black African victims both north and south, this has meant suffering, dehumanization, exploitation, denial of the meaningful and abundant life which Jesus Christ talks about—in short, anthropological pauperization.

The Socioeconomic Factor

According to Karl Marx:

Not to Have is not a mere category, it is a most disconsolate reality;
today the [one] who has nothing is nothing, for [one] is cut from
existence in general and still more from human existence. . . . Not to
Have is the most desperate spiritualism, a complete unreality of the
human, a complete reality of the dehumanized.[54]

Recent world events demonstrate the condemnation of Africa to poverty
by the world's powerful and the deprivation of black people of the responsibility of their own destiny. By the end of 1987, Africa's external debt had
risen to $218 billion. Discussing the crisis at the 1988 United Nations Spe-
cial Session on Africa, the continent was said to have come "on top of
existing social and economic deprivation" which, according to then Secretary General Javier Pérez de Cuellar, has meant "severe personal hardship
for hundreds of millions."[55]

The objective poverty of the African people stares the African church
and its theology in the face as both claim to bring these same people the
liberating message of Christ's gospel. To do theology in Africa today and
wink at the dehumanizing conditions of Africa's socioeconomic reality
involves what John Calvin called "nefarious perfidy," because this not only
constitutes a betrayal of the gospel itself, but also of the freedom of God's
own people.[56] As both independent and black South African societies
undergo painful transitions from rural to urban and from agricultural to
industrial, what Marx called the "reality of the dehumanized" poses tremendous theological challenges. These challenges range from poverty, hunger, diseases, poor housing, child and infant mortality, unemployment,
family disintegration, population explosion, inadequate or no health care
facilities and illiteracy to difficulties in transportation and inadequate communication systems.

A glance through the "economic literature" confirms the description of
Africa by EATWOT as the "continent of misery."[57] It appears underdevelopment is all that is developing in Africa, not growth. Prescriptions given
by developed countries, especially by such multilateral institutions as the
IMF and the World Bank, have always lacked the human dimension. It
seemed these Western-controlled institutions deliberately design their programs (conditions, in fact) to aggravate dependence, poverty, inequality,
subservience and vulnerability. These programs are designed without first
checking the social and economic impact they would have on human beings
with *Imago Dei*. They have neither a human face nor social concerns. They
are but designs to justify white dominance—the belief that black people
cannot govern themselves.

The general belief among African nationalists who led their respective countries to political independence was that the way economic problems would be tackled would depend on who had the political authority. This was the underlying notion of Kwame Nkrumah's biblico-political *"seek ye first the political kingdom"* and Sékou Touré's *"la primauté de la politique."* But as we have painfully come to realize, primacy in politics cannot solve Africa's acute social and economic problems in a world ruled and controlled by white supremacy.

Today, because of poverty, the very humanity of the black African in a white-controlled universe is condemned to death, as both South Africa and independent African countries have become the dumping grounds of dangerous Western nuclear and toxic industrial waste.[58] The theological reality of both independent and South African social and economic life today cannot be given any adequate interpretive analysis or be understood apart from the sociohistorical context within which black Africans have interacted with Europeans and their expansionist agenda for the past five centuries. There is "no way to understand the nature of our predicament except by confronting black experience in the various stages of the evolution of the capitalist world economy."[59]

One successive stage after another of the various ramifications of capitalist imperialism may appear to be less crude in methodology—since the dehumanization strategy acquired more sophistication in every subsequent stage—but as far as the exploitation of Africa is concerned, there has by no means been a reduction in magnitude. The *slave trade* may doubtlessly have been much more cruel and crude a method than the *colonialism* that followed it, but if the slave trade exploited African labor power outside Africa to develop the West, colonial imperialism exploited African resources *with* African labor within the African continent. And what about *neocolonialism* in postcolonial Africa, and the most hideous *racism* in the form of apartheid in post-1910 South Africa?

Racism in South Africa, like neocolonialism in the rest of Africa, is a legacy of slavery and colonialism. We have already mentioned how, according to Nkrumah, neocolonialism is worse than colonialism because it means power without responsibility and exploitation without redress. But what makes apartheid in South Africa the most heinous crime against humanity is the way it has been able to combine, successfully, all the ramification stages of capitalist exploitation to oppress its black victims: slavery, colonialism, racism and, with the creation of the "homelands," also neocolonialism. *Slavery*, because apartheid today exploits black labor outside the "Black nations"—the "homelands"—to develop white South Africa, leaving the black townships ghettoized. *Colonialism*, because apartheid exploits both the land it stole from blacks and black labor within blacks' own country. *Racism*, because apartheid discriminates against black people because of the color of their skin in terms of where to live, schools to attend, jobs to do and salary to receive, who to marry, and even in which cemetery to be buried. If in the United States, where unadulterated racism also thrives, the racial clauses are unwritten but not unspoken, in apartheid South Africa, the racial clauses are written and spoken. And finally, *neocolonialism*, because as it prevails in the rest of Africa, apartheid means white power without full responsibility for black existence and exploitation of blacks without full redress. Furthermore, the black petty bourgeoisie emerging from the "homelands" have become accessories to the exploitation of their own people by accepting as legitimate the oppressive economic status quo.

We must add as well that if in South Africa, race plays a crucial role in determining the class status with the white minority enjoying all the privileges, in neocolonial Africa, it is the very few ruling elite who, as a class, also enjoy ostentatious living. Indeed it is a theological fallacy to assume, as do some inculturationists, that the social and economic realities of South Africa have nothing whatsoever to do with the realities in independent Africa or vice versa; thus it is an error to conclude that African theology and Black theology should have nothing to do with each other.[60]

As an economic power, South African control over and menace to the frontline states is not much different from that of Western imperialist powers to the rest of Africa. For instance, just as France controls francophone Africa in the CFA franc monetary zone, so does South Africa control the rand monetary area of the Southern African Customs Union, which includes Lesotho, Botswana and Swaziland—countries whose currencies were pegged to the South African rand in 1974. The Southern African Development Coordination Conference (SADCC), whose major objective has been to reduce regional economic dependence on South Africa, has been able to draw attention in recent years to the inextricable connection between imperialist powers in the West and apartheid South Africa.[61] But since its formation in 1980, the SADCC has made very little progress toward achieving economic liberation, for two main reasons: the Western imperialist struggle for economic hegemony over Africa, especially Southern Africa, and the struggle of apartheid South Africa for regional hegemony. Margaret Lee affirms the inseparable link between these "two wars" as she writes: "These two wars, however, should not be viewed as mutually exclusive. In fact, they are one and the same since the whites in South Africa are inextricably connected with the West, both with regard to capitalism and to the belief in white supremacy."[62] This "inextricable connection" is self-evident. All Africans have suffered and continue to suffer from both apartheid South African and Western capitalist exploitation and its white-supremacy syndrome.

If SADCC states have gathered together to fight for "economic liberation" mainly from South Africa, the rest of Africa has no shortage of regional or subregional organizations devoted to bringing about what has been called "economic decolonization."[63] In West Africa, there is the Economic Community of West African States (ECOWAS), which also contains the *Communauté Économique de l'Afrique Occidentale* (CEAO) for the

French-speaking countries; in Central Africa, Economic Community of Central African States (CEEAC); and after the collapse of the East African Community in 1977, there is now the Preferential Trade Authority (PTA) for Eastern and Southern Africa. At the pan-African level, there is also the questioning of "the economic assumptions underlying the development recipe proposed by external actors" such as the IMF and the World Bank.[64] Hence, the proposal of the "Lagos Plan of Action" (LPA), which came out of the OAU economic summit in 1980 as an African alternative and approach to the crisis. All these regional and pan-African strategies came about because of the apparent failure of previous development programs drawn either by the developed *for* developing countries such as the United Nations Developing Decades, DD1 (1960s), DD2 (1970s) and DD3 (1980s)—or *between* developed and developing countries—such as the Lomé Conventions (Lomé I, II, and III) between the European Economic Community (EEC) and Africa, the Caribbean and the Pacific (ACP) countries. Most of these programs failed because they were "neocolonialist in intention and content."[65]

Presently, it is the IMF-inspired "structural adjustments" that are in vogue—Structural Adjustment Program (SAP) here, Economic Recovery Program (ERP) there, depending on the African country concerned. But since the same imperialist powers control the technology, capital, communications and other resources that could be used to maintain the economic status quo, one wonders whether an "adjustment" today or "readjustment" tomorrow within the same frame of the ongoing economic *dis*order would in themselves do anything to let loose the stranglehold. How then can Africa survive? An existential question! Would Africa perish if Africa were to *delink* its economic concerns from the conventional Western instruments that have produced no lasting solution to Africa's predicament? A probing question!

There is a serious need for an African-oriented approach to the crisis if recovery and growth, which have eluded the continent to date, are to begin. What role have theology and the church to play in guiding Africa out of these shackles? African theologians of EATWOT at the Oaxtepec Conference described Africa as the "continent of misery" and boastfully declared at that same meeting that "the African continent feeds a great part of the world with its cocoa, banana, coffee, tea, palm-oil, etc. [and], the African subsoil's abundant mineral and petroleum resources are fabulous: gold, diamonds, oil, gas, coal, uranium, iron, bauxite, manganese, etc."[66] Is this not proof that this misery of God's people in the continent is a human act, one that has been inflicted by human beings? Theology *in* Africa—African and Black theologies—must therefore grapple with this paradox.[67]

AFRICANIZATION, LIBERATION, AND THEOLOGICAL HERMENEUTICS

My attempt so far in this chapter has been to establish a link between the theological realities of blacks in South Africa and their brothers and sisters in independent Africa. Investigation of the religiocultural discussion has confirmed characteristics of cultural pluralism based on diversities in religion, ethnicity and language in both independent Africa and South Africa.[68] In the political and socioeconomic analyses—factors that have been the bone of contention between African and Black theologians—striking parallels have been drawn between the realities of the two theological areas. But do these striking similarities have implications for theological hermeneutics?

THEOLOGICAL HERMENEUTICS IN AFRICA BEGINS . . .

For African theologians, like their counterparts in Asia and Latin America, the hermeneutic presuppositions of the West are no longer considered normative in theology or praxis. Christians in Africa are seeking new ways of interpreting not only Scripture but also the human condition in their own cultural and political settings. Even among Western theologians today, the hermeneutic enterprise is not restricted to biblical exegesis or the hermeneutics of actual texts. Alongside this, they also advocate the construction of "a hermeneutic of the human world seen from various points of view as text-like, thus permitting a comparative study of the many forms of engagement of the gospel with the human situation."[69]

The hermeneutic enterprise is neither new nor unique to the field of theology. Modern hermeneutics began with Friedrich E. D. Schleiermacher, whose contribution marks a turning point in the development of hermeneutics. Schleiermacher not only epitomized the major hermeneutic theories and trends from the past, he also laid the foundation for a new beginning. Thus, hermeneutic philosophy as well as philological and historical hermeneutics are all indebted to him.[70] Schleiermacher's hermeneutics did not come out of a vacuum. In fact, it could be suggested that Schleiermacher's hermeneutics sprung from the European Romantic movement of the eighteenth and nineteenth centuries in a way similar to the process by which African theology grew from the Negritude movement or Black theology was based on the Black consciousness movement. In Europe, the *enlightened* spirit of the period "opened new dimensions and produced new tasks for hermeneutic thought."[71]

The very concept of interpretation poses a great problem in contemporary scholarship. As Paul Ricoeur has rightly observed, "There is no general hermeneutics, no universal canon for exegesis, but *only disparate and opposed theories* concerning the rules on interpretation."[72] Throughout the history of Christian theology, there has been diversity in theological hermeneutics and differing "schools" of interpretation—from the Alexandrian and Antiochene schools of late antiquity to the New Hermeneutics and Frankfurt Schools in the Western world and EATWOT in the Third World of the twentieth century. The contemporary theological scene is indeed saturated with diverse hermeneutic approaches and perspectives.

Therefore, the African search for a relevant theological hermeneutics is not only necessary for African Christian self-understanding and maturity, it is also a legitimate theological pursuit. Africans want to appropriate the riches of African insights into the human condition and the divine life, so as to enrich and enhance Christian life and thought. There are two main lines of thought regarding the character of African theological thinking. The first tends to look upon theology as "indigenizing in the sense of replacing the Western cultural incidents with African cultural elements."[73] This school of thought has come to be known as "Africanization" with different nuances in francophone and anglophone Africa and among Protestants and Roman Catholics. This hermeneutic approach emphasizes Africa's religio-cultural existence and finds expression in African theology. The second approach sets Africa's political and economic struggle within theological contexts and therefore emphasizes the sociopolitical and economic realities of the continent. This school of thought has come to be known as the "liberation" approach to theology in Africa, which also finds expression in South African Black theology.

Thus, like Rudolf Bultmann's existentialist program of *Entmythologisierung*, the two approaches of "Africanization" and "liberation" in African theological discourse are hermeneutic procedures that seek to interpret the gospel of Jesus Christ to the contemporary African in the light of the African condition. But, unlike Bultmann, the African theologian regards history as a serious part of theological hermeneutics, for it is history that guides and directs African theological action. Consequently, understanding Africa's historical reality is an integral part of the hermeneutic process. Besides, interpretation is not an end in itself, but rather a means to transform African society. The task of the theologian, like the philosopher, is not just to *interpret* reality but, as Marx reminds us with his theses on Feuerbach, to *change* it. "Africanization" and "liberation" then can be described as hermeneutic procedures that seek both *understanding* of the African cultural-political reality and *interpretation* of this reality in the light of the gospel of Jesus Christ, so as to bring about *transformation* of the oppressive status quo.

These hermeneutic models have evolved as a result of the African Christian's search for intellectual clarity and comprehensibility of the Christian faith. They are an attempt to do away with the basic Western theological frameworks, orthodoxy, liberalism and neo-orthodoxy. They evolved as a response to what the Pan-African Conference of Third World Theologians has described as Africa's need for "a new theological methodology that is different from the approaches of the dominant theologies of the West."[74] Africanization and liberation are to be seen as the Christian intellectual revolution standing behind the African revolution that is directed toward the total emancipation of African society. Both approaches find their weapons within the cultural and political environment of the living conditions of African people. The black African theologian is constantly reminded of

Kwame Nkrumah's insistence that before any social revolution can take place it must, first of all, have "standing firmly behind it an intellectual revolution, a revolution in which our thinking and philosophy are directed towards the redemption of our society."[75] The theologian is, in a sense, an intellectual activist in Africa's struggle for liberation. However, the theologian cannot identify with the struggle for liberation or claim to have solidarity with those suffering *until* both his or her intellectual and religious beliefs in the cross of Jesus Christ take on an existential dimension.

Africanization and liberation are thus new forms of theological hermeneutics developed by both African and black theologians to bring full humanity to black Africans. With these new hermeneutics, Africans have initiated a process of *theologicogenesis* in Africa—a new theological beginning that calls for an epistemological break in theological reflection. But Africans' determination to disentangle the gospel of Jesus Christ, as well as their Christian self-understanding, from Western cultural assumptions and intellectual framework began with doubts and suspicion of the ideology and the theological interpretation coming from those who have enslaved, colonized and exploited them. "Conscious suspicion" becomes an integral part of African theological hermeneutics; it is, in fact, its point of departure.

... WITH HERMENEUTICS OF SUSPICION

Behind every hermeneutics of suspicion is what Paul Ricoeur has called "truth as lying,"[76] and as the three masters of suspicion, Marx, Nietzsche and Freud, provided the destructive critique of the phenomenology of the "sacred" to clear the horizon for more authenticity, so also in our present generation Africans are calling for "a new reign of Truth." The theory of the hermeneutics of suspicion, according to Ricoeur,

> begins by *doubting* whether there is such an object and whether this object could be the place of the transformation of intentionality into kerygma, manifestation, proclamation. This hermeneutics is not an explication of the object, but *a tearing off of masks, an interpretation that reduces disguise.*[77]

The new critical questions that African Christians began to ask in the wake of the African revolution brought a new theological consciousness, an awareness that led to the suspicion of Euro-Christianity and its interpretation of Scripture.

In this awareness, Africans also began to doubt the authenticity of Western religiosity, as they realized that the missionary interpretation of the gospel did not take into account the oppressive conditions in which Africans were living under colonial administration. Rather, they saw missionaries as drumbeaters of colonialism. Nor has Euro-Christian interpretation of the gospel taken into account other factors such as the slave trade, racism, sexism and neocolonialism—factors that have contributed to Africa's underdevelopment and backwardness in world affairs.[78]

When Africans view Western theology through the lens of a hermeneutics of suspicion, it demonstrates two things. First, it portrays missionary or white theology as a specific interpretation of both the Bible and reality designed and imposed by the dominant or the privileged group in order to support and justify its own ideological interests and to maintain the oppressive status quo, albeit such intention may never be made explicit. Second, it obliges African Christians in both independent Africa and South Africa to expose and undermine Western theology and to transform theology into a weapon in the hands of the oppressed to reclaim the liberating heritage of the gospel of Jesus Christ.

History is replete with evidence that religion has been the most far-reaching and forceful instrument of legitimation. The Afrikaner civil religion attests eloquently to this fact. Since all legitimation "maintains socially defined reality," religion has been able to legitimate behavior or power so well because it "relates precarious reality constructions of empirical societies with Ultimate Reality."[79] Therefore, those engaged in the struggle for liberation must examine carefully the role in both independent and South African societies which religion has played and continues to play in legitimating oppression and domination in the areas of race, gender, class and culture. The liberation process thus begins with suspicion, raising critical questions about the oppressive elements in and interpretation of religion that have previously been taken for granted and examines how religion, when dissociated from domination, might help bring about liberation. This is the task of theologians in black Africa who, having been challenged by the liberating heritage of the gospel of Jesus the Christ, are struggling to attain full humanity for their people. But what forms has this theological struggle taken among Christians in both the north and the south?

NOTES

1. "Final Communiqué" of Pan African Conference of Third World Theologians in Kofi Appiah-Kubi and Sergio Torres, eds., *African Theology En Route* (Maryknoll, N.Y.: Orbis Books, 1979), p. 190.

2. The "African Report" presented at the Second General Assembly of EATWOT held in Oaxtepec, Mexico, in 1986 in K. C. Abraham, ed., *Third World Theologies: Commonalities and Divergences* (Maryknoll, N.Y.: Orbis Books, 1990), p. 47.

3. Ibid.

4. Ibid., p. 35.

5. See, for example, Engelbert Mveng, "Third World Theology—What Theology? What Third World?: Evaluation by an African Delegate" in V. Fabella and S. Torres, eds., *Irruption of the Third World: Challenge to Theology* (Maryknoll, N.Y.: Orbis Books, 1983), p. 220. Cf. Patrick A. Kalilombe, "Black Theology," in David F. Ford, ed., *The Modern Theologians: An Introduction to Christian Theology in the*

Twentieth Century (New York: Basil Blackwell, 1989), p. 194.

6. John S. Mbiti, *African Religions and Philosophy*, 2nd ed. (London: Heinemann, 1989), p. 15.

7. Cf. Kofi Asare Opoku, "Religion in Africa During the Colonial Era" in A. Adu Boahen, ed., *General History of Africa*, vol. 7: *Africa Under Colonial Domination 1880–1935* (Berkeley: University of California Press, 1990), p. 228.

8. The "African Report" to EATWOT VII meeting in Oaxtepec declares: "Islam is today the majority religion in the African continent. According to statistics of 1985, out of a population of 529,386,814 in Africa, 217,527,174 are Muslim, that is 41.09 percent. The total number of Christians was up to 149,318,991 or 28.20 percent. Muslims remain in the majority even in comparison to the followers of traditional religions, who number only 162,540,689 or 30.70 percent." See Abraham, *Third World Theologies*, p. 41.

Ali Mazrui has also shown how the number of Muslims in Nigeria (a black African country) alone is greater than the number of Muslims in any Arab country. He also added: "The Muslim population in the African continent is greater than the Arab population *outside Africa* by a ratio of two to one. Seventy percent of the Arab people and 65 percent of the Arab lands are now in Africa." However, two factors, according to Mazrui, continue to maintain Arab centrality in Islam, namely, the Arabic language and Mecca. See Ali A. Mazrui, *The Africans: A Triple Heritage* (Boston: Little, Brown & Co., 1986), p. 144, cf. pp. 138, 135.

9. Aloysius Pieris, "The Place of Non-Christian Religions and Cultures in the Evolution of Third World Theology," in Fabella and Torres, eds., *Irruption of the Third World*, pp. 113–14; cf. his *An Asian Theology of Liberation* (Maryknoll, N.Y.: Orbis Books, 1988), p. 87.

10. Edward W. Blyden, *Christianity, Islam and the Negro Race*, New Edition (London: Edinburgh University Press, 1967).

11. V. Y. Mudimbe, *The Invention of Africa: Gnosis, Philosophy, and the Order of Knowledge* (Bloomington, Ind.: Indiana University Press, 1988), p. 128.

12. Blyden, *Christianity, Islam and the Negro Race*, p. 309, cited in Mudimbe, *The Invention of Africa*, p. 126.

13. Mudimbe, ibid., cf. Blyden, ibid., p. 187.

14. See Kwame Nkrumah, *Consciencism: Philosophy and Ideology for Decolonization* (New York: Monthly Review Press, 1970), esp. Ch. 3.

15. Ibid., p. 70.

16. Ibid., p. 63. Emphasis mine.

17. AACC, *Engagement: Abidjan 1969* (Nairobi: AACC, 1970), p. 117.

18. R. H. Bates, "Modernization, Ethnic Competition and the Rationality of Politics in Contemporary Africa," in Donald Rothchild and Victor A. Olorunsola, eds., *State Versus Ethnic Claims: African Policy Dilemmas* (Boulder, Colo.: Westview Press, 1983), p. 153.

19. Ibid. For Bates, while "tribe" denotes a group "bound by traditional political structures to which people are linked by the mechanisms of traditional political obligations," ethnic groups "are based upon newly created organizations, forged in the competitive environment of modern nation-states" and need not be based on traditional political institutions.

20. For instance, in reference to Murdock's "Map of African Ethnic Units" which he produced in his book, *Africa* (1959), Schneider has pointed out how this ethnic map is also "commonly referred to as a tribal map." See Harold Schneider, *The*

African: An Ethnological Account (Englewood Cliffs, N.J.: Prentice-Hall Inc., 1981), p. 3; cf. the map on p. 5.

21. D. G. Morrison et al., *Black Africa: A Comparative Handbook* (New York: Free Press, 1972), p. 166.

22. Kevin Danahar, "Neo-Apartheid: Reform in South Africa," in David Mermelstein, ed., *The Anti-Apartheid Reader: South Africa and the Struggle Against White Racist Rule* (New York: Grove Press, 1987), p. 253.

23. Pieris, *An Asian Theology of Liberation*, p. 100.

24. Cf. AACC, *The Struggle Continues* (Nairobi: AACC, 1975), pp. 54f, where the ecumenical body denounced tribalism and gave recommendations as to how to combat this "unacceptable projection or application of tribalness."

25. Thus, Josiah Young could write: " . . . for [Desmond] Tutu and [Burgess] Carr, an *African* theology must emphasize liberation from . . . the ethnic and caste conflicts that fed the slave trade and, in certain cases, facilitated colonialism." See his *Black and African Theologies: Siblings or Distant Cousins?* (Maryknoll, N.Y.: Orbis Books, 1986), p. 101.

26. In Torres and Fabella, *The Emergent Gospel: Theology from the Developing World* (Maryknoll, N.Y.: Orbis Books, 1978), pp. 56-75.

27. Ibid., pp. 73, 65.

28. Burgess Carr, "The Engagement of Lusaka," *South African Outlook*, vol. 104, no. 1237, June 1974, p. 94. There are some political analysts who have also viewed ethnicity in terms of class struggle. See for example, Georg M. Gugelberger's introduction to his edited volume, *Marxism and African Literature* (Trenton, N.J.: Africa World Press, 1985), p. v, where we see his efforts to replace "the notion of ethnicity . . . with clear class consciousness."

29. This classification is first given by Joseph H. Greenberg. See his *The Languages of Africa* (Bloomington, Ind.: Indiana University Press, 1966) and also, *Studies in African Linguistic Classification* (New Haven, Conn.: Compass Publishing Company, 1955), both cited in Donald G. Morrison et al., *Black Africa*, pp. 15ff. Cf. J. Ki-Zerbo, ed., *General History of Africa* vol. 1: *Methodology and African Prehistory* (Berkeley: University of California Press/UNESCO, 1981, 1990), pp. 110f, 116ff; Roland Oliver and Brian M. Fagan, *Africa in the Iron Age: c 500 B.C. to A.D. 1400* (Cambridge: Cambridge University Press, 1975), pp. 2f; Harold K. Schneider, *The African*, p. 29.

30. Engelbert Mveng, "Black African Art as Cosmic Liturgy and Religious Language," in Kofi Appiah-Kubi and Sergio Torres, eds., *African Theology En Route*, pp. 137–38; see also his book with the same title as this article (2nd ed., Yaoundé: CLE, 1974); originally published as *L'Art d'Afrique noire. Liturgie et Langage religieux* (Paris: Mame, 1965).

31. Ki-Zerbo, *General History of Africa*, p. 5.

32. Ibid., p. 94.

33. Pieris, *An Asian Theology of Liberation*, p. 70. Cf. his article "Toward an Asian Theology of Liberation: Some Religio-Cultural Guidelines," in Douglas J. Elwood, ed., *Asian Christian Theology: Emerging Themes* (Philadelphia: Westminster Press, 1980), p. 241.

34. Ibid., p. 70, cf. Elwood, *Asian Christian Theology*, p. 241.

35. W. Heisenberg, *Physics and Philosophy* (New York: Harper & Bros., 1958), p. 200, cited in J. R. Carnes, *Axiomatics and Dogmatics* (New York: Oxford University Press, 1982), p. 1.

36. Bill Ashcroft, Gareth Griffiths, and Helen Tiffin, *The Empire Writes Back: Theory and Practice in Post-Colonial Literature* (New York: Routledge, 1989), p. 7.

37. *Swahili* is one of the two most widely spoken languages in Africa, the other being *Hausa*, spoken in West Africa. Both languages have been tremendously influenced by Arabic and Islam. Arabic has influenced other African languages as well, such as *Somali* in the East and *Wolof* in the West.

38. The "Africa Report," in Abraham, *Third World Theologies*, p. 37.

39. Cf. Audre Lorde, *Sister Outsider* (New York: The Crossing Press, 1984), pp. 110-13.

40. The "Africa Report" in Abraham, *Third World Theologies*, p. 28.

41. Adrian Hastings, *African Catholicism: Essays in Discovery* (Philadelphia/London: Trinity Press, 1989), p. 171.

42. Ibid.

43. Bernard Magubane, "The Political Economy of the Black World—Origins of the Present Crisis," in James Turner, ed., *The Next Decade: Theoretical and Research Issues in African Studies* (Ithaca, N.Y.: Cornell University Press, 1984), p. 283.

44. This notion of South Africa as a colonial state "of a special type" is a thesis developed by the South African Communist Party (SACP). According to this "colonialism of a special type" (CST) thesis, in the South African reality, "the substance of the colonial status of the Blacks" in the post-1910 period, "has remained intact even though its form may have altered." The SACP sees this reality as providing "a correct starting-point for grappling with the complex problem of the relationship between national and class struggle." See Joe Slovo, "The Working Class and Nation-building," in Maria van Diepen, ed., *The National Question in South Africa* (Atlantic Highlands, N.J./London: Zed Books, 1988), p. 148.

45. Nkrumah, *Consciencism*, p. 57. Emphasis added.

46. Allan Boesak, *If This Is Treason, I Am Guilty* (Grand Rapids, Mich.: Eerdmans/African World Press, 1987), p. 6.

47. Allan Boesak, *Black and Reformed: Apartheid, Liberation and the Calvinist Tradition* (Maryknoll, N.Y.: Orbis Books, 1984), p. 129; cf. ibid., p. 6.

48. The "African Report," in Abraham, *Third World Theologies*, p. 29.

49. Kwame Nkrumah, *Neo-Colonialism: The Last Stage of Imperialism* (New York: International Publishers, 1966), p. xi.

50. See David M. Smith, *Update: Apartheid in South Africa, 1987 Edition* (New York: Cambridge University Press, 1987), p. 35; cf. South Africa's *Official Yearbook* (RSA, 1983), p. 195.

51. Nkrumah, *Neo-Colonialism*, p. ix; cf. Patrick Masanja, "Neocolonialism and Revolution in Africa," in Torres and Fabella, eds., *The Emergent Gospel*, p. 10.

52. For the ideological differences between the ANC and the PAC, see Francis Meli, *A History of the ANC: South Africa Belongs to Us* (Bloomington, Ind.: Indiana University Press, 1988), pp. 137-40; Motsoko Pheko, *Apartheid: The Story of a Dispossessed People*, (London: Marram Books, 1984), pp. 140-80; Leatt et al., *Contending Ideologies in South Africa*, (Grand Rapids, Mich.: Wm. B. Eerdmans, 1986), pp. 89-119. For the debate between "race" and "class," see L. Sebidi, "The Dynamics of the Black Struggle . . . ," in I. J. Mosala and B. Thagale, eds., *The Unquestionable Right to be Free*, (Maryknoll, N.Y.: Orbis Books, 1986), pp. 15-19.

53. The term "Unificationist" here is used to represent Nkrumah's view which advocated for African unity a supranational federal system (Union government) of

African nations; the "Pluralists" were those countries including Nigeria, which advocated "a loose association of sovereign and equal member countries"; and the "Functionalists," led by Nyerere of Tanzania, advocated a system based on regionalism. See *West Africa*, no. 3695 (London), June 6, 1988, p. 1025.

54. Karl Marx and Frederick Engels, *The Holy Family or Critique of Critical Critique* (Moscow: Foreign Languages, 1956), p. 59.

55. See Patrick Smith's report on Africa's debt crisis, "The Slow Progress of Africa's Recovery," *West Africa*, no. 3710 (London), September 19-25, 1988, p. 1713.

56. John Calvin, *Institutes of the Christian Faith*, ed. John T. McNeill, trans. Ford L. Battles (Philadelphia: Westminster Press, 1960), IV. xx. 31.

57. See "African Report," in Abraham, *Third World Theologies*, p. 31.

58. The countries which have so far been identified include: Benin, Congo, Equatorial Guinea, Gabon, Guinea, Guinea Bissau, Nigeria, Senegal, South Africa and Zimbabwe. These dangerous chemical wastes came from the United States and Europe. See Obinna Ayadike, "Toxic Terrorism," *West Africa*, no. 3696 (London), June 20, 1988, p. 1109.

59. Magubane, "The Political Economy of the Black World . . . ," in *The Next Decade*, p. 285.

60. See, for example, John Mbiti, "An African Views American Black Theology," in Gayraud Wilmore and James Cone, eds., *Black Theology: A Documentary History, 1966-1979* (Maryknoll, N.Y.: Orbis Books, 1979), pp. 477-82.

61. The SADCC was formed in April 1980 by the nine independent nations in Southern Africa—Angola, Botswana, Lesotho, Mozambique, Tanzania, Zambia, Swaziland, Malawi and Zimbabwe.

62. Margaret Lee, "SADCC and Post-Apartheid South Africa," *TransAfrica Forum*, vol. 6, nos. 3 and 4, Spring-Summer 1989, p. 99.

63. See Charles Kwarteng, "External Influences on Africa's Economic Decolonization," in ibid, pp. 83-97.

64. Ibid., p. 84.

65. Adeolu Adegbola, "Christian Responsibility in the Political Economy of Africa," *The Ecumenical Review*, vol. 37, no. 1, January 1985, p. 91.

66. The "African Report," in Abraham, *Third World Theologies*, p. 31.

67. Ali A. Mazrui also has spoken of this which he calls "paradox of habitation" in his *The African Condition* (New York: Cambridge University Press, 1980).

68. I must point out that Islam, which is predominant in independent Africa, is not so popular among black South Africans. However, there is an Islamic presence in South Africa. See, e.g., Gail M. Gerhart, *Black Power in South Africa: The Evolution of an Ideology* (Berkeley: University of California Press, 1978), p. 203; also, Albert Nolan, *God in South Africa: The Challenge of the Gospel* (Grand Rapids, Mich.: Eerdmans/David Philip, 1988), p. 219.

69. Lewis S. Mudge, "Hermeneutics," in Alan Richardson and John Bowden, eds., *The Westminster Dictionary of Christian Theology* (Philadelphia: Westminster Press, 1983), p. 253. Cf. Paul Ricoeur, *Freud and Philosophy: An Essay on Interpretation* (New Haven, Conn.: Yale University Press, 1970), p. 26; Jürgen Moltmann, *The Crucified God: The Cross of Christ as the Foundation and Criticism of Christian Theology* (London: SCM Press, 1974), p. 292; David Tracy, *Plurality and Ambiguity: Hermeneutics, Religion, Hope* (San Francisco: Harper & Row, 1987), pp. 1-27.

70. The term "hermeneutic" occurred sporadically in antiquity; for example, it appeared as a title for one of Aristotle's works, *Peri Hermeneias*. In late antiquity,

hermeneutic endeavor was carried out by the Alexandrian School. It was also part of the theological culture of the Middle Ages. But it was not until the Reformation and after that hermeneutics "as a special discipline came into being." See Kurt Mueller-Vollmer, ed., *The Hermeneutic Reader* (New York: Continuum, 1990), p. 2. In addition to biblical exegesis (sacred hermeneutics), other tendencies that were instrumental for giving rise to modern hermeneutics include philosophy, philology and jurisprudence (legal hermeneutics).

71. Mueller-Vollmer, *The Hermeneutics Reader*, p. 9. For more on Schleiermacher's hermeneutic thought, see his *Hermeneutics, the Handwritten Manuscripts*, ed. Heinz Kimmerle, trans. J. Duke and J. Forstman (Sect A. Bibl) (Missoula, Mont.: Scholars Press, 1977). For a good introduction to Schleiermacher's hermeneutics, see his "Foundation: General Theory and Art of Interpretation," in Mueller-Vollmer's volume, pp. 72-97. Of Schleiermacher's contribution in this field, Mudge has commented that his work decisively "transformed the hermeneutic question from one of devising adequate 'rules' for accurate exegesis to realization that the real issue is how any understanding of another mind or culture through written communication is possible. Schleiermacher identified many issues still salient in discussion today." See Richardson and Bowden, eds., *The Westminster Dictionary of Christian Theology*, p. 251. It is also important to mention Schleiermacher's tremendous impact on Wilhelm Dilthey, whose hermeneutics has made a breakthrough in the human sciences concerning the discipline's theory and methodology.

72. Ricoeur, *Freud and Philosophy*, pp. 26f; cf. p. 20. Emphasis added.

73. Kwesi Dickson, *Theology in Africa* (Maryknoll, N.Y.: Orbis Books, 1984), p. 132.

74. See the "Final Communiqué" of EATWOT II meeting held in Accra in 1977, in Appiah-Kubi and Torres, eds., *African Theology En Route*, p. 193.

75. Nkrumah, *Consciencism*, p. 78.

76. Ricoeur, *Freud and Philosophy*, p. 32.

77. Ibid., p. 30. Emphasis mine.

78. Cf. Walter Rodney, *How Europe Underdeveloped Africa* (Washington D.C.: Howard University Press, 1982).

79. Peter Berger, *The Social Reality of Religion* (London: Penguin Books, 1973), p. 41.

3 | African Theology as Inculturation Theology

We believe that African theology must be understood in the context of African life and culture and the creative attempt of African people to shape a new future that is different from the colonial past and the neo-colonial present. ... African theology must reject, therefore, the prefabricated ideas of North Atlantic theology by defining itself according to the struggles of the people in their resistance against the structures of domination. Our task as theologians is to create a theology that arises from and is accountable to African people.
— Pan African Conference of Third World Theologians[1]

AFRICANIZATION AS INCULTURATION

THE ROOTS OF AFRICANIZATION

Africanization did not just begin with decolonization in the 1950s and 1960s. Neither was it exclusively an ecclesial nor theological phenomenon. In fact, the Christian church was not the first to use it. As a term, *Africanization*, like *liberation*, was first used in the political arena. It became associated with the nationalist movement as the structures of hegemony in the colonial states began changing hands from Europeans to Africans. As early as the mid-1920s, when tension was already growing between white control and African initiative in the Gold Coast (Ghana), then Governor Guggisberg was forced to adopt an "Africanization scheme" to put Africans in key positions in the civil service.[2] This transfer of leadership and management authority later affected every field where there was European presence or domination, including the church.[3]

It is not surprising, therefore, that in 1954 the Rev. Peter K. Dagadu of Ghana addressed the World Council of Churches' Second Assembly at Evanston on the urgent need to Africanize the church on the continent. He declared,

It is becoming increasingly necessary for the missionaries to hasten their Africanization policy so as to overtake the political advancement in certain areas where African leadership is an accepted feature of

63

life. The training for Christian leadership must now be a peculiar duty of the Church so as to capture the initiative from the secular forces. Many Africans identify Christianity with the white face, and when they see many Europeans and Americans living their lives contrary to what the European missionary demands from the African convert, they are confused.[4]

Certainly, such confusion was not absent among African church leaders themselves, as evidenced in *Des Prêtres noirs s'interrogent* (1956), the first theological attempt at Africanization—in which we find black Catholic priests "wondering" what, in the light of the black condition, the Christian faith was all about.

Thus in the 1950s and 1960s, both African Catholicism and Protestantism made daring attempts to reassess Christianity from a new perspective. For example, a post-Vatican II Catholic survey on Africa in the late 1960s showed that the main concern was "the Africanization of the church," in which the church, "must *adapt* herself to African conditions."[5] Two major problems were seen in this Africanization or adaptation process: "the lack of sufficiently numerous native clergy and of a trained Catholic laity." The task was therefore seen to be the need to train priests and lay folks to be the *cadres* of Africanization—the forerunners of new Christian Africa. Another emphasis in this process was African interpretation of Christianity which, according to this survey, meant "an African re-interpretation of the faith, and the attempt to find an African theology."[6]

Among Protestants, the problem of Africanization before the inauguration of the All Africa Conference of Churches in 1963 was discussed in relation to church unity and the new theological inquiry this called for. So, for the All Africa Churches Conference, which became the All Africa Conference of Churches (AACC) in 1963, the question of ecclesial union could best be approached within the framework of "the Church's confrontation with the world." Since this confrontation could be seen in a much more radical fashion in Africa than in the West, it was imperative, according to the churches conference, for African Christians "to make a daring attempt to reassess the traditional systems of theology from a new perspective." The Conference further noted that:

An uncritical acceptance of the theology developed in the West, and an equally uncritical rejection of anything different from it, are both signs of theological immaturity and intellectual irresponsibility in Christian obedience—obedience to the Gospel within the context of a given, concrete, social situation.[7]

It should therefore be understood why at its 1963 inaugural assembly in Kampala, AACC rejected North Atlantic theology as prefabricated and bankrupt and called for "an adequate and clear theology."[8]

During the same period, individual Protestant theologians, such as John Mbiti and especially Bolaji Idowu, began calling on the African church to come out with an "indigenized" theology. Thus, since the 1950s and 1960s, African Christians have come out with different approaches to promote Africanization. This effort did not affect just the area of theological investigation; it was also encouraged in evangelism, liturgy, pastoral work, and catechesis. What then are some of the well-known solutions that have been advanced to promote an authentic African interpretation of the Christian faith?

NUANCES OF AFRICANIZATION IN THEOLOGICAL REFLECTION

One of the visible areas of the church's Africanization process has been in the field of theology. In the last chapter, I discussed how, as a theologico-hermeneutical procedure, Africanization represents the beginning of a new theological trend toward a search for an authentically relevant African perspective on the Christian faith. In this search, different approaches and theories have been propounded to promote better understanding and knowledge of the faith, ranging from the "stepping-stone" theory (which presupposes the presence of certain conceptual tools within African culture which, if identified, could be useful in communicating the gospel message to Africans effectively) to different approaches such as adaptation, incarnation and indigenization employed by both Catholic and Protestant theologians.[9]

The discussion of Africanization as a theological reality has taken place mainly within the contexts of these different versions or nuances of the churches' Africanization programs, with African Catholicism having a more progressive but frustrating history, as dictates often came from Rome. In an effort to re-express the Christian message with African idioms and conceptual tools, expressions such as adaptation, accommodation, indigenization, translation, incarnation, localization, inculturation, interculturation and so forth have been employed to contextualize African theological discourse. Most of these expressions are used interchangeably.[10]

As we have pointed out, *Des Prêtres noirs s'interrogent*, which began the modern African theology movement, focused mainly on this trend.[11] Following "the idea of adaptation in vogue at the time, the writers proclaimed the need to Africanize Christian doctrine, cult, pastoral practices and art, basing them on African culture and religious tradition."[12] This line of thought, which later found support in the renewal from the *aggiornamento* of the Second Vatican Council (1962–1965), represents the thinking of African Catholic theologians in the 1960s and 1970s. This is illustrated in the works of Vincent Mulago, Tharcisse Tshibangu, Charles Nyamiti and others.[13]

However, a shift in theological thinking became evident among African Catholics in the mid-1970s, when they began to question the meaning of the concept of theological unity expressed in the term *adaptation*, which Vatican II as well as Pope Paul VI had encouraged.[14] The emphasis now shifted toward *incarnation* as African thinkers perceived that the theology of adaptation, which insisted on the Africanization of some external aspects, was, like the concept of indigenization among Protestants, an invention and imposition of Western missionaries and was only concerned with superficial and external trappings.[15] At the 1974 Synod of Bishops in Rome, African Catholics therefore rejected "theology of adaptation," which they considered to be "completely out of date" and accepted, rather, "theology of incarnation," which was open to the aspiration of African people.[16] *Incarnation* was preferable because it involved "immersing Christianity in African culture [so that] just as Jesus became man, so must Christianity become African."[17] Thus, after an authentic search and research, African Catholic Christians came out with a christologically oriented term deeply rooted in Scripture to describe the nature of their theological task.

However, for all its biblical foundation and christological connotation, *incarnation* was disapproved of by Pope Paul VI, even though Vatican II theology had taken the economy of the Incarnation as a point of departure for understanding the different cultures and philosophies of people.[18] The Pope's reply to the 1974 Roman Synod condemned as "dangerous" all diversified theologies and maintained that "the content of the faith is either Catholic or it is not" and urged the African bishops to find "a better expression of faith." In his own words:

> Thus we consider necessary a word on the need of finding a better expression of faith to correspond to the racial, social and cultural milieux. This is indeed a necessary requirement of authenticity and effectiveness of evangelization; it would nevertheless be dangerous to speak of diversified theologies according to continents and cultures. The content of the faith is either Catholic or it is not.[19]

If we all recognize the diversification of cultures in this world, it is difficult indeed to reconcile the papal statement, "the need of finding a better expression of faith to correspond to ... cultural milieux" with that which says it is "dangerous to speak of diversified theologies according to ... cultures." Certainly, this papal discourse undermines Vatican II theology and the Pope's own promise of the 1969 Kampala address. This discourse must be seen and evaluated as it really is.

Veritably, for the "parent Church of Europe,"[20] Africa is still an infant which must be spoon-fed theologically. Should there be any wonder that, more than two decades later, Cardinal Ratzinger, Secretary of the Congregation for the Doctrine of the Faith, could also dismiss African theology as "more a project than a reality"[21] and "harbor some anxiety" about the Ecumenical Association of African Theologians,[22] apparently because, as an ecumenical movement that includes Protestants, EAAT cannot be controlled or dictated to from Rome? With over a century of existence in the continent, the church (the people of God) in Africa must not grow to maturity but must still remain an infant—dependent and dominated. History is replete with ample evidence that the roots of Africa's suffering today not only lie in Washington, London, Paris or any of the capitals of the so-called Christian countries of the West, but also deep in the Vatican, Canterbury and Westminster.

If, as we have seen, *adaptation* and later *incarnation* had been the main preoccupation of African Catholic theologians in their Africanization efforts, in Protestant circles the common expression used had been *indigenization*. If the "theology of incarnation" had been very much favored among most francophone African theologians, among most anglophone African theologians, it had been the "theology of indigenization." And if among Roman Catholics, the Symposium of Episcopal Conferences of Africa and Madagascar (SECAM) has been the movement that has provided the context for the search and development of an authentic African theology, among Protestants, it has been the All Africa Conference of Churches (AACC).[23] But since *adaptation* had been utterly rejected by SECAM and *incarnation* by the Vatican, and it also appeared AACC was not so enthusiastic about the term *indigenization*,[24] then a new term had to be sought, if something other than the generic expression Africanization—which was used in African politics, as well—was to be preferred.

Certainly, the mid-1970s was a period of theological crisis and frustrating experience for African theologians in both Catholic and Protestant endeavors. If the "theology of incarnation" preferred by African Catholic theologians met Vatican disapproval, among English-speaking Protestants this was also a time when the spirit of alliance between North American black theologians and African theologians, which had begun as a result of the transatlantic dialogue between the two groups since 1971, was abruptly broken following Mbiti's publication of his article, "An African Views American Black Theology," which separated the two theological realities from each other.[25]

The event that both challenged African theological thinking and was timely to bring hope and new beginning was the Pan-African Conference of Third World Theologians (EATWOT II) held in Accra in 1977 which, for the first time, brought not only Roman Catholics and Protestants together, but also francophone and anglophone African theologians. This same event firmly placed the theme of liberation on the African theological agenda and prepared the ground for a new concept of theological unity that came to be expressed in the term *inculturation*. By the end of the 1970s, this term had gained currency, especially in Roman Catholic circles. Perhaps first used by Professor Joseph Masson of Gregorian University in Rome in 1962, but given much popularity in 1978 by the Jesuit Superior General, Father Pedro Arrupe, *inculturation*—a term derived from sociology and anthropology—has become a theological concept that has been added to the lexicon of contemporary theology.[26]

Ironically, the incarnation paradigm has played an essential role in defining the theological concept of inculturation. Discussants of this expression always use the economy of the Incarnation as its model, so that Jesus Christ is seen as "the subject-matter of inculturation"[27] and Jesus is regarded as "the model of incarnation and inculturation" who incarnated in one particular time and place, and whose life and ministry remain "the central paradigm for uncovering and inculturating gospel values of the kingdom into particular contexts."[28] Besides, Vatican II theology, which talked about "the economy of the incarnation"[29] but never used the expression *inculturation*, is [re-]interpreted as the point of departure for understanding inculturation.

With such reading of incarnation into the meaning of inculturation, it is therefore not surprising that although this new expression, which like adaptation was a dictation and an imposition from the West, nevertheless became attractive to Africans, despite the fact that some considered the word to be "ugly" and its sound to be "unromantic."[30] Inculturation then came to be seen as embracing the whole of Christian life and thinking, and not just "a question of liturgical adaptation or innovation, much less of the use of drums and materials." Rather, it involves "concepts, symbols, and a whole new way of thinking and doing things [demanding] imagination, courage and initiative."[31]

In theological terms, Justin Ukpong has eloquently described all that is entailed in the inculturation process:

> In this approach, the theologian's task consists in re-thinking and re-expressing the original Christian message in an African cultural milieu. It is the task of confronting the Christian faith and African culture. In the process there is inter-penetration of both. Christian faith enlightens African culture and the basic data of revelation contained in Scriptures and tradition are critically re-examined for the purpose of giving them African cultural expression. Thus there is integration of faith and culture, and from it is born a new theological reflection that is African and Christian. In this approach therefore, African theology means Christian faith attaining African cultural expression.[32]

Thus, by the mid-1980s inculturation was accepted by EAAT theologians as a theological concept in Africa and is used generically to embrace what is both known as *incarnation* in Roman Catholic circles and *indigenization* in Protestant circles. Inculturation has therefore become the common expression among African Catholics and Protestants, as well as among French- and English-speaking African theologians to pursue the phenomenon of Africanization.

TRENDS IN AFRICAN THEOLOGY

Before the inauguration of EAAT, some African theologians made attempts to map the trends of the African theological enterprise. For example, following the adaptation approach then in vogue in the early 1970s, Charles Nyamiti distinguished between three different trends: the "speculative school," with stress on philosophy; the "social and biblical school," with a more pragmatic and biblical approach; and the "militant school," with emphasis on liberation, as in South African Black theology.[33] Ngindu Mushete distinguished two stages in the development of African theology: "theology of adaptation" and "critical African theology."[34]

Following the Pan-African Conference[35] that injected the theme of liberation into African theology and EAAT's acceptance of inculturation as a theological concept, a sharp distinction began to be drawn within African theology itself between *inculturation theology* and *African liberation theology*. These two trends are to be distinguished from *Black theology* in its South African manifestation and from *African feminist or women's theology* among African women.[36] While the inculturation model continued the old way of seeking to integrate the Christian faith with African cultural life and thought forms, as shown in the works of John Mbiti, Harry Sawyerr, Bolaji Idowu, Kwesi Dickson, Edward Fasholé-Luke and others, the liberation approach took a new direction and began to set Africa's economic and political struggle within theological contexts, as seen in the writings of Jean-Marc Ela, Engelbert Mveng, Laurenti Magesa and others. While the inculturationists are mainly from anglophone Africa, the liberationists are mainly from francophone Africa. African women theologians include Mercy Oduyoye, Teresa Okure, Louise Tappa, Bette Ekeya, Thérèse Souga, Rosemary Edet, Rose Zoé-Obianga and others.[37] The four theological trends in Africa are based on the four interrelated issues which serve as well as points of departure for the respective systems: culture (inculturation theology); poverty (African liberation theology); gender (African women's theology); and race (Black theology).

Ngindu Mushete depicted the current trends well when he described theology in Africa as *"le grand combat pour un christianisme africain,"* with this struggle unfolding "in two characteristic directions which are intimately linked. One direction is the task of inculturation and the other is the task of social promotion and liberation."[38] Presently there are two major theological directions in Africa: *inculturation*, which stresses Africa's religiocultural realities and finds expression in the narrowly defined "African theology" (now inculturation theology); and *liberation*, with its emphasis on the continent's politico-socioeconomic realities, which finds expression not only in Black theology in South Africa, but also in African liberation theology and African women's theology. The future task of theologians in Africa is to develop a synthesis between these seemingly conflicting approaches, since the African theological reality cannot be reduced exclusively to the politico-socioeconomic or to the religiocultural existence of African life.

The recent writings of liberationists in independent Africa, especially Jean-Marc Ela, and of inculturationists in South Africa such as Gabriel Setiloane, indicate that even if it is remarkably reduced, the tension between the two approaches is not over.[39] I will examine two representative cases in African theology that exemplify the tension between inculturation and liberation. As a first case, I will choose the dependable *sources* that define African theology. Since no theological system that is as advanced as Christianity can evade the issue of christology and as Jesus Christ is seen as the subject-matter and the model of inculturation, I will select as a second case study, the African response to the christological question.

Since investigations have demonstrated that in Africa today the liberation boundaries are not confined to South Africa but extend to independent Africa, and also because the inculturation contours crisscross to South Africa, as the examples of Setiloane and Ela show, in dealing with the two case studies, I will not limit the analyses to liberationists in South Africa but will also include liberation-oriented theologians from independent Africa and inculturationists from both areas.

CASES OF THEOLOGICAL TENSION IN AFRICA

CASE ONE: SOURCES AND FOUNDATION OF AFRICAN THEOLOGY

It is important to remind ourselves always, when discussing the sources of African theology, that in the process of its development, African theology, has gone through different phases, and different definitions have also been offered.[40] The challenging orientation from the Pan-African Conference of EATWOT II continues to shape and direct African theological thinking. The "Final Communiqué" from this conference constantly reminds us to avoid holding a static view of African theological reality.[41] Obviously, the seemingly ambiguous "other African realities" included in the five sources mentioned by the communiqué is a clear indication that for EATWOT theologians, there is no single answer that would be valid for all time, and that in each situation a new answer ought to be sought.

Therefore, as we enter the twenty-first century, we must reexamine and rethink the raw materials, the formative factors and the dependable sources we use in defining African theology. It is to this end that I would like to mention—in light of Africa's anthropologico-religiocultural and politico-socioeconomic realities discussed earlier—the following four sources for critical analyses: 1. the Bible, Christian tradition and theological heritage; 2. African traditional religion, culture and philosophy; 3. African anthropology and other social sciences; and 4. African independent churches.

The Bible, Christian Tradition and Theological Heritage

The Bible, which is the primary witness of God's self-revelation in Jesus the Christ, is recognized by African theologians as the basic source of African theology. Accepted as the Word of God, the Bible is not only regarded as the source and norm of all Christian knowledge and the evidence of the divine will toward all humanity, but also as a diving board from which Africans "jump" into theology— a platform from which they delve deep into the waters of divine truth to search for, experience and celebrate God.

This search is also to know how the God of our ancestors has been experienced by other people of old. For instance, the Israelites' experiences of the divine in the Hebrew Scriptures and those of Jesus Christ's followers in the New Testament confirm that our experiences of God may vary or may even seem to contradict other people's experiences, which may result in tensions in our *theo*-logies. Nevertheless, we certainly deepen our understanding and knowledge about God as these various experiences demonstrate the different aspects of the total picture of God. Thus, no single *theo*logy, certainly not the inculturationist's or the liberationist's, for that matter, can present us complete *theo*-logical knowledge in Africa.

The experiences of Africans living under different conditions have demonstrated this diversity or tension in biblical hermeneutics. Differences in interpretation of Scripture become evident not just between African and South African black theologians, such as between Kwesi Dickson and Itumeleng Mosala, but also among African theologians themselves. Thus, while a theologian like John Pobee would emphasize biblical criticism and even *religionsgeschictliche Methode*,[42] for Ela, the Bible must be read correctly "in the context of African realities [and] in order to express our faith we must examine biblical *and African* symbols."[43] Whereas Dickson would unquestionably emphasize the cultural, theological hermeneutical continuity between the Bible and African life and thought,[44] a woman liberationist, such as Teresa Okure, would see the Bible and its interpretation as the embodiment of both oppressive and liberative elements.[45] For Mveng, "the Bible raises ... worrying problems," as certain concepts "can be extrapolated, twisted and manipulated to the advantage of oppressors."[46] The importance that African theologians attach to the Bible is shown not only through the publications of individual theologians,[47] but also through conferences purposefully organized on the Bible, such as the Ibadan Consultation in 1965 and the two congresses held in Jerusalem (1972) and Cairo (1987).[48]

Making Christian tradition and theological heritage part of the sources of African theology does not necessarily mean Africans are appealing to antiquity for legitimacy and recognition, nor are we sacralizing the ethnocentricity of Western thought patterns. Tradition is essential because it is "the bridge which connects Scripture with our contemporary situation."[49]

James Cone is right in pointing out that it is impossible for any student of Christianity to ignore tradition. The life and history of the Christian church go back to Jesus of Nazareth, whose meaning in Scripture is mediated through tradition. Like the Bible, tradition "opens our story of Christ to the stories in the past and thus forces us to move outside of the subjectivity of our present."[50] Tradition may contribute to biblical hermeneutics, as well, since it is possible to trace from Scripture the development of traditions.[51]

African theologians emphasize the importance of the Christian church's theological heritage because they believe it was largely shaped by Africans, among whom are included Origen, Cyprian, Tertullian, Clement of Alexandria, Athanasius and above all, Augustine. Thus, Africa has its own theological heritage which has not been fairly acknowledged by the West—a heritage that has its foundation in Scripture.[52]

African Traditional Religion, Culture and Philosophy

Together with the Bible, African traditional religion (ATR) is considered a major source of African theology. Seen also as a principal source for the study of the African concept and experience of God, ATR has become indispensable for theological hermeneutics and analysis.[53] The vitality and dynamism of ATR in contemporary African societies, despite an accelerated movement toward Islam and Christianity, is demonstrated by the fact that its underlying worldview and philosophy have never been part of the decline. It is still "the religious and cultural context from which most Christians come and in which many of them still live. . . . "[54]

Liberation-oriented African theologians of EATWOT take ATR as an important theological source because, according to them, it speaks concretely to African people in the idiom and language they understand and proposes replies to their existential questions in day-to-day life, whereas the Christianity brought from the West, with its "most elaborate theology, the most eloquent apologetics, and the most militant atheism [is] helpless."[55] In an article entitled "A Definition of a Future African Theology," Gwinyai Muzorewa has also contended that since Africans can better understand the Christian faith "through the framework of indigenous religious beliefs," traditional religious ingredients in the definition of African theology is a *conditio sine qua non*.[56]

The traditional religions have always been an inseparable part of African people's culture. Kofi Asare Opoku has described African culture as a God-given heritage which is to be understood as "the sum total of all the traditions, ideas, customs, modes of behavior, patterns of thought, ways of doing things and outlook on life that have been received from God, learned and passed on from one generation of Africans to the other."[57] After the colonial destruction of African indigenous values and religious culture, Africans all over the continent are claiming the cultural heritage of their ancestors. Examining the problems and prospects in the development of inculturation theology, Luke Mbefo has explained why Africans must redis-cover and rehabilitate the cultural heritage of their past. He writes,

> There is a widespread conviction that our ancestors had a certain self-understanding, a view of their world and of their place within it, a life-style that was their own making and in which they felt at home, a religious attitude that responded to their experience of the tran-scendence and that satisfied their expectation of the transcendent in the immanent . . . they [also] possessed a self-contained and indepen-dently developed cultural integrity that was sufficient for coping with the realities of their world of experience.

He then offers a thesis for the theological motive force behind this search;

> If we could reclaim such a cultural originality, we would be able to develop within its structural parameters a theology that is authenti-cally Christian and equally authentically [African]. The justification of this is grounded in natural theology: God had spoken to our ances-tors before the arrival of Christianity; our ancestors had responded to God's address before the arrival of Christianity. In other words, for Christianity to have meaning and relevance, it cannot come as totally alien and unconnected with the Word of God spoken to our ancestors through creation. . . . The task is to discover how this word was heard and its repercussions in the life of our ancestors. [African] theologians believe that Christianity should continue, through fulfill-ment, this original Word of God.[58]

We have also included African philosophy because, like ATR, it is an integral part of African culture. A philosophical formulation genuinely takes place within a cultural experience and a socio-historical context. The debate that ensued in the aftermath of Tempels' *La Philosophie Bantoue* (1948) — between the Belgian missionary Alexis Kagame and the disciples of the ethnophilosophical school and the anti-ethnophilosophers, or West-ern-style African philosophers such as Paulin Hountondji, Marcien Towa and F. Eboussi Boulaga — demonstrated beyond doubt that there is an Afri-can philosophy that emphasizes cultural analysis, as well as the right to demand what V.Y. Mudimbe has called "an anthropological dignity."[59] For instance, the various trends in the ethnophilosophical school of thought have shown not only how philosophy "underlies and sustains African cul-tures and civilization" or provides us with "an analysis and an interpretation of linguistic structures or anthropological patterns," but also how studies in this philosophy "could be used for the Africanization of Christianity"[60] (as exemplified in Mbiti's 1971 *New Testament Eschatology in an African Background*). In fact, part of the inculturation process is the attempt to find ways in which the Christian faith can seek understanding in the philosophy and wisdom of African people. The philosophical approach to theology in Africa is more pronounced among the neoscholastic-trained Catholic theologians, as seen in the works of Vincent Mulago, Tharcisse Tshibangu, Charles Nyamiti, O. Bimwenyi and others.

A student of African theology realizes that the way theologians employ ATR, traditional culture, and philosophy in theological analysis differs considerably, and that it is not all that easy to group theologians into clean, identifiable categories. One theologian may, for instance, use more than one methodological approach to the study of ATR. An example is the phenomenological-ontological approach of John Mbiti, not to mention his theological interests.[61] However, a close examination discloses a common approach in the inculturation endeavor and another among the liberation-oriented theologians: While among the former, the common approach tends to be phenomenological, among the latter, emphasis is placed on functional analysis.

The phenomenological approach sees religion as a symbolic manifestation of the sacred. Therefore, its task is to *describe*, not to reduce, and so it tends to remain "neutral." In other words, as a descriptive science, it "avoids evaluating the religious values of the data being analyzed."[62] However, African theologians such as John Mbiti and John Pobee, especially, would like to go beyond simple description and recommend the philosophical phenomenologies of such thinkers as E. Husserl. Pobee is therefore very much interested in Paul Tillich. On "our concern . . . with the revelation of African religion," writes Pobee, "we recommend the phenomenological approach. This is the analytical description originally pioneered by E. Husserl which was applied to theology."[63]

Functional analysis, used by liberationists such as Mosala in South Africa, Mveng in francophone Africa, as well as some African women theologians, holds the view that ATR must function to fulfill certain needs in society and the individual. For Mosala, for example, the God of ATR is a God who is actively involved in human struggle for liberation. The God of African religion, he writes, "is not simply a concept, a reality removed from the reality called the world . . . but terrifyingly present in the human struggle for survival."[64] Unlike Mbiti, who considers ATR a *praeparatio evangelica* and unsalvific, Mveng considers African religions as "religions of salvation" and the religious praxis in traditional Africa as totally centered on the liberation of human life.[65]

African Anthropology and Other Social Sciences

If anthropological poverty is the negative factor in the African struggle for full humanity, then the interlocutors of African theology must be the "anthropologically poor," whom Frantz Fanon has called "the wretched of the earth." In their search for anthropological dignity, African theologians must not just analyze the foreign factors that perpetuate this pauperization, they must as well delve deep into Africa's own anthropological understanding and how this self-understanding relates not only to the divine but also to the whole cosmos.

Recent researches in anthropological studies carried out by African scholars have been encouraging. This is reflected in the theological projects of such theologians as Mveng and Ela and some African women theologians. For Mveng, for example, the African concept of humanity must not be viewed as a monad—an individual without any concrete consistency—but must be viewed, rather, as a dialectic of the *monad*, *dyad*, and *triad*. It is two dimensions—male-female—he stresses, that constitute the human person, and not just individual. "Man without woman is nothing; woman without man is nothing. Put the two together, and you will have a person in the African sense of the word."[66] Furthermore, as a network of interpersonal relationships, this dialectic points to a corporate existence—a community.[67] It is also *cosmic*, since humanity is bonded firmly to the spiritual universe by the soul, and the material universe by the body.[68] Thus, for African theologians, "there is unity and continuity between the destiny of the human person and the destiny of the cosmos. . . . [And] the salvation of the human person in African theology is the salvation of the universe."[69] Such a unity in African anthropology, according to Mveng, has theological consequences that affect not just moral actions in society but also theological reasoning on the mystery of the Incarnation, the church and the Sacrament.[70]

The writings of African women theologians such as Oduyoye, Okure, Zoé-Obianga and others have shown contradictions between this systematic unity of view and male-female relationships in male-dominated African societies and even the Christian churches. As Mercy Oduyoye's research has shown, even among mother-centered societies as those of the Akan of Ghana,[71] there is what has been described as the "tension in male/female relationship."[72]

A major factor in Oduyoye's project is the clear and explicit anthropological vision that governs her theological efforts to heal the brokenness between men and women. She stresses mutuality between male and female, and unlike Greek metaphysics, her anthropological vision does not entail a duality between male and female, a division in which one modality is seen and regarded as superior or more human than the other, and thus closer to the divine.[73] With her anthropologico-theological vision, Oduyoye attempts not only to undermine the androcentric and patriarchal [mis]interpretation of the feminine modality of humanity, but also to retrieve in theological terms what it really means to be truly human.

The importance of the social sciences in theological hermeneutics cannot be overemphasized. To understand what God is doing in Africa today, this search for God's liberative act in history, to agree with AACC, "must receive help from the competent social scientists as [Christians] receive help from natural scientists in their search for God in nature." The African Church then concludes:

> Mere contemplation or meditation, however deeply grounded in Christian faith and devotion, is not enough, nor will biblical and theological studies alone be of much help. *Only through the collaboration of theology and social science can Christians find the answers to their questions.*[74]

Because African theology, especially as expressed in the inculturation approach, is not well informed by the social sciences, it does not have any impact on the social, political and economic life of the African masses. In his article, "Dangers de bourgeoisie dans la théologie africaine," Bénézet Bujo has shown how this lack of sociopolitical and economic impact has made African theology a kind of *l'art pour l'art*.[75] All the sciences relating to human existence are of value to theology; albeit, some may contribute more directly than others. There is no branch of scientific discipline that pertains to human life and existence to which the theologian can remain completely indifferent.

The African Independent Churches

The African independent churches, according to Kofi Asare Opoku, "have succeeded in stripping Christianity of its foreignness which has been a great handicap and have shown that Christianity can be expressed and meaningfully informed by the African religio-cultural reality."[76] The theological potentiality of the African independent churches (AICs) is acclaimed by inculturationists and liberationists alike; however, key theologians from both schools of thought have not seriously engaged the study of the movement, as they have of ATR. For example, Mveng approaches these churches as a theological locus;[77] and for Bonganjalo Goba, they not only provide "raw data for theological reflection," they should also be regarded as a point of departure for black theological reflection.[78] For Fashole-Luke, it is necessary to bring the AICs into theological focus because their innovative insights will not merely contribute toward the development of African theology, they will also prevent African theology from "becoming sterile academic exercises divorced from the life situation of . . . Africa" and from becoming a product only fit for Western consumption.[79] According to Muzorewa, the reason for considering the phenomenon as a dependable source for defining African theology is contained not merely in the fact that "it draws most of its insights from traditional religion and culture when it indigenizes the faith," but it is as well informed by "both the needs of the African soul and the Scriptures."[80]

Even though the AICs are regarded as the bearers of authenticity and have the most authentically Africanized Christianity,[81] they have not escaped scholarly criticism and derogatory remarks—from the relative deprivation theory of anthropologists and sociologists to theological epithets of "heresy," "syncretism" and "satanism."[82] Among African theologians, there is an observable tension between the inculturationists and the liberationists on their perception of the AICs. This was summed up well by Josiah Young when he wrote: "Whereas the old guard of African theology tended to correct what they perceive to be primitive and problematic syncretism in the African independent churches, the new guard asserts that these churches are the hope of African theology."[83] Evidence from Ela and Mbiti provides much plausibility for Young's conclusion. For Ela, the AICs bear African authenticity and, unlike the mission churches, reveal the liberative might of the gospel of Jesus Christ.[84] For Mbiti, the proliferation of these independent churches must stop. Speaking of the Kenyan experience, he says:

> Christianity . . . has mushroomed denominationally, and the mushroom has now been turned into a messy soup. This excessive denominationalism is absolutely scandalous. . . . This invites someone to call a halt, and if that someone is not the churches themselves, then it may well be the government. Christianity must not be allowed to become a cloak and cover for divisiveness.[85]

To some of us, the very praxis of the AICs should serve as an invaluable source for African theological analysis. Sometimes referred to as "spiritual churches" and also as "charismatic churches," most AICs stress the possession of the Holy Spirit and, in fact, bear that name. In their day-to-day life, members are "filled with the Spirit," which is revealed in *charisms* (or *charismata*) such as healing, glossolalia, prophecy and so forth. Also, "baptized in the Spirit" members of these churches usually come to a lived awareness of the distinction between the Persons of the Trinity, and the doctrine is *experienced* as living truth rather than a theological theorem.[86] So in most parts of the continent, these churches have "more exciting vistas of thought in pneumatology, ecclesiology and soteriology . . . than the 'historical' churches which still follow the hackneyed themes of their Godfathers in the West."[87] Victor Wan-Tatah has also demonstrated how salvation for the AICs is conceived of as liberation in both spiritual and material terms. He explains:

> It means social harmony and prosperity to the individual and his community. Spiritual salvation in this sense metamorphosizes into material results. In these churches, believers seek liberation from tangible misfortunes such as sickness, witchcraft and witches, barrenness . . . and impotence.[88]

If in the mission churches, Africans have been searching in vain for the Christian solution to the problem of suffering and evil, in the AICs, the emphasis on faith healing makes Africans come to find the Christian solution to suffering that has been available in the traditional African concept of healing.

The African independent churches, hailed as "the avant garde of African Christian authenticity"[89] in which "the theme of liberation is as irrepressible as traditional African spirituality,"[90] have been known to foster a combination of the various religious traditions in Africa in their search for more satisfactory answers to the plethora of problems facing contemporary life.[91]

The native prophets who gave rise to these independent churches, such as Simon Kimbangu, William Wade Harris, John Chilembwe, Simon Mpadi, Moses Tunolase, Lotin Same and Jemisimiham Jehu-Appiah, arose as individuals called by God with a message of liberation to their oppressed people.[92] It is indeed in these churches that we find "a more honest unsophisticated rebellion that is there deep down in [Africans'] hearts against Christianity as it has been handed to [them] . . . by the missionaries."[93] Still, the challenges these independent churches pose to Christianity as practiced by the mission churches and to theology in Africa are tremendous indeed.

CASE TWO: CONCEPTS OF CHRIST IN AFRICA

Who Is Jesus Christ for Africa Today?

African theology is, one often hears argued, in a "christological crisis," for Africans have difficulty integrating the person of Jesus Christ in their belief system. It is commonplace to come across, in both African and non-African writings, views ranging from the fact that Jesus' very essence is "incompatible with autochthonous religious conceptions,"[94] or that Christ is a "Guest" in Africa,[95] to the view that even the concepts of christology are nonexistent in Africa.[96]

Indeed, it is not surprising that such views are expressed about African Christianity, for the African church itself—the locus of christological reflection—has been in identity crisis since the Christian faith was planted by missionaries from Western Christendom. Kofi Appiah-Kubi strikes the right note with his lamentation that the "missionary dominated churches" in Africa basically accept conventional Western academic philosophical teachings about Christ, and therefore "Jesus Christ seems to be a spiritual intellectual or philosophical entity in the missionary churches instead of being a dynamic personal reality in all life situations. Thus, He seems to be absent in general crisis situations of the African life."[97]

How can the African integrate a colonial christ into his or her belief system? How can the African not regard a neocolonial christ as alien or as guest? Veritably, such christs do not exist in African folk Christianity. For a long time, the African theological landscape has been dominated by "Westernized" male theologians whose portrayals of Jesus, as those of the questers of the so-called historical Jesus, have told us more about themselves than about the real image of Jesus of Nazareth. With the view to indigenizing the person of Christ, most christologies of African intellectuals have been artificial constructions that have had no relevance to the context or situation in which the masses of African people live. For Gabriel Setiloane, the christ brought by the white man is elusive. In his theological poem he writes: "He eludes us still this Jesus, Son of Man."[98]

No theological system that is as advanced as Christianity can escape the christological problem, and therefore Jesus' question, "But who do you say that I am?" (Mk. 8:29) confronts the African Christian and especially the theologian, as he or she endeavors to interpret the Word of God within the context of suffering and despair and make concrete the abundant life promised to God's people (John 10:10). Any response to this christological question must begin with the acknowledgment of concrete human experience. An authentic christological inquiry in Africa cannot be divorced or separated from Africa's religiocultural, sociopolitical and economic contexts — that is, from the concreteness of everyday life within which we christologize. In fact, in today's Africa, the truth of the matter is contained not so much in the absence of christology and whether Africans are able to integrate the person of Christ in their belief system. The main issue is whether the questions that African theologians — predominantly male theologians — have been raising all these years *do concern* the ordinary woman and man. It is whether the paradigms that are used actually provide the framework within which oppressed women and men can conceptualize the person of Christ.

With the emergence of African women's voices in theology during the past decade or so, and following African theology's dialogue with other Third World theologies within the context of EATWOT, African christological discourse has changed. Like Asian and Latin American Christians, African theologians "do not hold the normal orthodox Christology of traditional Christendom as very meaningful and inspiring," and therefore reject all "the identification of Christ with the domination over the weak and poor, and male supremacy."[99]

It is therefore understandable why, in its reflection on the question, "Who do you African Christians say that I am?" the All Africa Conference of Churches could attempt, at its Fifth General Assembly, "to rescue Christology from the captivity of the Northern Churches" and endeavor "to bring Jesus Christ in the people's daily life."[100] In responding to the question Jesus poses in Mark 8:27–29, the church says:

> We must try to answer the question Christ is posing to us as Christians in Africa: some of our Churches have been operating for over 150 years. We have been able to tell the world what the early missionaries told us that Jesus was and is. The challenge to us here is after these years of work in Africa, what do we ourselves say that Jesus is?

This was 1987. AACC continues:

> In our attempt to answer the question, we must try to rescue Theology
> and therefore Christology from the shelves of universities and the
> sanctuaries of the Churches: and make it a living, dynamic, active and
> creative reality in our communities and among our people. If indeed
> Jesus has come and lived with us: He is our elder brother, liberator
> and healer.[101]

Again, that was the African church in 1987. But the voice of the church in
Africa, like that of any other Christian church—with the exception of some
African independent churches led by women—is a *male* voice; it does not
intend to speak for or address itself to African women's needs. That is why
there appears to be tension between African male and female theologians
on the issue of christology. For instance, in her article "An African Woman's Christ," Mercy Oduyoye asks whether there is such a thing as "women's
christology," since "christology is the church's word about Christ" and the
church is dominated by men. She therefore considers her contribution not
as "what the church says about Christ, but rather what one African woman
wishes the church could say about Christ."[102] In what follows, I examine
the christological tension between African male and female theologians. In
the discussion, I will as well bring out the christological differences between
the inculturationists and the liberationists.

Christologies of Inculturation and Liberation

In responding to the christological question, African male theologians
have mostly followed the New Testament pattern by conferring on Jesus
some African traditional religious and political titles and concepts that are
sometimes juxtaposed with New Testament concepts. This is what is mainly
followed in the two different approaches to theological reflection about
Jesus the Christ: the inculturationist approach, which uses mainly the traditional worldview, and the liberationist approach, which has a liberation
thrust.

The inculturationist or religiocultural approach to the christological
problem takes seriously Africa's pre-Christian and pre-Muslim religious
experience and knowledge. In this model, it is the traditional African epis-
temology that serves as a point of departure. Jesus' presence in Africa
today, the proponents of this model argue, cannot be acknowledged without
Africa's past religious knowledge and experience. For instance, the
responses that both the Jewish public and Jesus' disciples gave to the christological question(s) Jesus posed in Mark 8 indicate that people's previous
religious experience and knowledge in confessing the reality of Jesus Christ
are *sine qua non*. The answers that those confronted with Jesus' reality
gave—John the Baptist, Elijah, the (eschatological) prophet and, above all,

the Christ (Messiah) answer from Peter—were all Jewish religious and apocalyptic figures or tools.

Therefore, it is argued, there is no novelty in Peter's answer, for all he did was use an old religious (i.e., Jewish) expression for a new reality. It is this new reality that confronts all people and all ages, and, in confronting Africa, this new reality must be expressed from Africa's religious experience and knowledge. Thus, John Kurewa spoke for the theologians of the religiocultural school when he said that in responding to the question, Africans "cannot simply imitate Peter," but have to say "who Christ Jesus is from the African perspective—to express who He is and what He is doing in our midst. We cannot answer this question adequately without knowledge of our culture and our composite religious experiences as African people."[103] Again, most male theologians of the inculturation school would agree with Bolaji Idowu that if the God of our redemption is the same as the God of our creation, then, in constructing an African christology, the primal religions of Africa cannot be ignored.[104]

Certainly, for the inculturationist, Africans cannot christologize without consulting religiocultural continuities. It is to this end that some elements of African traditional religion and culture, such as ancestrology, chieftaincy, sacrifice, healing, anthropology, the concept of the family and so forth, provide the framework for constructing African christology.[105] Also, Charles Nyamiti has pointed out how, in the light of the African worldview, some African theologians such as Efoé-Julien Pénoukou have seen Jesus Christ as the fulfillment of the cosmotheandric relationship in the world—that is, a christological vision in which God, humanity and the world are united symbiotically.[106] Nyamiti has further identified two nuances in inculturation christology. He writes:

> A careful examination of the procedures undertaken by African christologists reveals two ways of approaching the subject. There are those who attempt to construct an African christology by starting from the biblical teaching about Christ and strive afterwards to find from the African cultural situation the relevant christological themes. Secondly, there are those who take the African cultural background as their point of departure for christological elaboration.[107]

The sociopolitical or liberationist approach to the christological question in Africa is held largely by South African black theologians. This model, which has been influenced by other liberation theologies of the Third World and of minorities in North America, is also preferred by African women. Faced with the realities of racism and other *isms* of oppression, the exponents of this model—Takatso Mofokeng, Allan Boesak, Bonganjalo Goba, Simon Maimela and other black theologians, as well as a few liberationists from independent Africa—claim that Jesus is the Liberator and hope of Africa, which epitomizes apostolic teachings about the significance of the

Christ-event. They therefore find as a legitimate pursuit the attempt to correlate "the liberation which is proclaimed in the gospel" to the plethora of problems that Africa is facing.[108] Jesus the Liberator is the underlying theological principle in Goba's *An Agenda for Black Theology*, in which he stresses that in the South African context, Jesus Christ is understood "as the liberator of the wretched and oppressed."[109] It is in Jesus' sharing of our common humanity, according to Goba, that Jesus opens the path of liberation in history,[110] a liberation process in which Christians are called to participate.

Another significant image, beside "Liberator," used by the theologians of this school to answer the christological question is "Black Christ" or "Black Messiah," thus taking inspiration from North American black theologians such as James Cone and Albert Cleage.[111] This approach portrays Jesus not only as the Oppressed One whose life so much reflects the life of the oppressed and marginalized black Africans, but also the One who would liberate them from their suffering and oppression.

African Women's Liberation Christology

With women's voices now being heard in theology, African christological discourse has taken on a new dimension. From the mere use of African titles to fit in New Testament concepts or the juxtaposition of African traditional symbols and biblical patterns which is understood as African christology, now stress is placed on structures in African society that oppress women and marginalize God's children and the role that Christ plays in liberating not only African women but also men. While accepting the liberation approach to christology, most women reject the cultural approach because they see African traditional culture included in the contemporary structures of oppression.[112]

Central to the christological reflection of African female theologians is the experience of women in patriarchal society and male-dominated churches. It is not surprising, therefore, that some African female theologians make women's experience the point of departure for christology. For example, Thérèse Souga writes, "We need a christology that takes into account the situation of women in the African world. Christology cannot be formulated without taking into account women and their place in church and society in Africa."[113]

In their jointly written article, "The Christ for African Women," two Ghanaian women, Elizabeth Amoah and Mercy Oduyoye, raise some important questions about women and christology,[114] one of which was whether there is such a thing as a "women's christology." Although they concede that it is the African men who have dominated the field of written theology and also allude to the fact that traditional statements of christology do not take into account women's experience of life, the authors believe that there are "some thoughts on the Christ from the perspective of African women" that could be shared with other Christians. Obviously, one has to agree with Amoah and Oduyoye that African women's christology has been there for a long time, since there have been female Christians on the continent whose christology can be ascertained not so much from the writings of African women as from the way they live and practice their Christian faith. This is evidenced not merely in the predominance of women in the churches, it is demonstrated also in women's activities in various church organizations, their contributions in Bible study, evangelism and teaching in the Sunday schools, as well as in preaching—especially in the independent churches. The tape-recording, translation from the African language into English and subsequent publishing of the prayers and praises to Jesus of an illiterate African woman belonging to the African independent church movement in Ghana clearly supports our point.[115]

According to Oduyoye and Amoah, even though African women generally "affirm the christological position of the African men, at times they go beyond it or contradict it altogether."[116] The main area where African women affirm their male counterparts' christologies is in the use of titles that are conferred on Jesus—titles such as Healer, Savior, Sacrifice, Lord, Christus Victor, and above all, Liberator. However, the interpretations that African women render to some of these titles "go beyond" those of the men. For instance, "Christus Victor" plays such a crucial role in the christologies of male theologians such as Emmanuel Milingo and John Mbiti,[117] as victory over Satan and evil spiritual forces in the world. The "Christus Victor" christology of the African women, however, is "the African women's Christ" who knows that evil is a reality in a male-dominated society, for "death and life denying are the experience of women."[118] Furthermore, the title of *Okyeame* (Go-between) that Pobee ascribes to Jesus is reinterpreted by Amoah and Oduyoye to include women: Whereas to Pobee, *Okyeame* can be nothing else but male, in the "Akan system of rule, the *Okyeame* can be either man or woman."[119]

But there are titles for Christ used by men that African women seem to reject. One of such titles is "Christ the King," which, as "a latecomer in christological imagery, does pose problems."[120] In their places new titles are substituted; the most outstanding and perhaps thought-provoking of them all is the ascription of the qualities of a woman to Jesus.[121]

The title that is given prominence in all African women's christologies is Jesus as "Liberator"—the one who liberates them from dehumanizing customs, taboos and traditions. For Oduyoye, Jesus is the One who "liberates women from the burden of disease and ostracism of a society ridden with blood-taboos of inauspiciousness arising out of women's blood."[122] Because of the inherent oppressive elements in African culture, most African women set Christ in opposition to all cultural systems that dehumanize and oppress them. For Bonita Bennet of South Africa, Jesus "did not only refrain from belittling women: He actually stood up to . . . His contemporaries to defend women."[123] According to Souga, Jesus bears "a message of liberation for every human being" and especially for those who are socially the most disadvantaged. Jesus therefore stands with the African woman today, as he did with the Jewish women of his time. Souga however laments that the church in Africa that is called by Jesus' Name has false images of women that have produced "certain negative kinds of behavior" towards women.[124] For her, the theological question about the role of women and the christological question cannot be separated. There is solidarity existing between Jesus and African women, who are the most marginalized in society.

African women reject the "Christ of dogma" or the doctrinal approach to christology that prevails in the male-dominated church. Instead, they accept the "Christ of history" who, according to Louise Tappa, defines his mission as a mission of liberation.[125] The African woman has therefore accepted Jesus as the Liberator who brings total liberation, embracing every aspect of life: "One cannot speak of physical liberation separated from spiritual liberation," for the spiritual encompasses the physical. The truly spiritual is that which embraces "all the material and physical life of the human being and our communities."[126] Tappa then challenges male supremacy in the African church and in theology. She writes: "Today it is impossible for African theology . . . to emerge and to bloom unless both African churches and African theology start out from, and develop around the situation of women in Africa."[127] Tappa reminds male theologians that the sexist is no different from the racist, for the principle that makes it possible for the one to profess Christianity while being a racist is the same principle that enables one to profess the faith while keeping women in a lower position than men. As long as African male Christians discriminate against women in the churches and in theology, she concludes, they have no moral obligation to demand liberation for blacks in South Africa, for the principle of apartheid is also preached when women are told they are not worthy to be ordained into the ministry of the church of Christ.[128]

Apparently, the emergence of African women's christology "from the underside" (Ekeya)[129] has indeed questioned the authenticity and relevance of the christologies of male theologians. Now the "crisis" is no longer the absence of christology, but rather an "irruption within the irruption" (Oduyoye) of African christological reflection.

The Ancestor-Liberator?

The question, "Who is Jesus Christ for us today?" confronts the African just like everyone else, and therefore the question, "What do Africans say Jesus Christ is?" is a legitimate one. Every christological inquirer sets out on the track of this Jesus with the inquirer's own questions and concerns in mind. For the African, these concerns and questions must be informed and shaped at the same time by Africa's worldview and thought forms and Africa's sociopolitical and economic realities. The African Christ must be able to answer this twofold concern of the oppressed and the anthropolog-ically poor, the majority of whom are women.

At the sociopolitical level, our question must be: What image of Jesus would solve Africa's multifaceted problems of poverty, racism, sexism, class-ism, colonialism, neocolonialism, imperialism, injustice, political dictator-ship and repression, imprisonment without trial, rampant coups d'état, hunger, drought, incurable diseases—in short, everything that tends to hinder the promotion of African full humanity.

At the religiocultural level, our interests should be more pneumatolog-ical (cf. 1 Cor. 12:3) to supplement the soteriological interests of the lib-erationist approach. We should search for an image that can answer our question of the nature of the Christ who, although not physically present with us today, is concerned with what happens in the human family and seeks to promote our full humanity. With these concerns, Jesus Christ could then be seen by both oppressed African women and men as Liberator and Ancestor.

As a liberator of Africa, Jesus is seen as our hope through whom, by whom and in whom God will deliver God's people from oppression and the forces of death: the One who frees women from male-dominated struc-tures in church and society, South African blacks from white supremacist domination, and the poor and the weak from the rich and the strong. For in him, there is neither Jew nor Gentile (racism), slave nor free (classism), male nor female (sexism). The liberating act of God in Christ, as it is summarized in the life and work of Jesus of Nazareth, tells us that the oppressor should never triumph over his or her victim. Our understanding of Jesus as the liberator therefore derives from both our understanding of biblical witness and the conditions within which we live in Africa today.

As an ancestor, Christ is still part of the human family. He does not live in a far distant heaven without relating to us. Never for a moment does he forget this world which gave him his being. He protects, guards and guides us. It is from Jesus the Christ that we, the whole tribes of God—we *Christ-ians*—have taken our name.

The ancestral figure as a christological reality for the African has been acclaimed by many key theologians, so that Jesus Christ has come to be seen as "the ultimate embodiment of all the virtues of the ancestors, the realization of the salvation for which they yearned."[130] Archbishop Milingo explicates and justifies the appropriateness of espousing Jesus with the ancestors.

> Giving Jesus the title of Ancestor is not just giving Him an honorary title. Jesus fits perfectly into the African understanding of ancestor. He is more than that, but we can find in Him all that we Africans are looking for in our ancestors. This is a very noble title, because when we consider Jesus as an ancestor, it means that he is to us an elder in the community, an intercessor between God (Mwari, the high god)

and our community, and the possessor of ethereal powers which enable Him to commune with the world above and with the earth. He is able to be a citizen of both worlds. This is the availability of Jesus.[131]

A significant dimension in the role played by the ancestors is how they are believed to transmit and safeguard life.[132] "As the Ancestors watch over life of their descendants and continuously strengthen it," writes François Kabasélé, "so does Christ continuously nourish the life of believers."[133] For Bénézet Bujo, the significant role that ancestors occupy in the life of Africans should stimulate theologians to construct something new and he insists, therefore, that the ancestral phenomenon be used "to find a new 'Messianic' title for Jesus Christ and work out a new theological way of speaking of him."[134] This "theology of ancestors" is seen not only as a starting point for a new christology but also as a point of departure for a new ecclesiology[135] and pneumatology.[136] If, as African theologians have contended, Jesus Christ the Liberator manifested in his earthly life "all those qualities and virtues which Africans like to attribute to their ancestors and which lead them to invoke the ancestors in daily life,"[137] then, in their establishment of a relationship with Jesus the Christ, Africans must keep in dynamic and creative tension their religiocultural and politico-socioeconomic concerns and see Jesus Christ as the Ancestor who liberates, or the liberating Ancestor.

NOTES

1. See the "Final Communiqué" of the Pan African Conference of Third World Theologians in Kofi Appiah-Kubi and Sergio Torres, eds., *African Theology En Route* (Maryknoll, N.Y.: Orbis Books, 1979), p. 193.

2. See Kwame Nkrumah, *I Speak of Freedom: A Statement of African Ideology* (New York: Frederick A. Praeger, 1961), p. 72; cf. Andrew Roberts, ed., *The Colonial Moment in Africa*: *Essay on the Movement of Minds and Material, 1900-1940* (New York: Cambridge University Press, 1990), p. 75.

3. Africanization took place in all areas of societal life; it included management and decision-making positions that governed operation of large firms, the economy, the military, ideologies such as capitalism and socialism, personnel in universities and research centers, and there was also a talk of "Africanization of the Sciences." See Mudimbe, *The Invention of Africa*, p. 169.

4. Cited in All Africa Churches Conference, *Africa in Transition*: *The Challenge and the Christian Response* (Geneva: WCC, 1962), p. 12.

5. Ernesto Gallina, *Africa Present: A Catholic Survey of Facts and Figures*, trans. Dorothy White (London: Geoffrey Chapman, 1969), pp. 12-13. Emphasis added.

6. Ibid., p. 14. Other areas to be Africanized, according to this survey, included ritual, liturgy and lay groups.

7. All Africa Churches Conference, *Africa in Transition*, p. 89.

8. AACC, *Drumbeats from Kampala* (London: Lutterworth, 1963), p. 38; cf. pp. 32ff.

9. See Ngindu Mushete, "The History of Theology in Africa: From Polemics to Critical Irenics," in Appiah-Kubi and Torres, eds. *African Theology En Route*, p. 28; O. Bimwenyi, "L'Inculturation en Afrique: attitude des agents de l'évangelisation," *Aspects du Catholicisme du Zaïre* (Kinshasa: Faculté de Théologie Catholique, 1981), pp. 263-81; Mudimbe, *The Invention of Africa*, p. 170.

10. For the meaning and relevance of each of these terms, see Peter Schineller, *A Handbook on Inculturation* (New York: Paulist Press, 1990), pp. 14-24; Aylward Shorter, *Toward a Theology of Inculturation* (Maryknoll, N.Y.: Orbis Books, 1988); Justin S. Ukpong, *African Theologies Now: A Profile* (Eldoret, Kenya: Gaba Publications, 1984), pp. 26f.; Dickson, *Theology in Africa*, p. 116.

11. Cf. Engelbert Mveng, "African Liberation Theology," *Concilium 199*, p. 22; Jean-Marc Ela, *African Cry* (Maryknoll, N.Y.: Orbis Books, 1986), p. 121.

12. Patrick Kalilombe, "Black Theology," in David F. Ford, ed., *The Modern Theologians: An Introduction to Christian Theology in the Twentieth Century* (New York/London: Basil Blackwell, 1989), p. 202.

13. See Vincent Mulago, *Un Visage africain du Christianisme* (Paris: Présence Africaine, 1965); T. Tshibangu, *Le Propos d'une théologie africaine* (Kinshasa: Presses Universitaires du Zaïre, 1974); cf. his *Théologie Positive et théologie speculative. Position traditionelle et nouvelle problématique* (Louvain-Paris: Béatrice Nauwelaerts, 1965); Charles Nyamiti, *The Way to Christian Theology for Africa* (Eldoret, Kenya: Gaba Publications, 1978).

14. See Pope Paul VI's Address to the All Africa Bishops' Symposium on July 31, 1969, in which he declared to the bishops that ". . . you may, and you must have an African Christianity," in *AFER*, vol. 10, no. 4, 1969, pp. 302-5. Following this address, African Catholic theologians began to explore "ways and means of articulating what this African Christianity is"; A. M. Lugira, "African Christian Theology," *African Theological Journal*, vol. 8, no. 1, 1979, p. 56.

15. Aylward Shorter, *African Christian Theology: Adaptation or Incarnation?* (Maryknoll, N.Y.: Orbis Books, 1977), p. 150; cf. AACC, *The Struggle Continues* (Nairobi: AACC, 1975), p. 52.

16. Shorter, *Toward a Theology of Inculturation*, p. 213; cf. ibid., p. 150.

17. Ukpong, *African Theologies Now*, p. 27.

18. Vatican II, *Ad Gentes*, no. 22. Unless otherwise stated, all references to Vatican II documents have been taken from Austin Flannery, ed., *Vatican II: The Conciliar and Post Conciliar Documents*, Revised Edition (Grand Rapids, Mich.: Eerdmans, 1988).

19. *L'Osservatore Romano*, n. 45, 7 November 1974, p. 9, cited in Shorter, *Toward a Theology of Inculturation*, p. 214.

20. Shorter, *Toward a Theology of Inculturation*, p. 247.

21. Ibid, p. 244.

22. Ela, *My Faith as an African* (Maryknoll, N.Y.: Orbis Books, 1988), p. 181.

23. There have, however, been other fronts beside these two ecumenical movements where theology in Africa has also developed, namely, the universities, seminaries and institutions of higher learning. Theology has also developed as a commitment to liberation struggles, especially in Southern Africa, where Black theology has emerged.

24. AACC, *The Struggle Continues*, p. 52.

25. Mbiti's article was first published in *Worldview*, vol. 17, no. 8, August 1974. See also Gayraud S. Wilmore and James H. Cone, eds., *Black Theology: A Docu-*

mentary History, 1966-1979 (Maryknoll, N.Y.: Orbis Books, 1979), pp. 447-82. More will be said on this later in Ch. 4.

26. For detailed information on the history and development of the term, see Shorter, *Toward a Theology of Inculturation*, pp. 10ff.; cf. Schineller, *A Handbook on Inculturation*, pp. 5ff. In a letter to the whole Society of Jesus, Father Arrupe defines inculturation as "the incarnation of the Christian life and of the Christian message in a particular cultural context, in such a way that this experience not only finds expression through elements proper to the culture in question, but becomes a principle that animates, directs and unifies the culture, transforming and remaking it so as to bring about 'a new creation'." See Pedro Arrupe, "Letter to the Whole Society on Inculturation," in *Studies in the International Apostolate of Jesuits* 7 (June 1978), p. 9; cited in Schineller, *A Handbook on Inculturation*, p. 6.

27. Shorter, *Toward a Theory of Inculturation*, p. 75.

28. Schineller, *A Handbook on Inculturation*, p. 7.

29. *Ad Gentes*, no. 22.

30. Shorter, *Toward a Theory of Inculturation*, p. 81.

31. Peter K. Sarpong, "Evangelism and Inculturation," *West African Journal of Ecclesial Studies*, vol. 2, no. 1, 1990, p. 8.

32. Ukpong, *African Theologies Now*, p. 30. Because the process has to do with the interaction or dialogue between the Christian faith and African culture, the term *interculturation* has also been suggested. See Joseph Blomjous, "Development in Mission Thinking and Practice 1959–1980: Inculturation and Interculturation," *AFER*, vol. 22, no. 6, 1980, pp. 393-98. For SECAM's interpretation of inculturation in all areas of the church's life — evangelism, catechesis, liturgy, pastoral work, as well as theological investigation, see the whole issue of *AFER*, vol. 33, nos. 1 and 2, February/April 1991.

33. Charles Nyamiti, "Approaches to African Theology," in Torres and Fabella, eds., *The Emergent Gospel*, p. 32.

34. Ngindu Mushete, in Appiah-Kubi and Torres, eds., *African Theology En Route*, p. 27.

35. The Pan-African Conference also distinguished among three different theological trends on the continent: (i) a theology which, while admitting the inherent values in the traditional religions, sees in them a preparation for the Gospel; (ii) a critical theology which comes from contact with the Bible, openness to African realities, and in dialogue with non-African theologies; and (iii) black theology in South Africa which takes seriously the black experience of oppression and the struggle for liberation. See Appiah-Kubi and Torres, eds., *African Theology En Route*, p. 192.

36. Cf. Justin Ukpong, "Theological Literature from Africa," *Concilium 199*, p. 67.

37. See Emmanuel Martey, "African Women and Theology in Africa and the Third World," *Voices from the Third World*, vol. 13, no. 2, December 1990, pp. 54-88; cf. Elizabeth Amoah and Mercy Oduyoye, "The Christ for African Women," in Virginia Fabella and Mercy Oduyoye, eds., *With Passion and Compassion: Third World Women Doing Theology* (Maryknoll, N.Y.: Orbis Books, 1988), pp. 3-65.

38. Marie J. Giblin, "African Christian Theological Resources," in Regina Bechtle and John Rathschmidt, eds., *Mission and Mysticism — Evangelism and the Experience of God* (Maryknoll, N.Y.: Maryknoll School of Theology, 1987), p. 17; cf. Ngindu Mushete, "Courants actuels de la théologie en Afrique," *Bulletin de*

Théologie Africaine, vol. 6, julliet-décembre 1984, pp. 247-52.

39. See Jean-Marc Ela, *My Faith as an African*, esp. Ch. 9 and 10; also see Gabriel M. Setiloane, *African Theology: An Introduction* (Johannesburg: Skotaville Publishers, 1986).

40. For example, for the different definitions that individual theologians and theological conferences have offered, see John Mbiti, "The Biblical Basis for Present Trends in African Theology," in Appiah-Kubi and Torres, eds., *African Theology En Route*, p. 83; John Kurewa, "The Meaning of African Theology," *Journal of Theology for Southern Africa*, no. 11, June 1975, p. 36; Kwesi Dickson, "African Theology: Origin, Methodology and Content," *The Journal of Religious Thought*, vol. 32, no. 2, Fall-Winter 1975, pp. 40f.; Muzorewa, *The Origins and Development of African Theology*, p. 96; also, AACC, *Engagement Abidjan 1969*, p. 114; EATWOT II in Appiah-Kubi and Torres, eds., *African Theology En Route*, p. 194. Cf. Mveng, "African Liberation Theology," *Concilium 199*, pp. 17ff., and Ukpong, *African Theologies Now*, p. 4.

41. The five sources of African theology given by the Pan-African Conference are in themselves "an indicative rather than exhaustive list" (Mveng). These include: (i) The Bible and Christian Heritage; (ii) African Anthropology; (iii) African Traditional Religions; (iv) African Independent Churches; and (v) Other African Realities. See Appiah-Kubi and Torres, eds., *African Theology En Route*, pp. 192f. The three major sources that all African theologians use are: (1) The Bible; (2) African Traditional Religion; and (3) African Independent Churches.

42. John Pobee, *Toward an African Theology* (Nashville: Abingdon, 1979), p. 20. And on this Pobee is supported by Setiloane, see his *African Theology: An Introduction* p. 32, where he also stresses the scientific methods of form, literary and textual criticism.

43. Ela, *African Cry*, p. 113. It must be emphasized that the liberationists as well stress scientific interpretation of the Bible but, for them, this is not an end in itself as seen in Mveng (*Concilium 199*, p. 27) and more especially among South African black theologians (e.g., Goba, Mosala, etc.) as we shall soon see.

44. Dickson, *Theology in Africa*, pp. 141ff., 19f. Cf. his "Continuity and Discontinuity Between the Old Testament and African Life and Thought," in Appiah-Kubi and Torres, eds., *African Theology En Route*, pp. 95-108; also his *Uncompleted Mission: Christianity and Exclusivism* (Maryknoll, N.Y.: Orbis Books, 1991).

45. Teresa Okure, "Women in the Bible," in V. Fabella and M. Oduyoye, eds., *With Passion and Compassion*, p. 52.

46. Mveng, "African Liberation Theology," *Concilium 199*, p. 27.

47. See Mbiti, "The Biblical Basis for Present Trends in African Theology," in Appiah-Kubi and Torres, eds., *African Theology En Route*, pp. 83-94, where he treats this in some detail.

48. For the Ibadan proceedings, see Dickson and Ellingworth, eds., *Biblical Revelation and African Beliefs*; for the proceedings of the First Congress on the Bible and Black Africa, see Engelbert Mveng and Zwi Werblowsky, *L'Afrique Noire et la Bible* (Jerusalem: Israel Interfaith Committee, 1974). The Second Cairo Congress under the theme, "Africa and the Bible," was organized by EAAT, August 14-21, 1987.

49. James Cone, *God of the Oppressed* (New York: Seabury Press, 1975), p. 113.

50. Ibid.

51. Cf. John Mbiti, ed., *Indigenous Theology and the Universal Church* (Bossey: Ecumenical Institute, 1979), p. 71.

52. See Lamin Sanneh, *West African Christianity: The Religious Impact* (Maryknoll, N.Y.: Orbis Books, 1983), Ch. 1.

53. The early well-known works on African traditional religion by both Africans and non-Africans which have contributed in this area include: Edwin W. Smith, ed., *African Ideas of God* (London: Edinburgh House Press, 1950); Geoffrey Parrinder, *African Traditional Religion* (London: Hutchinson's University Library, 1954); H. Deschamps, *Les Religions de l'Afrique noire* (Paris: Presses Universitaires de France, 1954); E. Damann, *Les Religions d'Afrique noire* (Paris: Payot, 1964); John Mbiti, *African Religions and Philosophy*; also his *Concepts of God in Africa* (London: SPCK, 1970); E. Bolaji Idowu, *African Traditional Religion: A Definition* (Maryknoll, N.Y.: Orbis Books, 1975); also his *Olodumare: God in Yoruba Belief* (London: Longmans, 1962).

54. Francis Cardinal Arrinze, "Pastoral Attention to African Traditional Religion: Letter of the President of the Secretariat for non-Christians to the Presidents of all Episcopal Conferences in Africa and Madagascar," *Bulletin*, 68, XXIII. 2, 1988, p. 102.

55. See "African Report" in Abraham, ed., *Third World Theologies*, p. 39.

56. Gwinyai Muzorewa, "A Definition of a Future African Theology," *African Theological Journal*, vol. 19, no. 2, 1990, p. 171.

57. Kofi Asare Opoku, "The Relevance of African Culture to Christianity," *Mid-stream*, vol. 13, nos. 3-4, Spring-Summer 1974, p. 153, cf. p. 155.

58. Luke Mbefo, "Theology and Inculturation: Problems and Prospects—The Nigerian Experience," *The Nigerian Journal of Theology*, vol. 1, no. 1, December 1985, p. 55.

59. Mudimbe, *The Invention of Africa*, p. 151. For more on this philosophical debate, see F. Eboussi Boulaga, "Le Bantou Problématique," *Présence Africaine*, 66, 2nd Quarter, 1968, pp. 3-40; Paulin Hountondji, *Sur la philosophie africaine* (Paris, Maspero, 1977), English tr. *African Philosophy: Myth and Reality* (Bloomington, Ind:. Indiana University Press, 1983); Marcien Towa, *Essai sur la problématique philosophie dans l'Afrique actuelle* (Yaoundé: CLÉ, 1971); cf. Alexis Kagame, *La philosophie bantu-rwandaise de l'être* (Brussels: Académie Royale des Sciences Coloniales, 1956).

60. Mudimbe, *The Invention of Africa*, p. 152.

61. Cf. Mbiti, *African Religions and Philosophy*, Ch. 2; cf. his *New Testament Eschatology in an African Background* (Oxford: Oxford University Press, 1971).

62. Jacob K. Olupona, ed., *African Traditional Religions in Contemporary Society* (New York: Paragon House, 1991), p. 29.

63. Pobee, *Toward an African Theology*, p. 21. E. Bolaji Idowu also used a pragmatic-description approach in his *Olodumare: God in Yoruba Belief* (London: Longmans, 1962).

64. Itumeleng J. Mosala, "African Traditional Beliefs and Christianity," *Journal of Theology for Southern Africa*, no. 43, June 1983, p. 22.

65. Mveng, "African Liberation Theology," *Concilium 199*, p. 28.

66. Ibid., p. 30.

67. Mveng, "Black African Art as Cosmic Liturgy and Religious Language," in Appiah-Kubi and Torres, eds., *African Theology En Route*, p. 139.

68. Mveng, "African Liberation Theology," *Concilium 199*, p. 30.

69. The Pan-African Conference's "Final Communiqué," in Appiah-Kubi and Torres, eds., *African Theology En Route*, p. 193.

70. Mveng, "African Liberation Theology," *Concilium 199*, p. 30.

71. See Mercy Oduyoye, "Feminism: A Pre-Condition for a Christian Anthropology," *African Theological Journal*, vol. 11, no. 3, 1982, pp. 193-208; also her "Christian Feminism and African Culture: The 'Hearth' of the Matter," in M. Ellis and O. Maduro, eds., *The Future of Liberation Theology* (Maryknoll, N.Y.: Orbis Books, 1989), pp. 441-49; cf. her *Hearing and Knowing* (Maryknoll, N.Y.: Orbis Books, 1986).

72. Giblin, "African Christian Theological Resources," p. 31.

73. Mercy Oduyoye, "Be a Woman and Africa Will Be Strong," in Letty Russell et al., eds., *Inheriting Our Mothers' Gardens* (Philadelphia: Westminster, 1988), p. 44.

74. AACC, *Africa in Transition*, p. 71. Emphasis added.

75. Cited by Per Frostin, *Liberation Theology in Tanzania and South Africa: A First World Interpretation* (Lund, Sweden: Lund University Press, 1988), p. 15. Cf. Bénézet Bujo, "Dangers de bourgeoisie dans la théologie africaine. Un examen de conscience," *Select*, 7 (1982), p. 10.

76. Kofi Asare Opuku, "Issues in Dialogue Between African Traditional Religion and Christianity," paper presented at WCC's Sub-Unit on Dialogue with People of Living Faiths Consultation, Kitwe, Zambia, September 22-25, 1986.

77. Mveng, "African Liberation Theology," *Concilium 199*, pp. 30f.

78. Bonganjalo Goba, *An Agenda for Black Theology: Hermeneutics for Social Change* (Johannesburg: Skotaville Publishers, 1988), pp. 53 and 54f. respectively.

79. E. W. Fashole-Luke, "Footpaths and Signposts in African Christian Theologies," *Scottish Journal of Theology*, vol. 34, no. 5, 1981, p. 401.

80. Muzorewa, "A Definition of a Future African Theology," p. 171.

81. Adrian Hastings, *African Christianity* (New York: Seabury Press, 1976), p. 53.

82. See Victor Wan-Tatah, *Emancipation in African Theology* (New York: Peter Lang, 1989), p. 155; also, Dean S. Gilliland, "How 'Christian' Are African Independent Churches?" *Missiology*, vol. 14, no. 3, July 1986, pp. 260, 264.

83. Josiah Young, "African Theology: From 'Independence' Toward Liberation," p. 46.

84. Ela, *African Cry*, p. 50.

85. Quoted in Hastings, *African Christianity*, p. 53.

86. Cf. Arnold Battlinger, ed., *The Church Is Charismatic* (Geneva: WCC, 1981), p. 125.

87. Wan-Tatah, *Emancipation in African Theology*, p. 157.

88. Ibid.

89. Hastings, *African Christianity*, p. 54.

90. Josiah Young, "African Theology: From 'Independence' Toward Liberation," p. 46.

91. Kofi Asare Opuku, "Changes Within Christianity: The Case of the Musama Disco Christo Church" in O. U. Kalu, ed., *The History of Christianity in West Africa* (New York/London: Longman Group Ltd., 1980), p. 319; cf. Richard Ray, "Christianity," in Andrew Roberts, ed., *The Colonial Moment in Africa* (New York/Cambridge: Cambridge University Press, 1986, 1990), p. 172.

92. Cf. Vittorio Lanternari, *The Religions of the Oppressed: A Study of Modern Messianic Cults* (New York: Alfred A. Knopf, 1963).

93. AACC, *Drumbeats from Kampala*, p. 32.

94. Matthew Schoffeleers, "Folk Christology in Africa: The Dialectics of the Nganga Paradigm," *Journal of Religion in Africa*, vol. 19, Fasc.2, June 1989, p. 157; cf. V. Neckebrouk, *Le peuple affligé* (Immensee: Neue Zeitschrift für Missionswissenschaft, 1983), pp. 306, who has cited a number of pertinent sources.

95. See E. B. Udoh, "Guest Christology," Ph.D. Dissertation (Princeton, N.J.: Princeton University, 1983).

96. John Mbiti, "Some African Concepts of Christology," in Georg F. Vicedom, ed., *Christ and the Younger Churches* (London: SPCK, 1972), p. 51.

97. Kofi Appiah-Kubi, "Jesus Christ—Some Christological Aspects from African Perspectives" in John Mbiti, ed., *African and Asian Contributions to Contemporary Theology* (Geneva: WCC, 1977), p. 55.

98. Gabriel M. Setiloane, "I Am An African," in Gerald H. Anderson and Thomas Stransky, eds., *Mission Trends No. 3—Third World Theologies* (New York: Paulist Press/Eerdmans, 1976), p. 130.

99. See EATWOT's Introductory Statement on "Christologies in Encounter," *Voices from the Third World*, vol. 11, no. 2, December 1988.

100. AACC, Report on the Fifth General Assembly—*A Compendium of Documents for Sections/Groups* on "Who do you African Christians say that I am?," GA/SEC.II (DOC.6), Lomé, August 1987, p. 1.

101. Ibid.

102. Mercy Oduyoye, "An African Woman's Christ," *Voices from the Third World*, vol. 11, no. 2, December 1988, p. 119.

103. J. W. Z. Kurewa, "Who do you say that I am?," *Voices from the Third World*, vol. 8, no. 1, March 1985, p. 9. For more discussions on African christology, see F. Kabasele et al., eds., *Chemins de la christologie africaine* (Paris: Desclée, 1986); J. N. K. Mugambi and Laurenti Magesa, eds., *Jesus in African Christianity: Experimentation and Diversity in African Christology* (Nairobi, Kenya: Initiative Publishers, 1989).

104. Bolaji Idowu, *Toward an Indigenous Church* (London: Oxford University Press, 1965), p. 25. Cf. Oduyoye, *Hearing and Knowing*, p. 75.

105. See, among others Pobee, *Toward an African Theology*, pp. 81ff.; Mbiti, "Some African Concepts of Christology," in Vicedom, *Christ and the Younger Churches*, pp. 51-62; Harry Sawyerr, *Creative Evangelism: Towards a New Christian Encounter with Africa* (London: Lutterworth Press, 1968); Muzorewa, *The Origins and Development of African Theology*, p. 19; Kurewa, "Who do you say that I am?," pp. 10-15.

106. Charles Nyamiti, "African Christologies Today," in Mugambi and Magesa, eds., *Jesus in African Christianity*, pp. 18f.; cf. E-J. Pénoukou, "Realité africaine et salut en Jesus Christ," *Spiritus*, vol. 23, no. 88, December 1982, pp. 374, also his "Christologie au village" in F. Kabasélé et al., eds., *Chemins de la christologie africaine* (Paris: Desclée, 1986), pp. 69-106.

107. Nyamiti, "African Christologies Today," p. 17.

108. See Simon Maimela, "Jesus Christ: The Liberator and Hope of Oppressed Africa," *Voices from the Third World*, vol. 11, no. 2, December 1988, pp. 143-44; cf. Takatso A. Mofokeng, *The Crucified Among the Crossbearers: Towards a Black Christology* (Kampen: J. H. Kok, 1983); Boesak, *Farewell to Innocence*, pp. 16ff.

109. Goba, *An Agenda for Black Theology*, p. 38.

110. Ibid., p. 39.

111. See Allan Boesak, *Black and Reformed: Apartheid, Liberation and the Calvinist Tradition* (Maryknoll, N.Y.: Orbis Books, 1984), pp. 10ff.; also his *Farewell to Innocence*, pp. 41-45; Goba, *An Agenda for Black Theology*, p. 40. Cf. James Cone, *God of the Oppressed*, pp. 133ff., also his *A Black Theology of Liberation*, 2nd ed. (Maryknoll, N.Y.: Orbis Books, 1986), pp. 119ff.; Albert Cleage, *The Black Messiah* (Trenton, N.J.: African World Press, 1968, 1989).

112. See Rosemary Edet and Bette Ekeya, "Church Women of Africa: A Theological Community," in Fabella and Oduyoye, eds., *With Passion and Compassion*, pp. 4ff.; cf. Anne Nasimiyu-Wasike, "Christology and an African Woman's Experience," in Mugambi and Magesa, eds., *Jesus in African Christianity*, pp. 123ff.

113. Thérèse Souga, "The Christ-Event From the Viewpoint of African Women: A Catholic Perspective," in Fabella and Oduyoye, eds., *With Passion and Compassion*, p. 29.

114. Ibid., pp. 35ff.

115. See Afua Kuma, *Jesus of the Deep Forest* (Accra, Ghana: Asempa Publishers, 1980). Afua Kuma's christological sayings in the Twi language were tape-recorded by Peter Ameyaw, written down by Vincent Adjepong and Michael Owusu, and were translated into English by Father Jon Kirby.

116. Fabella and Oduyoye, eds., *With Passion and Compassion*, p. 43.

117. See Emmanuel Milingo, *The World in Between* (Maryknoll, N.Y.: Orbis Books, 1984); Mbiti in *Christ and the Younger Churches*, pp. 54f.

118. Oduyoye, "An African Woman's Christology," *Voices from the Third World*, p. 123; cf. Fabella and Oduyoye, eds., *With Passion and Compassion*, p. 43.

119. Fabella and Oduyoye, eds., *With Passion and Compassion*, p. 43; cf. p. 41.

120. Ibid., p. 41.

121. Ibid., p. 44.

122. Mercy Oduyoye, "Women and Christology: An African Woman's Christ," a paper presented at the EATWOT Continental Consultation on Theology from the Third World Women's Perspective at Port Harcourt, August 19-23, 1986, p. 4; cf. ibid., p. 43.

123. Bonita Bennet, "A Critique on the Role of Women in the Church," in Mosala and Tlhagale, eds., *The Unquestionable Right to be Free*, p. 172.

124. Fabella and Oduyoye, eds., *With Passion and Compassion*, p. 25.

125. Louise Tappa, "The Christ-Event from the Viewpoint of African Women: A Protestant Perspective," in Fabella and Oduyoye, eds., *With Passion and Compassion*, p. 31.

126. Ibid., p. 32.

127. Ibid., p. 33.

128. Ibid., pp. 33f.

129. Bette J. M. Ekeya, "A Christology from the Underside," *Voices from the Third World*, vol. 11, no. 2, December 1988, pp. 17ff.

130. Bénézet Bujo, *African Theology in Its Social Context* (Maryknoll, N.Y.: Orbis Books, 1992), p. 81; cf. Charles Nyamiti, *Christ As Our Ancestor* (Gweru, Zimbabwe: Mambo Press, 1984); E. Milingo, *The World in Between*, pp. 78-80; John Pobee, *Toward an African Theology*, p. 94; Emilio de Carvalho, "What Do the Africans Say That Jesus Christ Is?" *African Theological Journal*, vol. 10, no. 2, 1981; François Kabasélé, "Christ as Ancestor and Elder Brother," in Robert J. Schreiter, ed., *Faces*

of Jesus in Africa (Maryknoll, N.Y.: Orbis Books, 1991), pp. 116-27.

131. E. Milingo, *The World in Between*, p. 78.

132. Kabasélé, "Christ as Ancestor and Elder Brother," p. 120; Bujo, *African Theology in Its Social Context*, pp. 18-21.

133. Ibid., p. 120.

134. Bujo, *African Theology in Its Social Context*, pp. 78-79.

135. Ibid., pp. 75-114.

136. Cf. Muzorewa, *The Origins and Development of African Theology*, p. 13.

137. Bujo, *African Theology in Its Social Context*, p. 80; cf. Milingo, *The World in Between*, p. 78.

4 | Black Theology as Liberation Theology

Liberation is not a theoretical proposition to be debated in a philosophy or theology seminar. It is a historical reality, born in the struggle for freedom in which an oppressed people recognize that they were not created to be seized, bartered, deeded, and auctioned. . . .

The significance of Black Theology lies in the conviction that the content of the Christian gospel is liberation, so that any talk about God that fails to take seriously the righteousness of God as revealed in the liberation of the weak and downtrodden is not Christian language.

—James Cone[1]

Black Theology, therefore, because it comes from a situation of oppression and suffering of a people who believe in God and who ask what the Gospel of Jesus Christ has to say about the situation, is also a theology of liberation.

—Allan Boesak[2]

In chapter 2, I demonstrated how, as a hermeneutic procedure, liberation has been Africa's acquisition of a new theological self-understanding. In the South African situation, liberation has emerged out of the specific context of apartheid and is based on the historical experience of black people under white supremacist domination.

In confronting the demonic power of apartheid, liberation, as a theological self-understanding, has both challenged black people to discover who they are as people with God's image and given them the determination to be participants in God's liberative activity. Black suffering and oppression, notes Bonganjalo Goba, have become "the medium through which God's promise of liberation manifests itself."[3] In this liberation promise, the oppressor, black theologians claim, will not overcome the victim; prior to any question of how God liberates in history is the biblical affirmation that God liberates. "Just as in the Old Testament," writes Allan Boesak, "the message of liberation forms the *cantus firmus* of the New Testament."[4]

Liberation as a theological category emerged because the situation in which South African black Christians found themselves was not an amorphous concept but "a reality which [was] experienced and analyzed as oppressive, killing, perverted" and through the "countless discriminatory laws and practices of the apartheid system [they were constantly] reminded of their inferiority and political immaturity from cradle to grave."[5] Liberation then came to the South African scene as "a direct aggressive response to a situation where blacks experience alienation at political, economic and cultural levels."[6]

Black theology developed from this new theological hermeneutic that seeks to emancipate oppressed blacks from white domination and to meet the challenges brought about by the vicious circle of apartheid in modern society. As the theological expression of Black consciousness, Black theology has called upon black people "to throw off the shackles of their own internal enslavement as a necessary precursor for throwing off the external enslavement."[7] Liberation, then, is the black theological choice for anthropological dignity over against anthropological poverty. It is a quest for true humanity.

LIBERATION AS THE QUEST FOR ANTHROPOLOGICAL DIGNITY

Since the anthropological medium out of which the pursuit of black theological reflection emerged has been that of deprivation and denial of human dignity, Black theology has concerned itself, first and foremost, with *liberation*, because liberation relates to the fullness of life in community. Liberation, Nyameko Pityana has explicated, "presupposes a search for humanity and for existence as a God-given being."[8] It is its struggle against this pauperization of black humanity that gives South African Black theology its authentic and peculiar African character and distinguishes it from other liberation theologies of the Third World.

In South African society, a society dominated and controlled by white supremacy, liberation, as a theological category and hermeneutic procedure, seeks to understand and interpret this black anthropological reality in the light of the gospel of Jesus Christ, to bring about a radical transformation of the dehumanizing status quo. Black theologians therefore insist that "a relevant message of the gospel is that which not only helps [blacks] to regain [their] self-confidence and respect as human being[s], but which focuses attention on the removal of the dehumanizing facets of modern life."[9] Steve Biko, for example, embraced Black theology not because he attended mission schools (Lovedale and Marianhill), for he was fully aware that these, like other Christian institutions including the churches, were "still swimming in the mire of confusion."[10] Rather Biko saw Black theology as a vehicle through which black problems could be solved and their God-created being restored. That is why he could write of Black theology as a theology seeking "to relate God and Christ once more to the black man and to his daily problems. It wants to describe Christ as a fighting God and not as a passive God who accepts a lie to exist unchallenged. It grapples with existential problems ... [and] seeks to bring God to the black man and to the truth and reality of his situation."[11]

Born out of black anthropological awareness, Black theology acknowledges the reality of the conflictual nature of the world in which both the oppressor and oppressed live. In their theological analyses, black theologians have demonstrated how this conflict-reality is symptomatic not only of the sinful alienation between God and humanity, but also of human brokenness at the horizontal level between races, classes and sexes.[12] South African society is a conflict-ridden society, a microcosm of what is happening now in our divided world. In South Africa this includes racial conflict, ethnic conflict, class conflict, ideological conflict, and conflict between the sexes. The situation out of which Black theology in South Africa emerged is a situation of conflicts. That is why black theologians would grapple with the question of "doing theology in a situation of conflict"[13] and Goba would write: "Black theological reflection is inclined to conflict theory, one which recognizes conflicting elements in society over the question of power resources."[14] For Simon Maimela, Black liberation theology attributes the alienated human existence to "injustice, oppression and the will to dominate — all of which individually and collectively breed conflict and polarization among people." He sees Black theology's liberation agenda as the attempt to bring radical transformation of the dehumanizing social system.[15]

As a theology of liberation, Black theology takes seriously the complete reality of the dehumanized, which it sees as a complete unreality of the human. Furthermore, it underscores the fact that it is the reality of the dehumanized that best reflects the conflict-reality of the South African situation. Understanding the South African reality as it really is must be done from the perspective of the oppressed; Black theology, like other liberation-oriented theologies, insists on the preferential option for the oppressed. This insistence, according to Maimela, is based not "on the compassionate feeling for the underdogs, but on ... biblical revelation." He then explains:

According to Black Theology, God has already taken sides with the oppressed, the outcasts and the despised when God elected to liberate Israel from Egyptian bondage. It is a preferential option for the poor which was brought to a new height in the coming of Jesus, who was himself a poor and oppressed man of sorrows, who suffered and was crucified as the criminal and the rejected outcast. ... [T]he preferential option for the poor is grounded on the fact that God has taken sides.[16]

Such a hermeneutic privilege of the poor and oppressed is the result of a *rereading* of the Bible and is emphasized by all liberation theologies. James Cone hammered home this biblical truth when, in his seminal work, he wrote: "In Christ, God enters human affairs and takes sides with the oppressed. Their suffering becomes his; their despair, divine despair."[17] "Oppressed peoples," Desmond Tutu adds, "must hear that, according to the Bible, this God is always on the side of the downtrodden. [God] is so graciously on their side not because they are more virtuous and better than their oppressors, but solely and simply because they are oppressed."[18]

However, in stressing the option for the poor and oppressed, Black theology, through its conscientization efforts, must seek to arouse and mobilize the oppressed blacks themselves to take a clear option against oppression and suffering and join the God of the Exodus and of Jesus the Christ to become instruments of their own liberation. The option for the poor, as Albert Nolan has observed, is not always the "commitment which the non-poor have to make to the cause of those who are oppressed. But what is far more fundamental in the Bible is the option of the poor for their own cause."[19] Apparently, the solution to the South African problem cannot be located in the gratuitous options of rich white liberals but in the revolutionary awareness of the oppressed blacks themselves.[20] It therefore follows that any God-talk in Africa today that fails to challenge marginalized women and men or exploited black workers to take a univocal option for their own cause and struggle for their own liberation is neither prophetic nor Christian.

But Black theology's emphasis on and analysis of the social reality in which oppressor and oppressed remain polarized and alienated from each other has soteriological implications. Salvation associated with the Fact of Christ is no longer perceived exclusively on an individual basis, and neither is it understood as an escape from an unjust and sinful world; rather, it is taken as a sociohistorical reality having to do with the liberation of God's people from dehumanizing and oppressive social structures. Sin then becomes not merely personal but also a collective concept, and is redefined to refer to all structural realities that are the negation of liberation. Salvation, Black theology insists, cannot be separated from sociohistorical liberation and, therefore, Maimela would contend that "salvation already achieved and promised in Christ is the precondition for historical liberation."[21] For Allan Boesak, the dilemma between liberation and salvation is totally unnecessary. This, he argues, must be rejected, because it is "a ploy of some Christians to escape the pressing challenge of the poor."[22]

Thus, while the ultimate salvation that awaits God's people at the eschaton remains a divine act, liberation—which has already been inaugurated and has begun in this world, as witnessed in the life and work of Jesus the Christ (the *Deus-Homo*)—is a joint task for both God and humankind. It is in this liberative task that we, as Christians, are called to participate to bring about the actualization of God's Reign. So, in the divine-human Jesus, black theologians believe, humanity and God have become *co-workers* in changing dehumanizing conditions and bringing about a radical transformation of the oppressive structures in this world. It is the task of Black theology, its exponents believe, to conscientize, teach and empower the oppressed blacks in a society controlled by white supremacy to join hands with the God of the Exodus and of Jesus Christ to be instruments of their own liberation.

CASES OF THEOLOGICAL TENSION

CASE ONE: EARLY SOURCES AND FOUNDATION OF BLACK LIBERATION THEOLOGY

In this section, I am going to concentrate on *early* sources and foundations of Black theology; therefore I will not discuss such essential topics as African traditional religion and the African independent churches, which are now important sources of South African Black theology. Apparently it was the exclusion of African religious culture from Black theology by its early exponents which, in the 1970s, invited criticisms from the inculturationists and later from black liberationists such as Takatso Mofokeng and Itumeleng Mosala. Mofokeng, for instance, "criticizes both Manas Buthelezi and Allan Boesak for ignoring the importance of culture in doing black theology." Like Steve Biko, Mofokeng recognizes "the existence of a damaged but thriving black culture."[23] Today, all would agree with Mokgethi Motlhabi that,

> African traditional religions and the African independent churches are some of the sources of African religious expression which need to be taken seriously in any positive search for the roots of Black theology in South Africa even as they are taken seriously in African theology itself.[24]

Since it was the early definition of Black theology that began the controversy between the inculturationists and the liberationists, I have selected four sources of nascent Black theology for examination. These include: the Black experience; Black consciousness; the Bible; and the Black American heritage.

Black Experience in History

All theological reflection and praxis takes place within a historical context, and in South Africa, the experience of black people is grounded in a history of racial oppression and economic exploitation that have left scars and wounds on the psyche and the essence of many black Africans. Black experience in South African history, as Nyameko Pityana observes, has been "a history of continuous plunder of land and cattle by the European invaders, of devastation and the decimation of peoples, followed by their economic enslavement. It is a story of treacherous deeds."[25] To be black in South Africa, Motlhabi reminds us, means "in the first place to be the victim of apartheid [and] the object of colonization, disinheritance and exploitation."[26]

Black experience under apartheid was a painful experience. It meant the denial of one's very humanity and the right to determine one's own life and future. Such an anthropological pauperization of black ontology is a blasphemous denial of the *Imago Dei* in humanity. It is out of this anthropological medium of deprived and dehumanized people that Black theology has emerged. Therefore,

> There is no truth for and about black people that does not emerge out of the context of their experience. Truth in this sense is black truth, a truth disclosed in the history and culture of black people. This means that there can be no black theology which does not take the black experience as a source for the starting point.[27]

Since Black theology developed as a conscious and systematic reflection on the black experience of suffering, it cannot be fully understood or appreciated apart from this experience, which serves as its hermeneutic point of departure.

As it reflects on what it means to be black in a hostile world controlled by white supremacy, Black theology, as James Cone has observed, attempts to "uncover the structures and forms of black experience because the categories of interpretation must arise out of the thought forms of the black experience itself."[28] In a similar vein, Simon Maimela has also pointed out how "Black theology as a conscious and systematic reflection on the black situation of racial oppression in South Africa, is born out of a historical experience of suffering, of domination and humiliation of the powerless by the powerful racial group."[29]

But this anthropological fact of "blackness" that black liberationists employ as a theological category has strongly been opposed by inculturationists from both independent and South Africa. For instance, although John Mbiti would concede that Black theology draws from the black experience and its concern for "blackness" is related to the circumstances of suffering, humiliation and racism, he condemns the concept because, for him, "racial color is not a theological concept in the Scriptures" and furthermore, theology does not arise from suffering but out of joy.[30] Unlike Desmond Tutu, who sees "black" as referring to all those "who are oppressed and are ready to apply the insights of black theology to their particular situation,"[31] for Mbiti, in reading Black theology "one becomes sated with color consciousness."[32] Mbiti makes little room (if any) for human experience in his theological enterprise, and therefore suffering has no theological import. In fact, suffering has no significance for the Christian faith, either, not even the cross of Jesus.

For Mbiti, the cross of Jesus Christ was just an ordinary event and an experience shared by all humankind. According to him, Jesus died on the cross because he was a perfect, complete, entire, mature and responsible man. ... It was as an ordinary man that Jesus died, and the great Christian *differentia* comes obviously from the fact of the Resurrection by which the Christian faith stands and falls. What happens before Easter is an experience which [human beings] share. What happens after Easter is the uniqueness of the gospel.[33]

Mbiti does not consider Jesus' death as primarily expiatory sacrifice but a symbol of a perfect human state. Elsewhere, he is equally provocative. Salvation, Mbiti declares, "is possible *without* the cross," and he considers Jesus "a Savior" not so much because of the cross but because Jesus is linked with God who, being Almighty, rescues and saves.[34] With such an interpretation of the cross, it is no wonder that for Mbiti, theology should arise out of joy.

Takatso Mofokeng sees the cross differently. For him, it is "the culmination and starting point of the way to liberation."[35] For Mofokeng, the cross has the immediate effect of making the world's victims new people who become new active subjects of their history. These victims, he stresses, are set free from all passivity and participate actively in the struggle for full humanity — a struggle that makes them "crossbearers" for true humanity. Mofokeng affirms the presence and suffering of God on the cross: It is an "event between the Son and the Father by the power of the Holy Spirit."[36] In it, God solidarizes with suffering humanity to the deepest point. In the same way, today Jesus Christ identifies and solidarizes with the poor and the oppressed in their suffering. Thus with the cross, Mofokeng concludes, Jesus raises new followers.[37]

Another inculturationist who opposes blackness as a theological category is Gabriel Setiloane. As a South African who has crossed boundaries, he compares the black experience in his country with the experiences of other black people throughout the world and concludes that the black experience has been that of poverty and oppression.[38] However, he opposes the view that theology should be "clouded by socio-political distractions."[39] Like Mbiti, he also criticizes Black theology's preoccupation with blackness. For instance, referring to Wole Soyinka's jejune remark that "a tiger does not proclaim its tigritude," Setiloane condemns Black theology for its engagement of the experience of blackness. He writes:

The tiger is not preoccupied with its tigritude, but just lives it. So also it is wrong for Africans to be preoccupied with their Negritude. Their calling is to live it. ... [As] soon as the Black vs. White scenario is over, there will be no need for Black theology any more.[40]

If, however, Setiloane is convinced that the black experience is that of poverty and oppression and he would define theology as verbalization of human experience of and with divinity,[41] then it is difficult indeed to imagine how black people — called to live their blackness — would disengage this existential experience from theological reality.

In point of fact, Setiloane undermines his own stance against the use of black experience in theological reflection when he writes, "We who were still left under white domination and still experience a constant negation of our humanness because of our color cannot help but experience and hear Divinity in the realms of Black vs. White."[42]

Black theology has arisen out of the black experience precisely because no theology emerges out of a vacuum. Making the black experience the starting point for black theological hermeneutics thus implies "a critique of the ruling ideology, combining epistemological, anthropological and theo-logical concerns."[43] It is, therefore, within the framework of the painful experience of black people in history that Black theology's emphasis on biblical truth — as expressed in theological statements such as "epistemological privilege of the oppressed" and "God sides with the oppressed" — is to be assessed and understood.

Furthermore, it is within the framework of this same black experience that Buthelezi's anthropological (over against the ethnographic) approach to theology in South Africa is to be understood and interpreted. For Buthelezi, blackness as an anthropological reality must be the point of departure for any meaningful theology, because that is the factor that determines and governs black people's daily existence.[44] Any God-talk outside this anthropological fact — this *black experience* — makes God's revelation in Christ ahistorical and the incarnation "becomes an abstract object of theological speculation instead of a living reality."[45]

Black Consciousness

Black consciousness, as a political concept, has evolved out of a community of people who have been deprived of their human dignity and denied every means of political self-expression and full intellectual development. As a political philosophy, black consciousness became the articulation of a new awareness, a new identity and a positive affirmation of black humanity which, as a result of white cupidity, has been denigrated and dehumanized. Black consciousness is therefore "an authentic intellectual product of the creativity of an oppressed people."[46]

The movement that the concept of black consciousness inspired had a tremendous impact on the thinking of young black students and seminarians, some of whom in the early 1970s were to become exponents of Black theology — the theological expression of black consciousness. Goba is therefore right in saying that the black consciousness movement "provided the context of black theological reflection in South Africa."[47] The most prominent figure behind the BCM was Steve Biko, who also saw an inextricable link between the concept and Black theology, which he described as "a situational interpretation of Christianity [which] seeks to relate present-day black man to God within the given context of the black man's suffering and his attempt to get out of it."[48]

A fundamental political motif of black consciousness was to bring an ideological change, with a new emphasis on black African values and rejection of values of oppression. The manifesto of the South African Student Organization (SASO) stated this succinctly:

> The basic tenet of black consciousness is that the black man must reject all value systems that seek to make him a foreigner in the country of his own birth and reduce his basic human dignity. The black man must build up his own value system, see himself as self-defined and not defined by others.[49]

Black consciousness, as pointed out earlier, increased Africans' awareness of their political oppression and economic exploitation. This awareness militated against ethnic particularism and led Africans (together with Coloreds and Indians) to think in terms of black solidarity. Black consciousness created a political atmosphere which made it possible for blacks to break ties with liberal whites in multiracial politics. It empowered black people "to do what is necessary to bring a halt to the white encroachments on black humanity."[50]

Black consciousness brought into being other groups committed solely to the black struggle for liberation; these included the Black Community Programmes (BCP) and the Black People's Convention (BPC). As blacks participated in these liberation-oriented programs, it consequently affected their interpretation and reflection of the gospel of Jesus Christ. Black consciousness radicalized black Christians and stimulated their critical thinking about social and political problems and thus created the intellectual atmosphere out of which both black theological reflection and sociopolitical activism of the black clergy were to emerge.

But black consciousness was not just an outward experience with a superficial meaning; it was more than that. It had and still has enormous outward repercussions on unjust South African capitalist society. It was above all an outburst of the inner dimension of black psyche which became the determinative structuring principle that began to govern oppressed black people's interaction with a hostile environment dominated and controlled by white supremacy. It was the irruption of that dimension of the divine image in black psyche which sought to negate and to say "NO" to white inhumanity to black humanity. Thus, while it affirmed the full humanity of black people as God's children, black consciousness undermined the apartheid structures that served only the interests of the white minority and denounced them as a complete unreality of the human.

It was because of black consciousness' quest for true humanity that the concept appealed to black Christians. According to Desmond Tutu, for example, black theological reflection "has become part of the black consciousness movement, which is concerned with the evangelical aim of awakening in blacks a sense of their intrinsic worth as children of God."[51] Allan Boesak's description of the concept is still helpful and can epitomize our discussion. He wrote:

> Black consciousness may be described as the awareness of black people that their humanity is constituted in their blackness. It means that black people are no longer ashamed that they are black, that they have black history and black culture distinct from the history and culture of white people. It means that blacks are determined to be judged no longer by, and adhere no longer to, white values. It is an attitude, a way of life.[52]

There is no gainsaying that black consciousness and Black theology, both of which arose out of the black experience, were regarded by black theologians as inextricably linked. Thus, Mosala and Buti Tlhagale spoke for all black liberationists when they commented: "Black theology is a child of Black Consciousness" and as an ideology of the black struggle, black consciousness has "provided a fundamental matrix for developing a black theological hermeneutic."[53]

However, not all theologians in Africa would associate black consciousness with Black theology. While all black liberationists would espouse the concept with theological reflection, some inculturationists would not. For instance, I have pointed out how, for Mbiti, racial color is both a nontheological and nonbiblical concept. He sees even further, and condemns "color consciousness" as idolatrous.[54] However, Mbiti regards black consciousness as a chief concern of "South African theology of liberation" (a term he prefers to Black theology), and sees it as "an important development which . . . has a bearing on the question of the theology of liberation."[55]

Gabriel Setiloane is perhaps the finest example here. He interprets black consciousness, within the framework of his understanding of theology, as the verbalization of the human experience of God, with this "experience" apparently confined to the racial boundary of the theologian. Unlike black liberationists, who see an inextricable link between black consciousness and Black theology, Setiloane views the two as having separate and different concerns altogether. For him, black consciousness seeks the total understanding of black humanity and verbalizes this, irrespective of the white person or his or her conceptualization—a thing Black theology cannot do, because "Black theology cannot do without the White man and his whiteness."[56] Setiloane does not see how black consciousness and Black theology can have the same concern if "whiteness" and Western conceptualization, which are irrelevant to black consciousness, are still exploited by Black theology.

While Setiloane feels that black consciousness as a concept has deepened the black experience of God and helped "the black man to go back to his roots as Man, African Man," he has doubts whether, in both its American and South African manifestations, Black theology is "seeking to verbalize the Black man's experience of Divinity outside his contract with the white man, or even being able to do so, if even it wanted to."[57] With such an effort to divorce black consciousness from Black theology, it is not surprising to see Setiloane identify black consciousness with "Africanization," and see "a kind of child-mother relationship between black consciousness and African theology."[58] Thus for Setiloane, black consciousness' theological motivation is but the belated expression of Negritude in francophone Africa and African Personality in anglophone Africa.[59]

The Bible

Biblical hermeneutics within Black theology itself has drastically changed since the early 1970s, which has been our main focus in this section. The 1980s onwards have seen such a high level of scholarly sophistication in the use of the Bible that black theologians themselves have been seriously challenged for drawing their biblical hermeneutical assumptions from white theological and intellectual frameworks.

Such a potent challenge has mainly come from Itumeleng Mosala.[60] For Mosala, Black theology has hardly become "an autonomous weapon" of oppressed blacks in their struggle for liberation. He contends that "unless black theologians break ideologically and theoretically with bourgeois biblical-hermeneutical assumptions, black theology cannot become an effective weapon of struggle for its oppressed people." Mosala then sets himself the task of developing "a distinctive biblical hermeneutics of liberation for black theology."[61] The effective analytical tool he employs to achieve this is the *historical materialism* associated with Karl Marx—a methodology which, ironically, is also rooted in Westernism.

It was with South African black theologians that a new biblical hermeneutics, which begins with a hermeneutics of suspicion, emerged on the African continent. In this new hermeneutic approach—one apparently akin to those of liberation theologies in the United States and Latin America—we see a prophetic and pertinent way of interpretation that engages social analytical tools in reading the signs of the times (Matt. 16:3). Like all liberation theologians, black liberationists lay much emphasis on the rereading of the Bible, a practice not found among African theologians of the inculturation school.

From the very outset, South African black theologians saw Black theology as "attempting to do ... precisely what the biblical authors were doing for their communities to which they addressed themselves."[62] Theology in the Bible, Tutu contends, is an *engaged* theology addressing specific situations, and it is this "biblical paradigm" that Black theology has meticulously followed.[63] Thus, from the beginning, black theologians emphasized

that Black theology was a biblical theology that expressed itself contextually.[64]

The bone of contention between liberationists and inculturationists in
this early period was therefore not limited to the issues of blackness and
liberation; it also extended to the use of the Bible. John Mbiti, for instance,
attacked nascent Black theology for its lack of scriptural backing. He under-
lined that although the theme of liberation that is emphasized in Black
theology has a strong biblical basis, "apart from a few instances, this theology of liberation does not use the Christian Scriptures to back it up."[65]
Basing his evaluation primarily on the British edition of the first publication
on South African Black theology, *Black Theology: The South African Voice*
(1973), Mbiti does not understand how, for instance, the exodus-liberation
theme, which features so prominently in North American Black theology —
a theological system from which South African blacks have drawn so
much — should not be "mentioned even once in the book."[66] Then referring
to South African Black theology and to AACC's interest in liberation, Mbiti
writes, "This neglect in Africa of the biblical backing of the theology of
liberation is a very alarming omission that calls urgently for correction;
otherwise that branch of African theology will lose its credibility."[67]

Inarguably behind the tension on this particular issue is the question of
how scripture is used in theology.[68] There are observable differences
between liberationists and inculturationists in the way they use the Bible.
A few examples should suffice.

Unlike inculturationists, whose interpretation of scripture is always
restricted to the text without much concern for any transformative praxis,[69]
liberationists emphasize that "hermeneutical praxis of biblical faith is not
simply confined to interpreting text and experience but concerned itself
with engaging in the transformation of society."[70] Whereas inculturationists
are obsessed with finding continuities and discontinuities between the Bible
and African cultural life and thought,[71] black liberationists acknowledge the
ambiguity of scripture and therefore contend that the Bible can be used as
a force for liberation or for oppression. Thus for Allan Boesak, even though
the biblical message is such "a powerful message of liberation and human
freedom that, once understood, it cannot but inspire those who are active
in the struggle for political liberation," the same Bible can be used as well
"to undergird [and] to justify political ideology and preservation of unjust
social structures."[72] However, Boesak does not tell how to deal radically
with these oppressive and unjust structures in theological hermeneutics and
praxis.

Again, unlike the inculturationists, who hold that the Bible must be
explored "against the background of traditional African life and thought"
without giving any regard to the ideological interests of the interpreter,[73]
black liberationists hold that biblical hermeneutics is never neutral but
always reflects the ideological interests and commitment of those engaged
in it.[74]

Black American Heritage

Strictly speaking, the tension between African inculturationists and black liberationists was an offspring of the dissent between African theologians and North American black theologians that began when they became partners in dialogue in the early 1970s. The tension in Africa arose when Black theology in South Africa (BTSA) was subjected to the same kind of criticisms as those levelled against Black theology in the United States of America (BTUSA).[75] The transatlantic dialogue began through the initiative of African Americans who felt they had something in common with their African brothers and sisters; notable among them were James Cone and Gayraud Wilmore.

To fully understand what we have called the inculturation-liberation tension, we must grasp what went on between African theology and North American Black theology in the early 1970s. In the series of meetings after the first formal consultation held in Dar-es-Salaam in 1971, African and North American black theologians explored the similarities and dissimilarities between the two theological systems. In all these meetings, theologians articulated the ways in which both Africans and black Americans were attempting to understand their own life situation as they pondered over the existential question: "What does it mean to be black and Christian at this point in history?"[76]

There were no doubts that when African and American black theologians came together in dialogue, both sides knew that they had much in common; what was not all that clear was whether the commonalities between them could lead them to a common theological point of view.[77] It was at the very first formal consultation in Dar-es-Salaam that the theological differences between African theology and North American Black theology were identified. While *liberation* was identified as the main theme of North American Black theology, with an emphasis on politics, *Africanization* was identified as African theology's main theme, with an emphasis on culture.[78] This differentiation over a liberation-political thrust and an Africanization-cultural leaning has since polarized the two theological systems, despite efforts toward alliance that were made in two subsequent consultations in New York City in 1973 and in Accra, Ghana, in 1974. The former was an informal consultation at Union Theological Seminary that sought to lay the ground rules for further discussion. Its aim was to explore the meaning of North American Black and African theologies as they were articulated in both academic and ecclesiastical circles.[79] At the Legon Conference in Accra, even though participants felt that "progress had been made in mutual understanding, if not toward synthesis," nonetheless specific plans were not made for continuation of the dialogue between African and American black theologians.[80]

It was not until the establishment of EATWOT that African and North American black theologians met under the auspices of the Pan-African

Conference of Third World Theologians in 1977 in Accra. EATWOT became the main context for theological dialogue between the emergent theologies of the oppressed people in the Third World and minorities in the United States. In 1986 black theologians in the United States resumed direct dialogue with black theologians in South Africa in a conference in New York City.[81]

In all the meetings between African and North American Black theologians, the question of liberation doubtlessly loomed large in the minds of participants,[82] and for black Americans, at least, their conviction was that "the two groups were indeed in the process of forming a strong alliance."[83] But the publications of some African theologians, especially John Mbiti's article, "An African Views American Black Theology," broke the spirit of an alliance that had not yet flowered and nipped it in the bud.[84]

In this article, Mbiti made a sharp distinction between African theology and American Black theology and concluded that "Black theology cannot and will not become African theology," because the two theologies "emerged from quite different historical and contemporary situations."[85] Although other African theologians have expressed similar views on Black theology, as we will come to see later, those of Mbiti were the ones that surprised and disturbed American black theologians, especially James Cone, who—having jointly taught a course on African and Black theologies at Union Theological Seminary in New York, where Mbiti was the Henry Emerson Fosdick Visiting Professor (1972–1973)—felt Mbiti had misrepresented Black theology.[86] Mbiti's critique drove black theologians both in America and in South Africa to a defensive extreme. For instance, Desmond Tutu's article "Black Theology/African Theology—Soul Mates or Antagonists?" was a direct response to Mbiti.[87]

When Black theology emerged in South Africa, blacks in that country never concealed their indebtedness to North American Black theology and to its exponents, especially James Cone. "As we wrestled with the challenge of Black Consciousness," recalls Bonganjalo Goba, "we were really influenced by the writings of James Cone. We discovered in his theological hermeneutic a fresh approach in engaging in the liberation struggle." Goba then concludes, "I can remember how Cone's ideas dominated our Black theology seminar at Wilgespruit in 1970 and became a useful basis for developing a Black theology arising out of the South African context."[88] Blacks in South Africa saw Black theology as standing "with one leg in Africa and the other in black America."[89] For them, it was a combination of African theology and American Black theology. The editor of the first book on South African Black theology wrote:

Black Theology in South Africa . . . is a unique combination of the theology of disinheritance and oppression and the theology of culture. It is North America's Black Theology and independent Africa's African Theology in which politics and 'culture' are deeply and inextricably intertwined.[90]

For the South Africans, therefore, although it drew much theological insight from North American Black theology, South African Black theology has its own distinctive character and, as such, exhibits peculiar African characteristics.

Desmond Tutu has emphasized how, in their struggle, South African blacks have been motivated by the accomplishments of black Americans, whose influence has also stimulated the creation of South African Black theology. In his own words,

> In Southern Africa, black theology was inspired by its North American counterpart, which existed for so long implicitly in the Negro Spirituals that gave heart to black slaves in the heavy days of their bondage and which became more articulate and explicit during the civil rights campaign.[91]

Like most blacks in his country, Tutu has observed how, although they are oppressed, blacks in the United States have made some successful strides toward freedom which, according to Dwight Hopkins, have "inspire[d] blacks in South Africa to acknowledge the inherent divine gift in their ontology."[92]

But such a link incurred the displeasure of African inculturationists. John Mbiti wrote yet another article, which focused this time exclusively on South African Black theology. As in his earlier article, Mbiti separated the theological realities of the situations of blacks in South Africa and blacks in North America. He avoided applying the term "Black theology" to black theological reflection in South Africa; instead, he chose to call it "South African Theology of Liberation" so that "it is not confused with its wider application in North America."[93]

But Mbiti is not the only African who determined to separate theology in Africa from North American Black theology. Harry Sawyerr, E. W. Fashole-Luke and Gabriel Setiloane have all expressed similar views, albeit in different ways. Whereas for Sawyerr, *Theologia Africana* "must not be based on such contemporary factors brought about as in the United States of America,"[94] for Fashole-Luke, African Christian theologies must be raised "above the level of ethnic and racial categories and emphasis."[95]

Gabriel Setiloane took the argument further by disavowing Black theology of its American origin and relocating it in the African setting. According to him, the sentiment expressed by American black theologians in 1969 had already come about (though in less polemic terms) at the AACC Youth Assembly in Nairobi seven years earlier. Setiloane defined "Black theology" as a term used "in reference to the whole area of theological thinking by the Black Man in the World."[96] He then declared, "My own point of view is that Black theology, as I have tried to define it above, did not begin in the United States."[97] In drawing a distinction between what he called "American Black Theology enthusiasts and the Africans," one is left in the dark as to whether or not Setiloane was writing as a South African black living under a political system called apartheid. For him, whereas the Americans "do their theologizing in the dust and heat of political warfare, hence their militancy and impatience . . . we can claim to work in an atmosphere of political freedom [*sic!*] and comparable calm."[98]

CASE TWO: THE LIBERATION CONTROVERSY REEXAMINED

Black theology in South Africa, I have emphasized from the beginning of this chapter, is a theology of liberation. This liberation, I have also maintained, presupposes a black search for full humanity—a God-given personhood. Differently put, a critical concept in Black theology is that liberation is the process through which oppressed blacks are seeking to bring about radical transformation of oppressive social structures and relationships.

Through their encounter with the gospel of Jesus Christ, black theologians have come to acknowledge the biblical truth that the basic thrust of the gospel message is liberation. The Bible, they claim, testifies to the liberation of oppressed people that began with God's liberative act in the Hebrew Scriptures and found fulfillment in Jesus the Christ in the New Testament.[99]

Like their counterparts in North America and the rest of the Third World, South African black theologians have insisted that liberation *is* the gospel of Jesus Christ and not just consistent with it. Taking a clue from James Cone's hermeneutic insights, they have contended that *liberation is the content of theology*.[100] Other Third World theologians have emphasized as well the validity of liberation in this regard. For instance, the Asian theologian Aloysius Pieris has demonstrated how "liberation is the *sole* concern of Christ and His Church," and therefore, "theology is none other than the attempt on the part of the Church to spell out this concern in theory and practice."[101]

It has been suggested that even the expression *theology of liberation* is "tautological as there cannot be a nonliberational theology," for it is *liberation* that "ultimately determines the validity of any theology." Thus, for Pieris, "a theology is valid if it *originates, develops*, and *culminates* in the praxis/process of liberation."[102]

But how has this significant truth of the theological reality been perceived in Africa? Obviously, it is not hard to answer this question: While the liberationists see liberation as the content of theology, the inculturationists feel that theology "cannot be reduced to one such theme alone without undue narrowing and impoverishment."[103]

The initial reaction of African theologians to Black theology's emphasis on liberation came in the early 1970s, during their dialogue with American black theologians. James Cone has shown how in each of their meetings with African theologians the latter "have shied away from the term 'liberation,' because they say that the gospel is not political [and] not an ideology of the oppressed."[104]

John Mbiti is a good representative of the Africans who have systematically shied away from the theme of liberation. For example, on this issue, he wrote:

> As a theology of the oppressed, every concern in Black theology has some bearing on the question of liberation. What I view as an excessive preoccupation with liberation may as well be the chief limitation of Black theology. When the immediate concerns of liberation are realized, it is not at all clear where Black theology is supposed to go.[105]

In Mbiti's opinion, Black theology has not given an adequate definition to the eschatological reality. "There is no clue," he says, "as to when one arrives at the paradise of 'liberation'." Black theology, according to Mbiti, has mythologized the concept of liberation and therefore avoids other main theological issues which do not relate directly to the liberation concept.[106] Unlike Desmond Tutu and J. N. K. Mugambi, who see liberation not as just one of the issues but rather that "all issues are aimed at liberating Africans from all forces that hinder them from living fully as human beings,"[107] Mbiti, like Nyamiti, sees liberation as "one of [African theology's] many themes."[108] Furthermore, according to Mbiti, what blacks in South Africa need is liberation, *not* a theology of liberation.[109] "To declare," he further argues, "that Jesus Christ is a liberator and 'a fighting God,' does not automatically make Him bring an immediate end to the suffering for the Africans."[110]

With such a scathing attack on Black theology's "preoccupation with liberation," it did not come as a surprise when John Mbiti did not include liberation as one of the "six chief concerns" of South African Black theology, whose message has stressed liberation and to set the downtrodden free.[111] Even though the theme of liberation runs through *Black Theology: The South African Voice* (1973) — the book Mbiti was evaluating — Mbiti saw christology, man [sic!] and humanity, the church, Black consciousness, authority, and God and *not* liberation as the major thematic concerns of South African Black theology.[112]

John Mbiti does not see how liberation can be discussed in Black theology and leave out white Christians in South Africa: "Isn't liberation also a concern for them?" He then concludes, "Surely, ultimate liberation would have to benefit both White immigrants and indigenous Africans in South Africa. ... Theology cannot be the exclusive exercise of any single group of people, be they male or female, Africans or Europeans."[113] In point of fact — as evidence suggests — either Mbiti was unaware that South African Black theology has not excluded whites in its discussion of liberation, as is, for instance, seen in Manas Buthelezi's emphasis on the theology of racial fellowship over against the theology of separate development,[114] or else he did not like what black theologians have said or are saying about this particular theme. For one thing is clear: No black liberationist in South Africa would make "white immigrants" the first beneficiaries of what Mbiti has called "ultimate liberation," whatever that means. Most would insist — as Desmond Tutu has done with his relational theology — that "no one in South Africa will achieve liberation *until* blacks attain emancipation by exercising 'their God-given personhood and humanity'."[115]

Dwight Hopkins has reminded us how, as early as 1973, Manas Buthelezi had emphasized that "the gospel of liberation will free black and white simultaneously but each in distinct ways."[116] Buthelezi himself had contended that "South Africa urgently needs the Gospel of liberation, a Gospel that will liberate the whites from the bondage inherent in the South African way of life — a way of life that chokes brotherhood and fellowship between black and white."[117]

In his relational theological hermeneutics, Desmond Tutu has structured "a complementary approach in both the method toward and the goal of liberation."[118] Black theology, Tutu submitted in 1974, "declares that the liberation of the black man is the other side of the coin of the liberation of the white man — so that it is concerned with human liberation."[119] Dwight Hopkins epitomizes Tutu's relational hermeneutics:

> Briefly put, the goal of black and white liberation complement one another. Though Tutu believes in white liberation through the forgiveness generated by black liberation's "participation in the economy of salvation," he never sanctions a cheap forgiveness. On the contrary, in its pardon of white oppression black liberation does not rule out militant confrontation and demands repentance in order for white liberation to materialize; for Jesus Christ, in his own pardon to both liberate and unite humanity, died on the cross.[120]

In the inculturation camp, there is another perspective on liberation that deserves attention. If Mbiti has systematically shied away from the theme of liberation and has refused to accept the concept as a theological-hermeneutical category, the case is apparently different with Gabriel Setiloane who, as a South African, is confronted *daily* with the reality of the black struggle for liberation. However, as with Mbiti and inculturationists in general, sociopolitical liberation is completely nonexistent in Setiloane's theological hermeneutics. Rather, he talks about a liberation that is not explicitly defined. In fact, the kind of liberation in the "African theology" that Setiloane advocates in the South African context is not without ambiguity. In his own words,

The liberation African theology strives for is that of the very "Soul of Africa" from the imprisonment in the vaults of Western conceptualism and discourse, from cerebration and pseudo scientific-ness to human-ness, Botho, Ubuntu, authenticity born out of a living practical experience of MODIMO, Qamata, Lesa, uMvelinqangi is the totality of life. It is diffused in and permeates.[121]

If what Setiloane is saying is that liberation as a concept is all-encompassing and that it embraces every dimension of human life, then one wonders why such an existential belief should not be translated into theological reality and praxis.

Inevitably, this last statement brings us to the most crucial question: If liberation, as the liberationists have contended, is the content of theology, then in which areas have they unequivocally expressed this theological reality? What different expressions of liberation have been rendered in theological reflection in Africa?

Expressions of Liberation

Whether John Mbiti is to be commended for shying away from the theme of liberation and for condemning the concept as a theological category or he is to be censured for not seeing far enough has been, in my opinion, best judged by history. Indeed, history has rendered its verdict on the relevance and validity of liberation theology in Africa. Since Mbiti's controversial essay appeared in 1974, two liberation-oriented theologies have emerged in independent Africa: African liberation theology and African women's feminist theology. These two theological perspectives have evidently been influenced in no small way by Black theology.

Therefore, of the four major theological strands in Africa, only African theology, or more precisely, inculturation theology, as narrowly defined by the "Old Guards," shies away from liberation. The rest — South African Black theology with black feminist theology, African liberation theology, and African women's theology — have a liberation orientation.

Initially, each of these liberation-oriented theologies defined liberation largely by the oppression it experiences and opposes and, consequently, that particular definition becomes its point of departure. Thus, whereas *race* became the point of departure for Black theology and *gender* for women's feminist theology, *poverty* became the starting point for African liberation theology.

But among African liberation theologians such as Jean-Marc Ela and Engelbert Mveng, and black liberationists (especially those whom Dwight Hopkins has described as "the members of the black cultural theology trend,"[122] such as Bonganjalo Goba and Itumeleng Mosala), there have been emphases on *cultural* liberation as well as on *political* liberation. These liberationists believe as well that part of colonial oppression and racial domination has been the deprecation of African culture; for them, therefore, liberation should not only be political, but also a cultural achievement.

In African theological reality, liberation has been explicitly expressed in four different areas: liberation from race oppression; liberation from gender oppression; liberation from class oppression and liberation from cultural oppression.

However, by becoming partners in dialogue (especially dialogue that has taken place mainly within the contexts of the Ecumenical Association of African Theologians [EAAT] and the Ecumenical Association of Third World Theologians [EATWOT]), these liberation-oriented theologians have been exposed to the fact that those who suffer under one form of oppression may themselves be responsible for imposing another form of oppression on another group, as the case of women demonstrates in both neocolonial Africa and racist South Africa.

Thus, while male theologians in independent Africa are radical when it comes to the issue of colonialism, and male South African black theologians are even more radical when it comes to the issue of racism, both African and black theologians are very conservative when it comes to the issue of sexism. As Mercy Oduyoye has succinctly stated, African male theologians (like their Asian and Latin American counterparts) have demonstrated that "antisexism is not their priority."[123] On the issue of sexism, Oduyoye further unveils the chauvinistic idiosyncrasies of her male counterparts:

> At times they have even said it is not an issue in their world, where men and women *know their place* and *play their role* ungrudgingly and no one feels suffocated by society's definition of femininity and masculinity. Issues of sexism are supposed to belong to a minority of disgruntled, leisure-saturated, middle-class women of the capitalist West.[124]

Unlike John Mbiti and Kwesi Dickson, who do not take a critical view of the oppressive patriarchal structures in both church and society, Mercy Oduyoye (like Rose Zoé-Obianga from francophone Africa [Cameroon][125] and Dorothy Ramodibe from racist South Africa)[126] takes a very critical look at the oppressive gender relations in both church and society, as well as elements in African religious culture that dehumanize women.

Although Mbiti acknowledges that African women suffer from male supremacist domination and that behind most of the African proverbs and myths "is the wish and practice on the part of male [men] to dominate women," yet he fails to grapple with the oppressive patriarchal status quo.[127] Kwesi Dickson, like Mbiti, also enumerates oppressive structures in African societies which subordinate women and relegate them to a secondary position. Nevertheless, Dickson still declares: "In my opinion, such words of comparison as inferior and superior are out of place in the African context;

they represent the importation of Western attitudes into a context to which they do not belong."[128]

Most inculturationists do not provide the basic framework within which to explore the issues affecting women. In fact, the inner logic of the inculturation approach to theology in Africa (which emphasizes culture, in which sexism is firmly entrenched, but shies away from liberation) is not antipatriarchal.[129]

Like the inculturationists, black liberationists in South Africa are equally guilty when it comes to women's issues. As far as gender relations are concerned, the record has not been impressive. Frank Chikane highlighted the contradictions within black theological reflection when he wrote,

> The contradictions . . . within the South African Black theology movement of protesting vehemently — and even violently — against racial, cultural, and politico-economic oppression, while continuing to oppress and exploit *women*, emerged more during the first part of the 1980s, causing serious embarrassment to the "revolutionaries" of the day.[130]

Consequently, liberationists have come to recognize the interconnectedness not only of the various forms of oppression, but also of the different expressions of liberation. They have come to the painful realization that oppression cannot be effectively and successfully combatted or eradicated piecemeal, because all its various dimensions — the *isms* of oppression — are interrelated. This multidimensionality of oppression demands a movement for liberation that is as encompassing as the oppressive structures of domination against which theologians in Africa are obliged to struggle.

NOTES

1. James Cone, *God of the Oppressed*, p. 155, and his "Black Theology and Black Liberation," in Basil Moore, ed., *The Challenge of Black Theology in South Africa* (Atlanta: John Knox Press, 1974), p. 52.

2. Allan Boesak, "Liberation Theology in South Africa," in Appiah-Kubi and Torres, eds., *African Theology En Route*, p. 173.

3. Goba, *An Agenda for Black Theology*, p. 36.

4. Allan Boesak, "The Relationship Between Text and Situation, Reconciliation and Liberation in Black Theology," *Voices from the Third World*, vol. 2, no. 1, June 1979, p. 35; cf. his *Farewell to Innocence*, p. 20.

5. Theo Witvliet, *A Place in the Sun* (Maryknoll, N.Y.: Orbis Books, 1985), p. 76.

6. Buti Tlhagale, "Towards a Black Theology of Labour," in Charles Villa-Vicencio and John de Gruchy, eds., *Resistance and Hope: South African Essays in Honour of Beyers Naudé* (Grand Rapids, Mich.: Eerdmans, 1985), p. 126.

7. Basil Moore, ed., *The Challenge of Black Theology in South Africa*, p. viii.

8. Nyameko Pityana, "What Is Black Consciousness?" in Moore, ed., *The Challenge of Black Theology in South Africa*, p. 63.

9. Manas Buthelezi, "An African Theology or a Black Theology?" in Moore, ed., *The Challenge of Black Theology in South Africa*, p. 34.

10. Steve Biko, "Black Consciousness and the Quest for a True Humanity," in Mokgethi Motlhabi, ed., *Essays on Black Theology* (Johannesburg: University Christian Movement, 1972), p. 23; cf. his *I Write What I Like*, p. 94.

11. Ibid., p. 23; cf. his *I Write What I Like*, p. 94.

12. See Simon Maimela, "Current Themes and Emphases in Black Theology," in I. Mosala and B. Tlhagale, eds., *The Unquestionable Right to be Free*, pp. 102–5.

13. See e.g., Frank Chikane, "Doing Theology in a Situation of Conflict," in Villa-Vicencio and de Gruchy, eds., *Resistance and Hope*, pp. 98–102.

14. Bonganjalo Goba, "Doing Theology in South Africa: A Black Christian Perspective," *Journal of Theology for Southern Africa*, no. 31, June 1980, p. 29.

15. Maimela, "Current Themes and Emphases in Black Theology," p. 104.

16. Ibid., pp. 105-6.

17. James Cone, *Black Theology and Black Power* (Minneapolis, Minn.: Seabury Press, 1969), p. 36.

18. Desmond Tutu, "The Theology of Liberation in Africa," in Appiah-Kubi and Torres, eds., *African Theology En Route*, p. 166.

19. Albert Nolan, "The Option for the Poor in South Africa," in Villa-Vicencio and de Gruchy, eds., *Resistance and Hope*, p. 192.

20. Cf. Tlhagale, "Towards a Black Theology of Labour," p. 130.

21. Simon Maimela, "Black Theology," *AACC Magazine*, vol. 2, no. 1, May 1984, p. 5; see also his "Current Themes and Emphases in Black Theology," p. 110.

22. Boesak, "The Relationship Between Text and Situation, Reconciliation and Liberation in Black Theology," p. 36.

23. Hopkins, *Black Theology USA and South Africa*, p. 136.

24. Motlhabi, "The Historical Origins of Black Theology," p. 50.

25. Pityana, "What Is Black Consciousness?," p. 59.

26. Mokgethi Motlhabi, "Black Theology: A Personal Opinion," in Motlhabi, ed., *Essays on Black Theology*, p. 56.

27. Cone, *God of the Oppressed*, pp. 17-18.

28. Ibid., p. 18.

29. Maimela, "Current Themes and Emphases in Black Theology," p. 102.

30. John Mbiti, "An African Views American Black Theology," in Wilmore and Cone, eds., *Black Theology*, p. 478.

31. Desmond Tutu, "Black Theology," *Frontier*, 17, Summer, 1974, p. 74.

32. Mbiti, in Wilmore and Cone, *Black Theology*, p. 478.

33. John Mbiti, "Some African Concepts of Christology," in G. F. Vicedom, ed., *Christ and the Younger Churches* (London: SPCK, 1973), p. 57.

34. John Mbiti, "ο σωτηρ ημων as an African Experience," in B. Lindars and S. S. Smalley, eds., *Christ and Spirit in the New Testament* (Cambridge: Cambridge University Press, 1973), p. 412, cf. p. 402. Emphasis added.

35. Takatso A. Mofokeng, *The Crucified Among the Crossbearers: Towards a Black Christology* (Kampen: J. H. Kok, 1983), pp. 259ff., cf. pp. 92ff.

36. Ibid., p. 261.

37. Ibid., p. 263.

38. Gabriel Setiloane, "Black Theology," *South African Outlook*, vol. 101, no. 1197, February 1971, p. 28.

39. Gabriel Setiloane, "Theological Trends in Africa," *Missionalia*, vol. 8, 1980, p. 49.

40. Ibid.

41. Ibid., p. 47; cf. his *African Theology*, p. 35.

42. Ibid., p. 49.

43. Per Frostin, *Liberation Theology in Tanzania and South Africa*, p. 103; cf. Boesak, *Black and Reformed*, p. 4.

44. Buthelezi, "An African Theology or a Black Theology?," p. 33; cf. his "Toward Indigenous Theology in South Africa," in Torres and Fabella, eds., *The Emergent Gospel*, pp. 56ff.

45. Witvliet, *A Place in the Sun*, p. 77.

46. Malesela J. Lamola, "The Thought of Steve Biko as the Historico-Philosophical Base of South African Black Theology," *Journal of Black Theology in South Africa*, vol. 3, no. 2, November 1989, p. 1.

47. Goba, *An Agenda for Black Theology*, pp. 32f; cf. his article, "The Black Consciousness Movement: Its Impact on Black Theology" in Mosala and Tlhagale, eds., *The Unquestionable Right to be Free*, pp. 58ff.

48. Biko, *I Write What I Like*, p. 59.

49. See Pityana, "What Is Black Consciousness?," pp. 60-61.

50. James Cone, "Black Theology and Black Liberation," in B. Moore, ed., *The Challenge of Black Theology in South Africa*, p. 52.

51. Tutu, "The Theology of Liberation in Africa," p. 163.

52. Boesak, *Farewell to Innocence*, p. 1.

53. Mosala and Tlhagale, eds., *The Unquestionable Right to be Free*, p. 57.

54. Mbiti, "An African Views American Black Theology," pp. 478–79.

55. John Mbiti, "The South African Theology of Liberation: An Appreciation and Evaluation," in Samuel Amirtham, ed., *A Vision for Man: Essays on Faith, Theology and Society* (Madras, India: The Christian Literature Society, 1978), p. 349.

56. Setiloane, "Theological Trends in Africa," pp. 49-50.

57. Ibid., p. 50.

58. Setiloane, *African Theology*, p. 45.

59. Setiloane, "Theological Trends in Africa," p. 50.

60. Itumeleng J. Mosala, *Biblical Hermeneutics and Black Theology in South Africa* (Grand Rapids, Mich.: Eerdmans, 1989), p. 5.

61. Ibid., p. 3.

62. Tutu, "Black Theology," *Frontier*, 17, Summer, 1974, p. 75.

63. Tutu, "The Theology of Liberation in Africa," in *African Theology En Route*, pp. 164-65.

64. Cf. Muzorewa, *The Origins and Development of African Theology*, p. 102.

65. Mbiti, "The South African Theology of Liberation," p. 356.

66. Ibid., p. 356.

67. Mbiti, "The Biblical Basis for Present Trends in African Theology" in Appiah-Kubi and Torres, eds., *African Theology En Route*, p. 89.

68. See Charles Villa-Vicencio, "The Use of Scripture in Theology: Towards a Contextual Hermeneutics," *Journal of Theology for Southern Africa*, no. 37, December 1981, pp. 3-22, which points out not just the differences, but also the confusion and ambiguity of theology's appeal to scripture.

69. Cf. E. W. Fashole-Luke, "The Quest for African Christian Theology," *The*

Journal of Religious Thought, vol. 32, no. 2, Fall-Winter, 1975, pp. 78-80.

70. Frank Chikane, "Doing Theology in a Situation of Conflict," in Villa-Vicen cio and de Gruchy, eds., *Resistance and Hope*, p. 99.

71. See Dickson, *Theology in Africa*, pp. 141ff., and his "Continuity and Dis continuity Between the Old Testament and African Life and Thought," in Appiah Kubi and Torres, eds., *African Theology En Route*, pp. 95ff.

72. Allan Boesak, "Civil Religion and the Black Community," *Journal of The ology for Southern Africa*, no. 19, June 1977, pp. 35-36.

73. Kwesi Dickson, "The African Theological Task," in Torres and Fabella eds., *The Emergent Gospel*, p. 47.

74. Cf. Bonganjalo Goba, "The Use of Scripture in the Kairos Document, *Journal of Theology for Southern Africa*, no. 56, September 1986, p. 61.

75. For a detailed discussion on this transatlantic dialogue, see James Con and Gayraud Wilmore, "Black Theology and African Theology: Considerations fo Dialogue, Critique, and Integration" in Wilmore and Cone, *Black Theology*, pp 463-76; cf. Josiah Young, *Black and African Theologies*, pp. 86-105; Dwight Hopkins *Black Theology USA and South Africa*, pp. 148-59.

76. See, e.g., Charles Shelby Rook's "Introduction" to the Ghana Consultatio Report, *The Journal of Religious Thought*, vol. 32, no. 2, Fall-Winter, 1975, p. 7.

77. See, e.g., Charles H. Long, "Structural Similarities and Dissimilarities i Black and African Theologies," *The Journal of Religious Thought*, vol. 32, no. 2, Fal Winter, 1975, esp. p. 9.

78. The 1971 Dar-es-Salaam meeting was sponsored by the African Commissio of the NCBC in the United States and the Christian Council of Tanzania. It wa named "Conference of Black Churchmen" and had as its theme "Black Identit and Solidarity and the Role of the Church as a Medium for Social Change." Th three major issues on which the consultation focused were: (a) economic deve opment, (b) education and (c) theology. All three issues were taken and treated i relation to each other. The papers presented have since been published under th title, *Black Faith and Black Solidarity*, edited by Priscilla Massie (New York: Frienc ship Press, 1973). Also on this conference, see Cornish Rogers, "Pan-Africanis and the Black Church: A Search for Solidarity," *Christian Century*, November 1 1971, pp. 1345-47; E. E. Mshana, "The Challenge of Black Theology and Africa Theology," *Africa Theological Journal*, vol. 5, December 1975; Wilmore and Con *Black Theology*, pp. 447ff.

79. Wilmore and Cone, *Black Theology*, p. 448. This Union Consultation, spor sored by the Society for the Study of Black Religion (SSBR) and the AACC, wa held June 7–9, 1973.

80. See Gayraud Wilmore, "African and Black Theology—Ghana Consultatio A Summary Report," *The Journal of Religious Thought*, vol. 32, no. 2, Fall-Winte 1975, p. 108. The conference was under the auspices of AACC and the SSBl Papers presented were published in *The Journal of Religious Thought*, vol. 32, n 2, Fall-Winter, 1975.

81. This conference, which took place at Union Theological Seminary (UT in New York City, was sponsored by UTS's Ecumenical Center and Theologic Field, the Institute for Contextual Theology (ICT) and EATWOT. The essays pr sented at this conference have since been published under the title, *We Are O Voice: Black Theology in the USA and South Africa*, edited by Simon Maimela ar

Dwight Hopkins (Johannesburg: Skotaville, 1989); cf. Dwight Hopkins, *Black Theology USA and South Africa*, pp. 162ff.

82. Mshana, "The Challenge of Black Theology and African Theology," pp. 23f.

83. Josiah Young, *Black and African Theologies*, p. 87.

84. See Wilmore and Cone, *Black Theology*, pp. 477-82. Mbiti's article first appeared in *Worldview*, vol. 17, no. 8, August 1974, pp. 41ff. just before the Accra Consultation in December 1974.

85. Ibid., p. 481.

86. James Cone, "A Black American Perspective on the Future of African Theology," in Appiah-Kubi and Torres, eds., *African Theology En Route*, p. 177; see also Wilmore and Cone, *Black Theology*, p. 493.

87. Desmond Tutu, "Black Theology/African Theology—Soul Mates or Antagonists?," *The Journal of Religious Thought*, vol. 32, no. 2, Fall-Winter, 1975, pp. 25-33; also, in Wilmore and Cone, *Black Theology*, pp. 483-91.

88. Goba, "The Black Consciousness Movement: Its Impact on Black Theology," p. 62.

89. Motlhabi, "The Historical Origins of Black Theology," p. 45.

90. See Motlhabi's "Foreword" in his edited volume *Essays on Black Theology*, p. 1.

91. Tutu, "The Theology of Liberation in Africa," pp. 163-64.

92. Hopkins, *Black Theology USA and South Africa*, p. 142.

93. Mbiti, "The South African Theology of Liberation: Appreciation and Evaluation," in S. Amirtham, ed., *A Vision for Man*, p. 350. Cf. an earlier article of Mbiti entitled, "African Theology," *Worldview*, August 1973, esp. pp. 37-38, where he also attacked South African Black theologians for being superficial and imitating James Cone.

94. Harry Sawyerr, "What Is African Theology?," *African Theological Journal*, vol. 4, August 1971, p. 22.

95. Fashole-Luke, "The Quest for African Christian Theology," *The Journal of Religious Thought*, vol. 32, no. 2, Fall-Winter, 1975, p. 87.

96. Gabriel Setiloane, "Black Theology," *South African Outlook*, vol. 101, no. 1197, February 1971, p. 28.

97. Ibid.

98. Ibid., p. 29.

99. Cf. Boesak, "The Relationship Between Text and Situation, Reconciliation and Liberation in Black Theology," p. 30.

100. See Cone, *A Black Theology of Liberation*, pp. 1ff.; cf. Boesak, *Farewell to Innocence*, p. 9.

101. Pieris, *An Asian Theology of Liberation*, p. 111.

102. Ibid.

103. Nyamiti, "Approaches to African Theology," in Torres and Fabella, eds., *The Emergent Gospel*, p. 43. Specifically, Nyamiti also cautions against "reducing Black theology to the theme of liberation from white segregation."

104. James Cone, "Reflections from the Perspective of U.S. Blacks: Black Theology and Third World Theology," in Fabella and Torres, eds., *Irruption of the Third World*, p. 242.

105. Mbiti, "An African Views American Black Theology," in Wilmore and Cone, *Black Theology*, p. 479.

106. Ibid., pp. 479-80.

107. Desmond Tutu, "Black Theology/African Theology—Soul Mates or Antagonists?" in Wilmore and Cone, *Black Theology*, p. 486; cf. *World Student Christian Federation Dossier*, no. 5, June 1974, pp. 41f. for Mugambi's view.

108. Mbiti, "The South African Theology of Liberation," in S. Amirtham, ed., *A Vision for Man*, p. 358.

109. Mbiti, "An African Views American Black Theology," p. 481.

110. Mbiti, "The South African Theology of Liberation," p. 356.

111. Motlhabi, "The Historical Origins of Black Theology," in Mosala and Tlhagale, eds., *The Unquestionable Right to be Free*, p. 46.

112. Mbiti, "The South African Theology of Liberation," pp. 350-55.

113. Ibid., p. 357.

114. Manas Buthelezi, "The Christian Institute and Black South Africa," *South African Outlook*, October 1974, p. 163; cf. Dwight Hopkins, *Black Theology USA and South Africa*, p. 98.

115. Hopkins, *Black Theology USA and South Africa*, p. 140; cf. Desmond Tutu, "The Theology of Liberation in Africa," in Appiah-Kubi and Torres, eds., *African Theology En Route*, p. 167.

116. Ibid., p. 99.

117. Manas Buthelezi, "Change in the Church," *South African Outlook*, August 1973, p. 130; cf. ibid., p. 99.

118. Hopkins, *Black Theology USA and South Africa*, p. 141.

119. Tutu, "Black Theology," *Frontier*, p. 74.

120. Hopkins, *Black Theology USA and South Africa*, p. 140; cf. Desmond Tutu, *Hope and Suffering* (Grand Rapids, Mich.: Eerdmans, 1984), p. 38; also his article, "Spirituality: Christian and African," in Villa-Vicencio and deGruchy, eds., *Resistance and Hope*, p. 164.

121. Setiloane, *African Theology*, p. 45.

122. Hopkins, *Black Theology USA and South Africa*, p. 121.

123. Mercy Oduyoye, "Reflections From a Third World Woman's Perspective: Women's Experience and Liberation Theologies," in Fabella and Torres, eds., *Irruption of the Third World*, p. 249.

124. Ibid.

125. See, e.g., Rose Zoé-Obianga, "Les Femmes Africaines et la Libération de l'Afrique," *Bulletin de Théologie Africaine*, vol. 6, no. 12, juillet-décembre 1984, 319-23. See also her article, "The Role of Women in Present-Day Africa," in Appiah-Kubi and Torres, eds., *African Theology En Route*, pp. 145-49.

126. See Dorothy Ramodibe, "Women and Men Re-creating Together the Church in Africa," *Voices from the Third World*, vol. 13, no. 2, December 1990, pp. 42-53.

127. John Mbiti, "Flowers in the Garden: The Role of Women in African Religion" in J. K. Olupona, ed., *African Traditional Religions in Contemporary Society* (New York: Paragon House, 1991), p. 61; cf. pp. 63ff.

128. Dickson, *Theology in Africa*, p. 64.

129. Cf. Martey, "African Women and Theology in Africa and the Third World," pp. 56-57; see also my article, "Church and Marriage in African Society: A Theological Appraisal," *African Theological Journal*, vol. 20, no. 2, 1991, pp. 136-47.

130. Chikane, "EATWOT and Third World Theologies: An Evaluation of the Past and Present," in Abraham, *Third World Theologies*, p. 148.

5 | Dialectics of the African Theological Paradigm

Inculturation and liberation, rightly understood, are two names of the same process!

—Aloysius Pieris[1]

African societies are being summoned to a global rethinking of their culture, to developing a new culture from a point of departure in current challenges. These challenges provoke us to a cultural invention.

—Jean-Marc Ela[2]

Rather there has been an emergence of dynamic cultural experience grounded in the immediate past and grappling with the present contemporary situation. Our culture in other words provides an orbit of meaning, one which synthesizes our past and present. It is a kind of a dialectical process which affirms and negates certain crucial and unimportant aspects of our cultural experience.

—Bonganjalo Goba[3]

In the previous chapters, I have been developing what I called the dialectic case for African theological reality. The discussions of African theology as "inculturation theology" and Black theology as "liberation theology" and the respective case studies examined clearly demonstrate that the inculturation-liberation polarity cannot be defined simply *between* African theologians *and* black theologians; it must also be defined *among* African theologians north of the Zambezi and *among* black theologians in South Africa. Each group of theologians should have some awareness of the other and each, in a way, should include the other.

Differently put, there is an appreciable dialectic between African theology and Black theology that makes the proponents of the two theological systems participants in the continent's sociohistorical reality. This means that the two theological hermeneutics—inculturation and liberation—find themselves concerned with the cultural as well as the political aspects of the African theological reality.

It is out of these cultural and political concerns that both African and black theologians have been inspired to embark upon a new theological

121

hermeneutics that makes the theologian an instrument of cultural and political emancipation—emancipating Christian theology itself from theological
methodology in which the discipline is seen as having nothing to do with
human history or the social conditions in which the poor people of God
live.

In Africa, inculturation and liberation, like any other theological concept, language or affirmation, have become symbols that mediate to black
African consciousness the reality in which Africans, as a struggling people
of God, live and the reality they are striving to attain. The two theological
hermeneutics not only mediate to us the complete "reality of the dehumanized" brought about by human greed and sin but, above all, they point
to the "complete reality of the human" created in God's image, an inherent
divine gift that black Africans are striving to achieve.

By contrasting the situation in which black Africans live with the situation in which they ought to live, the epistemologies of both inculturation
and liberation represent the most profound structure of theological symbolism which, through the reality of their pauperized ontology, manifests
to the world the divine reality and will for authentic human existence.

The dialectical character of theology that inculturation and liberation
symbolize is best represented in the central symbol of the Christian faith,
Jesus Christ. It is in the attempt to reflect this dialectical quality of the
mystery of the incarnation that the classical Chalcedonian formula, following Nicaea, affirmed—albeit in a very abstractionist fashion—Jesus Christ
as *vere Deus* and *vere homo*. It therefore appears that this dialectical tension
is a fundamental principle of the theological enterprise, which must be
confronted if the subject matter of Christian theology is not to be misrepresented.

If this be the case, then, the failure of most African and black theologians
to acknowledge and deal creatively with such a dialectical nature of the
theological enterprise reveals, in my opinion, a dangerous paralysis of theological analysis in Africa. Since in both the "inculturationist thesis on
liberation" and the "liberationist thesis on inculturation," this paralysis or
one-dimensional analysis of the African theological reality has been evident, it is important to lay out some key elements in these theses.

PARALYSIS OF UNIDIMENSIONAL ANALYSIS

INCULTURATIONIST THESIS ON LIBERATION

Fundamental to the inculturationist thesis is that Black theology, which
concerns itself with liberation, cannot be an expression of African theology
because it engages sociopolitical issues at the expense of indigenization and
therefore ignores the culture of the very people it claims to defend.[4] Black
theology is therefore seen as "a ready-made Western theology turned into
a consumption commodity for Africans." Since it ignores African culture

but chooses to exploit the conceptualization and methodology of Western theology, Black theology, it is contended, still does theology "within the field of Western European Graeco-Roman-rooted thought-forms and *Weltanschauung.*"[5]

Because the hermeneutic approach of the liberationists fails to include cultural analysis of the African reality, the inculturationists have argued that liberation is not and cannot be the only viable theological option for contemporary Africa.[6]

In my opinion, to restrict the African theological reality to the political plane is to oversimplify the complexity of the African liberation struggle for full humanity. The liberation struggle is also a struggle for the retrieval, conservation and survival of the cultural values of black Africans. The primary phase of an authentic liberation struggle begins with the cultural challenge posed by the oppressed group against their oppressors. Thus, for Amilcar Cabral, for example, the African struggle for liberation is "the most significant cultural factor in the life of African peoples."[7] Cabral further elaborates on this significant truth when he views liberation as "an act of culture." Cabral then substantiates:

> Study of the history of liberation struggles shows that they have generally been preceded by an upsurge of cultural manifestations. . . . Whatever the conditions of subjection of a people to foreign domination and the influence of economic, political and social factors in the exercise of this domination, it is generally within the cultural factor that we find the germ of challenge which leads to the structuring and development of the liberation movement.[8]

It is doubtful, indeed, whether the liberationists would bring total liberation to the poor and the oppressed, whom they claim to defend but whose culture they tend to ignore. A dangerous paralysis in black theological praxis is exposed in Itumeleng Mosala's statement that "Black theology's inability to connect adequately with the culture of resistance of the oppressed and exploited black people needs to be considered in the light of the class bases and commitments of the black theologians."[9]

LIBERATIONIST THESIS ON INCULTURATION

For the liberationist, the inculturationists' disengagement from the critical questions raised by the political and economic realities of the continent points to a precarious dimension of that strand of theology.[10] Liberationists also fault African theologians for failing to take the racial component seriously.

The inculturationists' methodological obsession with culture so dominates their range of vision that it becomes impossible to employ other dimensions of the African theological reality. It is not enough, maintains

Desmond Tutu, for the inculturationists to show that Africa has had an authentic religious and cultural heritage; rather, African theology "must now begin to address itself more seriously to present-day issues of the modern African and grapple with the enormous problems that have followed political independence."[11] For Manas Buthelezi, the inculturationists' reification of the African cultural past has meant a digression from today's critical social issues.[12]

Bonganjalo Goba also takes the old guards of the inculturation school to task. For him, Charles Nyamiti's stress on adaptation "tends to be very abstract without providing a praxis," and Bolaji Idowu's indigenization approach also "underestimated the forces of Western ecclesiastical domination and neocolonialism which continue to be a disturbing force on the continent of Africa."[13] The inculturationists, it is further argued by Chikane, ignore the reality of oppression not only in the areas of race and gender, but also of class, because they "fail to see the class culture they have identified with."[14] Bénézet Bujo is equally critical of the inculturation model: "The theology of inculturation, so often preached triumphantly in African churches," he writes, "is a pompous irrelevance, truly an ideological superstructure at the service of the bourgeoisie."[15] African theologians are therefore urged to become aware of the "reality gap" between them and the masses of the people, between their writings and the situation in which people live.

In my opinion, it is doubtful whether true inculturation can take place if most theologians who are enthusiastic about African culture are themselves alienated from that culture. As an alienated or culturally rootless class, they become unaware of the cultural resistance of the African masses, which has always been an integral and determining part of Africa's struggle for liberation. As Cabral maintained, before such culturally alienated intellectuals begin talking about Africanization, they themselves must undergo "re-Africanization" — a reconversion experience that can take place only through daily contact with the grass-roots masses and peasants and the communion of sacrifices the liberation struggle demands.[16]

True inculturation takes place in the reality of human experience. Certainly one must heed Bujo's warning that "a theology which preache[s] the necessity of inculturation, but simply ignore[s] the surrounding social misery" must be avoided.[17] The African church cannot be truly inculturated if only one dimension of the totality of African experience is taken seriously and other aspects of existence ignored. Inculturation cannot occur in an oppressive and exploitative environment. It only happens in an atmosphere of freedom. An inculturated church in Africa is a church emancipated from Western imperialism and domination. Just as an authentic liberation cannot take place without inculturation, so also a true inculturation cannot take place without liberation. Africa needs both emphases.

The African church, therefore, cannot be truly inculturated if it continues to be dictated to from Rome or any other city of the West. "The faith that will be able to say anything to these generations," observes Jean-Marc Ela, "will not content itself with an Africanization of Roman ecclesiastical models."[18] Unless there is an ecclesiological revolution that will radically transform the parent-child relationship between North and South, inculturation cannot be achieved.

PITFALLS IN THE INCULTURATION-LIBERATION APPROACHES

The realities of contemporary Africa should remind both African and South African black theologians of the boundaries they have imposed upon their own theological reflection. The black African cry today for liberation, arising from the voices of the dehumanized poor, the yelling of exploited workers, and the groaning of suffering peasants, denounces not just the contradictions within African societies, but also the disintegrative and myopic vision of both African and Black theologies.

Lack of such a unitary hermeneutical vision debilitates the efforts of both African and black theologians. It leads to a dearth of theological praxis that paralyzes Black theology in its work among the black working class in the face of capitalist South African society. It also deactivates African theology's commitment to the challenges of African women facing patriarchal African societies and male-dominated churches.

An attempt must be made to critically examine the common limitations of the premises upon which both inculturationists and liberationists construct their theological edifices. Otherwise, a unitary perception of inculturation and liberation cannot challenge us in our search for an integrative vision of the two theological systems.

A first observable weakness in the two theological approaches becomes evident in the lack of awareness of what constitutes *culture* in the African context. Discussion of African culture in both African and Black theologies is often superficially understood to mean only the traditional worldview, symbols, customs and art. It is this narrow definition of culture that inadvertently leads to theological parochialism.

Such a microcultural perspective of the contemporary African scene has dangerous hermeneutical consequences. On the one hand, it has led inculturationists to disregard present sociopolitical and economic issues in their theological agenda. On the other hand, liberationists seem unaware that their sociopolitical and economic concerns are a semiotic domain of culture. Perhaps we need to heed James Ngugi's warning not to confuse culture with irrelevant traditionalism. A meaningful culture, he insists, is "the one born out of the present hopes and especially the hopes of the impoverished peasantry, and that of the growing body of urban workers."[19] For Frantz Fanon, it is around the struggle of oppressed African people—the wretched of the earth—for full humanity that the black African culture "takes on substance, and not around songs, poems or folklore."[20]

The current African scene is marked by *both cultural continuity and change*. It is not just things of the precolonial past that constitute culture in contemporary Africa. The entirety of African culture cannot be limited to traditional symbols. Culture is not made only of symbols but also of praxis.

A thorough study of African culture cannot take place unless the power structures in African societies and the forces that offer resistance to these powerful structures are well understood. Analysis of contemporary African culture cannot therefore be limited to "traditionalism." It must include the whole totality of African existence—politics, economics, religion, precolonial worldview and thought forms, philosophy, language, ethnicity, music, arts, sexuality, and changes brought about by modern science and technology that have had impact on African people. These are not separate parts of the whole African existence, but, rather, they are *intersecting dimensions* of the African experience and African existence.

One theologian may, for the purposes of analysis, emphasize one or more of these many dimensions, depending on the theologian's main focus, but even whenever the focus is on a particular dimension, the theologian must consciously realize that the other dimensions are unyieldingly present. In point of fact, the legitimate and complementary role of each must be stressed for a relevant theology and for a universally authentic Christianity. African theology's concern for just the African past and customs must rapidly give way to a macrocultural level of African reality that encompasses as well the sociopolitical and economic aspects of life.

Culture is not an unchanging or static reality; culture is dynamic. An African theorist who has emphasized this dynamic nature of culture is Amilcar Cabral. He holds that "no culture is a perfect, finished whole"; like history, culture is "necessarily an expanding and developing phenomenon."[21] Cabral then makes an indestructible connection between culture and socioeconomic realities: "Even more importantly," he writes, "we must bear in mind that the fundamental characteristic of culture is its close, dependent and reciprocal connection with the economic and social reality of the environment, with the level of productive forces and the mode of production of the society which created it."[22]

In discussing African culture in theological hermeneutics, it is necessary to understand and acknowledge the general processes of cultural dynamics—of change and stability in culture. Unquestionably, culture varies from one group to another, but it is also true that culture changes from one period of time to another within one single group. Thus,

If culture changes, if culture is dynamic, it must be studied in its historical dimension as well as in terms of the relationship among its components. Where new influences impinge on any society, a student of culture is at once confronted with the problem of how much of the pre-existing body of custom and belief is discarded, how much is modified, and how much is retained.[23]

Reference to the dynamism of culture brings us to yet another limitation of both African and Black theologies, especially in the way they interpret African culture. Most key African and South African black theologians tend to regard culture as a *past-oriented* reality and therefore speak of African culture as if it were a static commodity that can and should be salvaged from the shrines of the past and brought onto the modern stage to be exhibited.

Such a simplistic interpretation among inculturationists is seen in Kwesi Dickson's attempt to answer the self-imposed question as to whether African theologians have meaningfully defined the given situation by limiting their discussion to the area of culture. "Now," Dickson writes, "no one would deny that there is a cultural reality in Africa which colonial rule and the more recent influences of urbanization, technology, etc. have not been able to destroy."[24]

The implication here is obvious: For Dickson, African "cultural reality" is what existed *before* colonialism and modernization, and therefore has nothing to do with modern social changes and vice versa. It is clear here also that there has not been any regard for the process of cultural dynamics, namely, that there is stability as well as change in culture over time. Even E. W. Fashole-Luke has strongly challenged his own inculturationist colleagues whether they "may not choose a wrong point of departure, if they regarded Africa's rural past as a frame of reference for African Christian theologies."[25]

This past-oriented reality given to culture in theological hermeneutics is even more pronounced among liberationists. Allan Boesak displays this hermeneutic bondage when he argues his case for Black theology as a contextual and authentic theology:

An authentic situational theology is prophetic, critical, not merely excavating corpses of tradition; but taking critically those traditions from the past that can play a humanizing and revolutionary role in our contemporary society. It is taking from the past that which is positively good, thereby offering a critique of the present and opening perspective for the future.[26]

Perhaps Manas Buthelezi's critique of indigenization provides the finest example of what we mean by rendering culture a past-oriented connotation.

[T]here are many Africans who still live according to the precepts of [the] "past". . . . There is a difference between psychologically "living in the past" in order to compensate for the virtually existential emptiness of the present, thereby trying to mitigate the conscious awareness of the horror of its oppressive destitution, and "living in the past" because it is able to offer something substantial within the framework of the concrete realities of the present, as much as it used to. Who can blame those who have the feeling that missionaries, with their right hands, are diverting our attention to our glorious past so that we may not see what their left hands, as well as those of their fellow whites, are doing in the dehumanization of our lives in the present? Who can blame a person who sees no wisdom in "writing theological poetry" about the past era while our human dignity is being systematically taken from our lives every day in the present?[27]

Buthelezi's consternation over the concerns of indigenization that emphasize culture is that the "African past" may be romanticized and conceived of in isolation from present realities. This "past," which is perceived as a worldview, Buthelezi contends, is nothing more than a historical abstraction of "what once was."[28]

Undeniably, Buthelezi has good reason to be concerned about the tendency of the indigenization approach to romanticize the past while people suffer in the present. This is an obvious danger that has manifested itself in the theological hermeneutics of indigenization, whose deliberate refusal to engage the critical issues of sociopolitical and economic realities has constituted an enormous obstacle to the liberation of Africa. Jean-Marc Ela has perceptively pointed out how precarious it is "to call the past something that it is not," and falsify or distort it just to support an orientation.[29] Such a narrow view of culture, or even the misconception of it as something belonging only to the past, explains liberationists' erroneous position that African culture cannot be relevant to the present African situation.

In point of fact, culture to the African is *life*; therefore our perspective on culture must be holistic—embracing every dimension that regulates societal life and not just traditional symbols or customs excavated from the night of precolonial past. Theology is neither archaeology nor anthropology.

Admittedly, no people "can truly come into a position of maturity and responsibility without a sense of continuity with their own past and respect for the value of their own attainment."[30] However, harking back to "the good old days" is no solution to present problems. Today most black African youth are so highly politicized that their political consciousness will no longer tolerate African leaders who evade their responsibilities and exploit the goodwill of African people by telling them to go back to their traditional support systems, many of which are now broken or changed beyond recognition. Our world today is no longer that of our ancestors. There is a need to redefine contemporary African culture which is veritably not exhaustible by "traditionalism."

Culture should not only be symbols but also praxis; Africa's political and economic realities are *de facto* inseparable parts of contemporary culture. If this be the case, then, are both inculturationists and liberationists not guilty of oversimplifying the complexity of the African theological reality and the African condition?

What implications does this process of cultural dynamics have for the future of theology in Africa? Where do we go from here? Do we have to see the two hermeneutical foci—inculturation and liberation—as complementary? Or does the thrust of one exclude the other? Or should we perhaps search for and work toward a position beyond both?

TOWARD A SYNTHETIC INTERPRETATION

In an effort to redefine African culture, I have demonstrated the need for a holistic view of culture. In the African situation, this *macro-culture* encompasses the sociopolitical and economic, as well as the religiocultural dimensions of human existence, and therefore of the African theological reality.

It is to this end that I postulate South African Black theology as a theology which seeks to analyze and engage the politico-socioeconomic dimension of contemporary African culture or, more precisely, the ongoing African cultural revolution. As evidence suggests, there is such a trajectory of thought among black theologians. For instance, Bonganjalo Goba shares this assumption when he writes:

> Black theological reflection is by sheer necessity grounded in our historical cultural experience. It attempts to relate to our cultural context not in a static way but in the context of the dynamic cultural revolution that is currently going on in Africa. It must reflect the tension between the past and present in our cultural experience, between the Christian mythos and the present African contemporary experience.[31]

For Goba, as for some of his colleagues, Black theology is a new way of expressing theologically the ongoing African cultural revolution—a revolution in which God's goal of liberation is manifesting itself.

Dwight Hopkins has insightfully pointed out the "cultural theological trends" in Black theology, both in its South African and North American manifestations.[32] Unlike Kwesi Dickson, Hopkins recognizes the dynamism of culture, and when discussing the cultural themes on which the Black Consciousness Movement in South Africa rested, he does not limit this to "traditional, indigenous culture" but extends it to include "self-reliance" and what he calls "new values and black pride," which were also political and economic themes in the Black Consciousness Movement.[33]

On the other hand, an African theology of inculturation needs to be reminded once more that "part of colonial oppression has been the belittling of the culture of the oppressed. Liberation is not only political; it must also be a cultural achievement, a reassertion of the validity of spiritual and intellectual continuity with the precolonial past." Therefore, "[t]he central theme of African theology is then itself a theme of liberation and a significant element within a black theology context."[34] That is why theologians such as Desmond Tutu, James Cone and others have stressed that the relation between the two perspectives does not have to be antagonistic; they are rather complementary, and both emphases are needed. Gwinyai Muzorewa's explanation of this point is illuminating:

> Black and African theologies are closely related although African theology has a particular focus on Africanization as the manifestation of their liberation from foreign dominating powers, both in ecclesiastical and secular terms. Therefore Africanization is a form of liberation *from* a colonial mentality, *to* a full humanity. It is also liberation from cultural limitations and deprivation.[35]

In Africa today, the "theological dilemma" is no longer a quandary between "liberation" and "inculturation," which is, in fact, a false dilemma. Rather, Africa's problem "is in *the battle for the liberation to which a new culture is called to give birth in dominated societies.*"[36] In this liberation struggle, the African church "must find its ways of expressing its faith in a basic articulation between popular culture and the liberation of the popular masses, which have remained close to their mores and traditions."[37]

Today, Africa's main challenge is to be found in its struggle for liberation—a struggle that confronts black African theologians from every angle of contemporary African culture. It is also a struggle which, because of the paralysis of Africa's theological and cultural analyses, lacks integrative vision, solidarity, mobilization of the masses and transformative praxis.

Theologically, this struggle for liberation is thus to be fought on two fronts. The first is the struggle for liberation in the socioeconomic and political realms of life. Focusing on these dimensional realities in Africa, a relevant, contextual and authentic theology has to grapple with all the political and socioeconomic structures that tend to oppress, exploit, impoverish, dehumanize and dominate the black African. Such a prophetic theology must uncompromisingly face the realities of colonialism, classism, racism, neocolonialism, sexism, capitalist imperialism, ideological conflicts, disunity and underdevelopment, and everything that militates against the realization of social justice based on equality. It is precisely here that we find African theology, as narrowly defined in inculturation theology, to be inadequate. A reappreciation of traditional religious culture will have no meaning if it does not contribute to African people's awareness that they are the victims of a diabolical form of oppression, or that their very cultural ontology is being incessantly pauperized by suffocating structures.

Second, the struggle for Africa's liberation is also in the religiocultural spheres of life. Here, theologians not only have to make use of the African worldview and thought forms to open "the door for people's creative participation in the interpretation of the Gospel for their life situation";[38] they must also struggle against foreign cultural domination and against the belittling of African culture that has eroded African cultural pride. The liberation struggle must include a religiocultural struggle that seeks to liberate black Africans from dehumanizing customs and other traditional practices that oppress people, especially women. Furthermore, it has to grapple with the problems of ethnic conflicts and linguistic barriers, as well as the problems of religious pluralism that have resulted in the loss of lives in some parts of Africa.

The importance of people's religious culture cannot be overemphasized. To deprive a people of their culture is to deprive them of "God's gift and what is authentic in their being."[39] That is why African theologians are struggling against "anthropological poverty," the denial of their cultural ontology. It is here also that Black theology needs to be reminded that "fostering pride in one's ancestral culture and religion [is] . . . an indispensable part of the liberation process."[40]

Religion is an integral part of people's culture; it also has to do with their being and existence. John Mbiti has described religion as "an ontological phenomenon" for the African, and he is right.[41] Mérard Kayitakibga has succinctly described the importance of traditional religion for the African existence:

African religion intimately penetrates all aspects of social life from birth through death. According to traditional religious concepts, there is no separation or division between the visible and the invisible. The African blends with the hereafter in a normal way. The invisible world is present in the visible world. The universe is sacred. It forms a unitary and dynamic whole of which certain parts are visible and other parts, more important and more determinative, are invisible.[42]

A relevant, contextual and authentic theology for Africa must have a unitary perception of inculturation and liberation. Such a dynamic definition of inclusive theology would lack *neither* an appreciation for traditional religious culture—the context from which the overwhelming majority of Christians in Africa come, and in which many of them still continue to live—*nor* refuse engagement in dialogue with the critical issues raised by contemporary political and economic factors—factors that are the main reasons for Africa's crisis and backwardness in world affairs.

Today, the African call is earnest and powerful because of the sociopolitical liberation it aims to achieve and the religiocultural dignity it seeks to attain. It demands a response, a *theological* response that must be at once political and cultural. It is upon the pillars of both culture and politics that a meaningfully relevant theological hermeneutics would emerge that can radically face the challenges of the future.

It is when both the liberationist and inculturationist analyses of African theological reality are integrated that we arrive at a new perspective in the creation of a unified theology of cultural and political liberation.

BLACK AFRICAN THEOLOGY EN ROUTE . . .

A theology that synthesizes South African Black theology of liberation and African theology of inculturation must at once be *black* and *African* to be able to address the concerns of both politico-socioeconomic and religio-cultural realities. The search for such an integrative vision will be found in a new theological project that does not nullify the uniqueness of either South African Black theology or African theology, but which advocates a reciprocal action between liberation and inculturation. Such a new theological enterprise becomes imperative because it seeks to preserve the unitary vision of cosmic reality which characterizes the wisdom of traditional Africa and eliminates the polarity and conflict between black and African theologians, and also because it links two theological systems and provides a total experience for African people in a world dominated by white supremacy.

A theology with such a synthetic interpretation of the two foci is what I envision as Black African theology. As a theology of political and cultural liberation, Black African theology underlines *blackness* in doing theology with a liberation-political thrust and also accentuates *Africanness* in doing theology with an Africanization-cultural leaning. Thus, Black African theology is a theology of political and cultural liberation jointly created by South African Black theology and African theology for the total emancipation of African people.

This synthetic interpretation of theology in Africa has already been stressed by both black and African theologians, albeit in different ways. For instance, Desmond Tutu, Bonganjalo Goba and Itumeleng Mosala have all emphasized the need to draw insights from African traditional religion and culture for South African Black theology. These theologians and others like them have already suggested the need for a synthesis of the two foci. Dwight Hopkins has also found the common denominator between the Black theology in North American and South African Black theology to be "the gospel of political and cultural liberation."[43] There is therefore an agreement among black theologians that the gospel message of Jesus Christ brings political as well as cultural freedom to poor and oppressed black people.

Furthermore, African theologians such as Engelbert Mveng, Burgess Carr, Kofi Appiah-Kubi, Jesse Mugambi and others have also stressed themes of both liberation and indigenization. By maintaining that the two themes converge, these theologians have carried into the attempts at synthesis perspectives which are the concerns of both African theology and Black theology.

Indeed, Burgess Carr is one of the few African theologians or church leaders to have a unitary perception of liberation and inculturation. For example, in responding to the call for a new world order, he insists that "African theology is influenced by the radical politics of 'Liberation' and

... 'Incarnation'."[44] Burgess Carr underscores the fact that, although liberation and incarnation represent the heart of the gospel, this significant truth has not been "the normative theological point of view current in the Church, not even in the African Church." Rather, he continued, it has been for those who have committed themselves to the struggle against the evil forces of modernism to liberate the Christian faith itself from the imperialist "monoculture" of the Western world.[45]

The call for a synthetic interpretation of the two main theological-hermeneutical directions on the African continent is in line with the visionary perspective expressed by the Pan-African Conference of Third World Theologians for the future of theology in Africa. The African situation, declares the conference, demands a new theological methodology that is accountable to Africans—a theology understood in the context of African cultural life and the creative efforts of African people to shape a new and different future.[46]

The contextuality and relevance of this new theological-hermeneutical project becomes evident in its engagement of both the political and cultural realities of black Africa, which has had a long history of slavery, colonial exploitation, racism and sexism and is still faced with the dangerous threats of classism, neocolonialism, hunger, diseases, rampant coups d'état, repressive regimes, denial of human rights and so on.

Therefore, the context of Black African theology "is the life of our states, our peoples, our churches with the numerous challenges which they have to face: political, economic, cultural and religious," and in our religiocultural and socioeconomic and political struggles for liberation. This theology—which may also draw insights from black African poets, novelists, artists, dramatists, political scientists, anthropologists and sociologists— becomes therefore "a spiritual mobilization to help God's people to face these challenges."[47]

... WITH MULTIDIMENSIONAL ANALYSES

The social arrangements of both neocolonial (i.e., independent) Africa and racist South African societies do not encourage mutuality. Both racist and neocolonial relationships in Africa are structured on the basis of greed and injustice. To make the Christian story meaningfully pertinent in the light of these unjust and oppressive conditions, theology in Africa must be responsive to the demands of all the situations it seeks to address.

In their efforts to gain full understanding of the social situation in contemporary Africa, certain theologians in both independent and South Africa have already begun to explore Africa's historical and structural relationships. This social analysis of the African reality not only serves as an effective instrument to discern the situation in which the poor black African masses live, but it also becomes an indispensable step toward a liberative theological praxis. In this regard, the significant contributions of Itumeleng

Mosala from South Africa and Jean-Marc Ela from Cameroon deserve to be mentioned.[48]

Like most oppressed people in Asia and Latin America, black Africans today see the world in a state of conflict — conflict not merely in terms of *class*, as Karl Marx saw it, but also in terms of *race, sex* and *culture*. This is why, when it comes to a searching discernment into the African situation and experience, Marx's perception of the sociohistorical reality *alone* becomes too narrow and rigid and does not provide us with the much-needed answers concerning racial, gender and cultural oppression.

Surely Marxist social criticism, which brings to light the economic exploitation of workers, is indispensable for Black African theological hermeneutics. As Africa continues to make the painful transition to industrialization, Marx's understanding of power in modern industrial society as consisting of "a group's participation in the decision-making processes of the major institutions that affect their destinies"[49] will help arouse the consciousness of black African working classes to insist on participating in the decision-making processes of institutions of production that play such significant roles in their lives. Multinational corporations, generally based in the United States, Western Europe and Japan, have enormous economic, political and cultural powers of exploitation and domination in Africa.

In addition, African and black theologians cannot ignore Marxist social criticism in seeking to understand the global economic order, capitalist exploitation and poverty; the more they do this, the further they distance themselves from the fundamental reasons for black African economic exploitation and domination, as well as from effective weapons to combat this exploitation.

However, the black African theologian's complete and fanatic dependence upon orthodox Marxist class analysis of society, which sees only the oppressive and negative components in culture and religion but does not appreciate the importance of popular cultural resistance against oppression and domination, rather complicates the problem. This is why one must agree more with Cornel West that, "*some form of Marxist analysis* is indispensable to understand the international economic order, capitalist societies and the perpetuation and preservation of gross inequalities and injustice in those societies."[50] Certainly, there are different nuances of Marxism, some of which do not downplay the significance of popular culture, such as that of Antonio Gramsci or Amilcar Cabral.[51]

The term *Marxism* comprises not only the theory and practice of Marx, but also the theoretical and practical modifications introduced in the course of time, under circumstances unforeseen by Karl Marx and Friederich Engels. George Lichtheim is correct in saying that *Marxism* as a term has come to stand for many different things.[52]

The inadequacy of orthodox Marxist class analysis in dealing with the issues of sex and race and with the religiocultural realities of the African world has been pointed out by many writers and theologians. As far as the gender question is concerned, some theorists have concluded that "neither Marx nor the Marxist tradition is able to develop an adequate understanding of patriarchy."[53] Isaac Balbus has cogently argued how Marx assumed that the inner logic of capitalism is antipatriarchal and, therefore, Marx never anticipated the problems that face contemporary feminist theorists, namely, how to make a revolution at once anticapitalist and antipatriarchal.[54]

According to Balbus, feminist Marxists—in their search for another approach that will treat "the formation of sexual identity as problematical and therefore worthy of independent theoretical attention"—are turning to Sigmund Freud and the Freudian tradition "for the illumination of the problem of patriarchy that Marx does not, and cannot, provide." However, this Freudo-Marxist theory of patriarchy is also seen to be ultimately incoherent.[55]

In point of fact, the contradictions in African societies demand that African women redefine the tasks and questions of theology from a different perspective—from their own concrete and experiential perspective. Like their counterparts in the rest of the Third World, African women must determine their own theological methodology and agenda. EATWOT VI affirms this when it declares:

> The oppression of women is a stark reality in the Third World where many cultures are strongly patriarchal. But to what extent this is an issue for Third World women is to be determined by the Third World women themselves. Neither Third World men nor First World women can determine the Third World women's agenda.[56]

On the religiocultural realities of African existence, the Marxian tradition has also been found to be ineffective. For instance, Frank Chikane writes,

> [T]he Marxist tools of analysis are not adequate to deal with the religio-cultural realities of Africa. . . . A radical, revolutionary approach to culture and religion should, therefore, start from the concrete reality that there are such things as culture and religion; that both are ambivalent phenomena; that they have both a reactionary and revolutionary potential. What we need to do as theologians is to discover this revolutionary potential of both culture and religion in the course of the struggle for the *basileia* or the new order.[57]

The Marxian tradition fails to recognize that cultural and religious attitudes and values have their own life and logic which are not completely accountable to class analysis. For Cornel West, orthodox Marxist analysis of culture and religion is to be rejected not because it is wrong, but because of its narrowness, rigidity and dogmatism.

It views popular culture and religion only as instruments of domination, vehicles of pacification. It sees only their negative and repressive elements ... [and] refuses to acknowledge the positive, liberating aspects of popular culture and religion, and their potential for fostering structural social change.[58]

What about the issue of race and class analysis? Perhaps this is the most controversial aspect of the analytical debate, especially in South Africa, where racism thrives and black theologians also take Marxist class analysis more seriously.

In South Africa, it is not all that easy to draw a demarcation of where race ends and class begins or vice versa. The agreement among many theorists is that racism is a tool of economic exploitation. Although this may be the case, in South Africa, racism has become an ideology of its own that tends to lead an independent life but, in turn, influences economic and political relationships.[59]

In fact, the oppressive structure of South African society is, as Kwame Nkrumah has described it, a "racist class structure,"[60] and racism and classism have "to be fought concurrently, at one and the same time."[61] Buti Tlhagale has also observed how in South Africa "the relations of production are presented in racial terms in order to safeguard the material and political interests of both the white ruling class and the white working class."[62]

If this be the case, then is not the dilemma between analysts who view race as a determinative classification of understanding and analysts who take class as the only factor for analyzing South Africa a false one? As a matter of fact, neither class nor race alone can determine the reality and the complex nature of South African society. It would be very ineffective, indeed, for a theologian to rely completely on orthodox Marxist analysis as the only weapon needed to battle all the social conflicts and forms of oppression.

This is the main flaw of Itumeleng Mosala's impressive and challenging 1989 book, *Biblical Hermeneutics and Black Theology in South Africa*. By employing historical materialism associated with Marx as the sole analytical tool in biblical and theological hermeneutics, Mosala has inadvertently exposed himself to the dangers we have been talking about.[63] For instance, it is not surprising that despite Mosala's acknowledgment of class, cultural, gender and racial struggles in the Bible,[64] his materialist reading only allows him to effectively analyze and explain the biblical class struggle. The other struggles—culture, gender and race—are left without effective analysis and explication.

Furthermore, Mosala's materialist reading of South African society enables him to locate the ideological and class positions of black theologians and identify three nuances in Black theology corresponding to these class locations.[65] However, he is unable to exorcise the sexist and chauvinistic idiosyncrasies of male black theologians; neither does he give any effective analysis of culture, which plays such an important role in his hermeneutics. If, as he has observed elsewhere, the apartheid ideology in South Africa "seeks separateness because it posits the superiority of one culture and the inferiority of the other,"[66] then cultural analysis must be taken seriously on its own merit.

In Africa today, the major patterns of social conflict cohere around four organizing principles: race, class, sex and culture. In the struggle for liberation and anthropological dignity, it is necessary to make an analytical distinction between these different but interrelated forms and experiences of oppression.

As a theological enterprise that takes social analysis seriously, Black African theology would wisely advocate the utilization of the following four models of analysis and stress their dialectical relations: 1) the *race model* against racism; 2) the *sex model* against gender oppression; 3) the *class analysis model* or Marxist and neo-Marxist tools of analysis against classism; and 4) the *religiocultural model* of analysis against cultural oppression.

All these models of analysis should inform black African theological hermeneutics, along with our interpretation of scripture. For as much as we emphasize the theme of liberation in scripture, we also are aware of the oppressive elements in the Bible. We should take seriously the theological findings of African women that the Bible is a patriarchal book,[67] as well as Mosala's conclusion that the Bible "is a ruling class document and represents the ideological and political interests of the ruling class."[68]

The experiences of black Africans in a patriarchal, racist and unjust society provide the epistemological lenses for our interpretation of the Word of God contained in scripture. Therefore, *rereading* of the Bible plays a crucial role. Consequently, in our interpretation of scripture, Black African theology of political and cultural liberation should take hermeneutics of suspicion seriously.

This applies equally to our use of Christian heritage and tradition as a source of theology. Black African theology makes a sharp distinction between what religion — especially Christianity — has sought after as an ideal, and what the actual result of its influence on the lives of its adherents has been. We have to say farewell to the days when the imperialist came masquerading in missionary clothing and when missionary reports were written to draw tears, sympathy and funds from Western Christians who wanted "Ethiopia to stretch forth her hands to God."

NOTES

1. Pieris, *An Asian Theology of Liberation*, p. 111.
2. Ela, *African Cry*, p. 128.
3. Goba, *An Agenda for Black Theology*, p. 14.
4. For John Mbiti, for example, Black theology with liberation as a main concern is "a specifically American phenomenon" and has nothing to do with African the-

ology. See Mbiti, "An African Views American Black Theology," in Wilmore and Cone, *Black Theology*, pp. 480-81.

5. Setiloane, "Theological Trends in Africa," p. 48.

6. Charles Nyamiti, for example, sees the militant tone of Black theology and its emphasis on the theme of liberation as an attitude which may "lead to lack of objectivity and to distortion of the facts." See his "Approaches to African Theology," in Torres and Fabella, eds., *The Emergent Gospel*, p. 43.

7. Cabral, *Unity and Struggle*, p. 148.

8. Ibid., pp. 142-43.

9. Mosala, *Biblical Hermeneutics and Black Theology in South Africa*, pp. 24-25. Mosala has as well demonstrated how the black struggle, which sets Black theology's agenda, also "tends to falter wherever and whenever it ceases to be informed by a critical reading of its own history and culture" (p. 85).

10. See Desmond Tutu, "Black Theology/African Theology—Soul Mates or Antagonists?" in Wilmore and Cone, *Black Theology*, p. 490. For Tutu, because of this lack of engagement, African theology has failed "to produce a sufficiently sharp cutting edge . . ." and he urges it "to recover its prophetic calling."

11. Tutu, "Black Theology," p. 76.

12. Buthelezi, "Toward Indigenous Theology in South Africa," in Torres and Fabella, eds., *The Emergent Gospel*, pp. 56-75.

13. Goba, *An Agenda for Black Theology*, pp. 11 and 12 respectively.

14. Frank Chikane, "EATWOT and Third World Theologies . . ." in Abraham, *Third World Theologies*, p. 161.

15. Bénézet Bujo, *African Theology in Its Social Context*, p. 71.

16. Cabral, *Unity and Struggle*, p. 145.

17. Bujo, *African Theology in Its Social Context*, p. 70.

18. Ela, *African Cry*, p. 102.

19. James Ngugi, "National Culture," in Minogue and Molloy, eds., *African Aims and Attitudes*, p. 243.

20. Frantz Fanon, *The Wretched of the Earth*, p. 235.

21. Cabral, *Unity and Struggle*, p. 149.

22. Ibid.

23. William R. Bascom and Melville J. Herskovits, eds., *Continuity and Change in African Cultures* (Chicago/London: University of Chicago Press, 1959), p. 2.

24. Dickson, *Theology In Africa*, p. 134; cf. pp. 47f.

25. Fashole-Luke, "Footpaths and Signposts to African Christian Theologies," p. 404. Unlike most African theologians, Fashole-Luke recognizes that "African cultures present problems of the past, present and future," and therefore asks on which of these three moments African theologians should base their theologies.

26. Boesak, "Coming in out of the Wilderness," p. 83.

27. Buthelezi, "Toward Indigenous Theology in South Africa," p. 62.

28. Ibid.

29. Ela, *African Cry*, p. 127.

30. Ralph Dodge, *The Unpopular Missionary* (Westwood, N.J.: Fleming H. Revell Co., 1964), p. 44.

31. Bonganjalo Goba, "Doing Theology in South Africa: A Black Christian Perspective," *Journal of Theology for Southern Africa*, no. 31, June 1980, p. 26.

32. Hopkins, *Black Theology USA and South Africa*, p. 165.

33. Ibid., pp. 27f. Cf. Leatt et al., *Contending Ideologies in South Africa*, pp. 109f.,

where the authors talk about Black Communalism, the political and economic policies of the BCM, which "is said to be rooted in traditional African culture."

34. Adrian Hastings, "On African Theology," *Scottish Journal of Theology*, vol. 37, no. 3, 1984, p. 368; cf. his *African Catholicism*, p. 91.

35. Gwinyai Muzorewa, "A Definition of a Future African Theology," *African Theological Journal*, vol. 19, no. 2, 1990, p. 177.

36. Ela, *African Cry*, p. 130. Emphasis added.

37. Ibid.

38. James Cone, "A Black American Perspective on the Future of African Theology," in Appiah-Kubi and Torres, eds., *African Theology En Route*, p. 184.

39. S. O. Abogunrin, "The Church and Cultural Renewal in Africa," *Indian Missiological Review*, vol. 10, no. 3, July 1988, p. 240.

40. Matthew Schoffeleers, "Black and African Theology in Southern Africa," *Journal of Religion in Africa*, vol. 18, Fasc. 2, June 1988, p. 101.

41. Mbiti, *African Religions and Philosophy*, p. 15.

42. Mérard Kayitakibga, "L'Eglise Catholique en Afrique Face aux Traditions Religieuses Africaines," *Bulletin — Secretariatus Pro Non Christianis*, 22/3, 69, 1988, p. 207.

43. Hopkins, *Black Theology USA and South Africa*, p. 166.

44. Burgess Carr, "An African Christian Response," in J. G. W. Ryan, ed., *Christian Faith and the New World Order* (Washington D.C.: Interreligious Peace Colloquium, 1978), p. 202.

45. Ibid.

46. In Appiah-Kubi and Torres, eds., *African Theology En Route*, p. 193.

47. Mveng, "African Liberation Theology," *Concilium 199*, p. 18.

48. For Mosala's significant contribution to contemporary theological hermeneutics, see his *Biblical Hermeneutics and Black Theology in South Africa* (1989); for Ela's, see his *My Faith as an African* (1988), as well as his *African Cry* (1986). With these works, the two theologians have challenged both the African church and its theology to live up to the liberating heritage of Jesus' gospel.

49. Cornel West, "Black Theology and Marxist Thought," in Wilmore and Cone, eds., *Black Theology*, p. 558.

50. Cornel West, "The Challenge of the Non-Latin Americans," in Sergio Torres and John Eagleson, eds., *The Challenge of Basic Christian Communities* (Maryknoll, N.Y.: Orbis Books, 1981), pp. 255-56. Emphasis added.

51. See Cornel West, "Black Theology and Marxist Thought," in Wilmore and Cone, eds., *Black Theology*, p. 562, where he describes Antonio Gramsci as "the most Marxist theorist of culture in this century"; cf. Gramsci's writing in Q. Hoare and G. Nowell Smith, eds., *Selections from the Prison Notebooks of Antonio Gramsci* (New York: International Publishers, 1971). For Amilcar Cabral, see his *Unity and Struggle*, esp. pp. 138-54.

52. George Lichtheim, *Marxism: An Historical and Critical Study* (New York: Frederick A. Praeger, 1961), pp. xiiif. It is precisely for this reason that one must give a qualification as to which particular nuance of Marxist analysis one is referring, especially in the African context. Here, my main critique is directed against orthodox Marxism as put forward by Marx. Therefore the kind of Marxist analysis I am advocating here is one which has been tested on African soil and does not downplay the importance of popular culture, as, for instance, in Amilcar Cabral's analysis, which sees liberation as an act of culture.

53. Isaac D. Balbus, *Marxism and Domination* (Princeton, N.J.: Princeton University Press, 1982), p. 169.

54. Ibid., pp. 63ff.

55. Ibid., pp. 169-70.

56. See the Final Statement of EATWOT VI Conference in Virginia Fabella and Sergio Torres, eds., *Doing Theology in a Divided World* (Maryknoll, N.Y.: Orbis Books, 1985), p. 186.

57. Frank Chikane, "EATWOT and Third World Theologies . . .," in Abraham, *Third World Theologies*, p. 158.

58. West, "Black Theology and Marxist Thought," in Wilmore and Cone, eds., *Black Theology*, p. 560.

59. See S. M. Bengu, "A Social and Political Analysis of Apartheid/Racism from a Black Lutheran Perspective," in Albert Pero and Ambrose Moyo, eds., *Theology and the Black Experience* (Minneapolis: Augsburg Publishing House, 1988), p. 145; cf. Theo Witvliet, *A Place in the Sun*, p. 85. Steve Biko also perceived the complexity of the situation when he said: "In South Africa, after generations of exploitation, white people on the whole have come to believe in the inferiority of the black man, so much so that while the race problem started as an offshoot of the economic greed exhibited by white people, it has become a serious problem on its own." Biko, *I Write What I Like*, p. 88.

60. Kwame Nkrumah, *Class Struggle in Africa* (New York: International Publishers, 1970), p. 27. Another expression that is often used is "racial capitalism," which, according to Lebamang Sebidi, "tries to come to grips with the whole South African reality. South Africa is both a racial oligarchy as well as a capitalist society. But the two do not run parallel; they are mixed and intertwined. Even the protagonists in the game do not know when they are being racially motivated, or when capitalistically impelled." Sebidi, "The Dynamics of the Black Struggle . . .," in *The Unquestionable Right to be Free*, p. 31.

61. Sebidi, in Mosala and Tlhagale, eds., *The Unquestionable Right to be Free*, p. 28.

62. Buti Tlhagale, "Towards a Black Theology of Labour," in Villa-Vicencio and de Gruchy, eds., *Resistance and Hope*, p. 132.

63. See Mosala, *Biblical Hermeneutics and Black Theology in South Africa*, pp. 4f.

64. Ibid., pp. 16, 185, 193.

65. Ibid., p. 191. According to Mosala, these trends are: (a) bourgeois-oriented Black theology; (b) a Black theology which emerged from the perspective of middle-class, mission-trained blacks; and (c) a Black theology which draws insights from the perspective of the black working class.

66. Itumeleng J. Mosala, "The Theology of Ideology and the Ideology of Theology in the Black and White Church Struggle in South Africa" (Pretoria: HSRC, 1988), p. 307.

67. Cf. Teresa Okure, "Women in the Bible," in Fabella and Oduyoye, eds., *With Passion and Compassion*, p. 54; Louise Tappa, "God in Man's Image," in Pobee and von Wartenberg-Potter, eds., *New Eyes for Reading*, pp. 101ff.

68. I. J. Mosala, "The Use of the Bible in Black Theology," in Mosala and Tlhagale, eds., *The Unquestionable Right to be Free*, p. 196; cf. his *Biblical Hermeneutics and Black Theology in South Africa*, p. 121.

6 | Conclusion

In the African theological reality, the dialectic character which both inculturation and liberation have come to symbolize beckons us to new insights and to a new theological direction that goes beyond the tension and polarity between African and Black theologies. It points us beyond dissent to integrative vision and reminds us of the holistic implication of the gospel of Jesus Christ as a gospel of religiocultural and sociopolitical and economic liberation.

The pursuit of an integral synthesis of the African theological reality is, therefore, the legitimate one for our time. The supposition that this is so is suggested even more strongly by the recent changes and developments in South Africa—developments which have ramifications for the African church and its theology. Certainly, recent events in South Africa provide much plausibility for the contention that that country is not an island on its own and is by no means separated from the rest of the continent. Compared with other African countries, the effects of colonialism and capitalist imperialism may seem more severe on black South Africa, but neither these nor any other factor can "dis-Africanize" South Africa.

The black struggle against white supremacist domination in South Africa—like the Kenyan struggle against the British, the Algerian struggle against the French or the Angolan struggle against the Portuguese—is part and parcel of the irruption of the wretched of the earth against anthropological poverty. The liberation agenda and the inculturation agenda are therefore closer than originally thought. As I have maintained throughout this study, they are two names of the same process toward anthropological dignity or the meaningfully abundant life that Jesus the Christ has promised (John 10:10). It is this message that must provide Africans with the lens as they probe the scriptures for an understanding of the doctrines of creation, incarnation, salvation and the church.

As black Africans, we must always press the issues that confront us in terms of our theology. As blacks and Christians living in a hostile world dominated and controlled by white supremacy, it is our suffering experience and our knowledge of the suffering God that empower us. It is this suffering which becomes the epistemological lens through which we scrutinize all the various dimensions of our existence.

This experience of enslaved and dehumanized people is affirmed by the biblical witness to the pain and struggles of the oppressed of Yahweh and the humiliating suffering of the crucified Son of God. Although the Bible may not supply direct solutions to all our problems, it nonetheless promotes critical consciousness and questions our social reality or the oppressive status quo. It is in the Bible that we come to know what God through Jesus Christ has intended for our living in this world. We therefore ask critical questions whenever God's people are denied their full humanity.

It is in the pursuit of anthropological dignity therefore that the search for integral synthesis of the African theological reality becomes indispensable. It is through the movement toward a unitary perception that each theological approach discussed in this study will develop a holistic understanding of the African reality to overcome its own conflicts and thus contribute to integral liberation.

It is to this end that the African church's pursuit of the process of inculturation "cannot be limited to the religious sphere but must penetrate all the areas of African life."[1] Africa today is in political and economic disarray but, long before colonialism, Africans had developed political systems of their own that worked, as evidenced, for example, among the Ashanti or the Zulu.

What has theology to say to African countries which still look to foreign models as a solution to their political fragility?

It has been over three decades since most African countries attained political independence from their colonial overlords and, so far, none of the imported constitutional experiments from outside the continent has worked. Too often these are destroyed by another colonial legacy—the military—with the power of the gun. African soldiers have often been able to take control of African politics, but they have not been able to take full control of its economy.

Evidently, in its inculturation praxis, the African church and its theology have an important role to play in giving rise to a new society which will evolve out of a new harmony forged between traditional Africa and modernity. For instance, the church must show positive leadership in the task of analyzing the sources of Africa's constitutional ills and remind politicians and military regimes that a solution to the continent's political predicament does not lie in foreign models. "The crisis of contemporary Africa can be solved only by those who have understood its historical roots and can see them in the light of the actual situation. Only thus can a new society arise which is both African and truly modern."[2]

The analysis of modern African political and social structures and how these function within the developing economy of African states must necessarily be rooted in the nature of traditional African societies.

If, as I have endeavored to demonstrate, the political and economic issues are also the concerns and, indeed, the demands of inculturation praxis, then the process of inculturation cannot be divorced from the concept of liberation. As a term and a concept, liberation is not anything new that blacks in South Africa imported from the Americas. If in African ecclesial or theological circles the quest for liberation has been a recent phenomenon, in African politics, it is not.[3] The African search for liberation never ended with decolonization or independence. Liberation in Africa, ex-president Julius Nyerere of Tanzania has cogently argued, should not be "a single action which can be completed and then celebrated as a past event." Rather it should be understood as *a historical process* with four different dimensions, namely: freedom from colonialism and racism; freedom from external economic domination; freedom from poverty and from injustice and oppression imposed on Africans by Africans; and mental freedom.[4]

These aspects of the liberation process, together with the various dimensions of African traditional life, are indeed ascertainable realities of Africa's modern history. These historical realities determine the content of our theological reflection, and theology must seek to affect these realities, either by affirming them or opposing them. The theologian must therefore raise up a prophetic voice that is at once committed to the truth about African historical reality and the truth about the gospel of Jesus Christ in a world community where truth and justice have often been withheld by false prophets "who cry peace! peace! where there is no peace."

But how well has Africa fared in these aspects of the liberation process? The answer to such an existential question is not far to seek. Apparently independence from colonial domination has not guaranteed total liberation for the African masses. Surely it has not brought the envisioned freedom and justice. Decolonization, as we have painfully come to realize, is more than sending a new delegation to the United Nations or establishing diplomatic offices abroad.

The nominally independent African countries today are more dependent economically on the outside world than ever before. The continent's capacity to grapple with the development of its people is hampered by the very state of global economic relations. In a world dominated and controlled by imperialist capitalism, political decolonization is of little substance. If to African nationalists political independence was a relatively easy task, definitely the "political kingdom" in Africa has not seemed capable to add "all other things . . . as well." One must, above all, cross the wilderness of economic dependency before one can reach the promised land of sovereignty and self-determination.

It is only when Africa is economically independent and interdependent that other races can give black Africans the respect that is due to them in a world where "independence is governed by availability of capital."[5] This is even more so with blacks in South Africa, where unadulterated racism still thrives despite the near end of apartheid. Independence and sovereignty in our world today have become economic and military functions. The weaker a country is economically or militarily, the more fragile is its independence.[6] Indeed "economic independence *strengthens* a country's sovereignty and delivers it from plunder by other countries."[7]

What then is the way out for postindependence Africa still harassed and ransacked by neocolonialism, that external economic demon? What role does the church or the theologian have to play in Africa's future?

Africa in the postapartheid and post-cold war era needs to search for an authentic African tool which will provide the theoretical frame that will articulate the consciousness of the poor masses. One does not have to be a Marxist to analyze society or "to see the fundamental importance of the economic basis for the political and ideological superstructure of a society."[8] This search must be willing to engage the combined presence of traditional Africa, Islamic Africa and Euro-Christian Africa — the triple heritage that has helped to shape contemporary Africa. Any theoretical framework, in order to be relevant or understood, must be read in the light of the historical or practical realities that help produce it.

It is in this regard that postindependence African theorists like Kwame Nkrumah and Amilcar Cabral ought to be taken seriously not only in political strategies but also in African theological hermeneutics and praxis. With their contributions to political and cultural liberation and the theoretical foundation they have laid for economic decolonization in Africa, Cabral and Nkrumah have left much to future generations.[9] For those interested in the theology of political and cultural liberation, the contributions made by these two theorists will provide an opportunity for a more resourceful theological enterprise.

But the liberation struggle in Africa is not just directed against powerful external forces of domination and exploitation; it is as well a struggle against internal forces of oppression. Differently put, the struggles against colonialism, racism and neocolonialism do not exhaust the list of the African liberation agenda. Oppression of Africans by Africans is shamefully present in every part of the continent. Substituting a tyranny and atrocity of the indigenous ruler for those of the foreigner is not attaining freedom. Furthermore, oppression of women by men is ubiquitous.

After decades of independence, hopes of many Africans have been shattered and disillusionment and public apathy have led to uncaring governments. Today in most countries women, men and children have been condemned to poverty, servitude and sometimes torture and murder. Human rights violations and abuses, curbs on freedom of speech, detention without charge or trial, together with hunger, refugee problems, unemployment, illiteracy, lack of access to social welfare and health care, make the life of Africans the most miserable. Fenner Brockway's depiction of hopelessness in postindependent Africa two decades ago still deserves attention. He has noted that contrary to the hopes and aspirations that African societies would be transformed, still

> mass poverty continued, appalling housing and primitive sanitation in towns remained, unemployment increased. A gulf grew between the people and the European-American educated elite who became the

Political Establishment; new indigenous rulers tended to become bureaucrats and sometimes dictators. Corruption poisoned the regimes, ministers becoming rich and living in mansions which rivalled those of the previous European masters. . . . Power by dominant political cliques was strengthened, one party states were decreed . . . opposition leaders were imprisoned; governments were overthrown by army coups . . . supported in the background by [foreign] agencies.[10]

But if the educated elite performed badly as rulers, the soldiers who ousted them through coups, in most cases, aggravated the situation, as they were preoccupied with consolidating their position in power and amassing wealth at the expense of the peasants, workers and the poor. The masses became imprisoned by hopelessness and destitution. Things grow from bad to worse under successive regimes: Why should the price of a loaf of bread be more than a worker's two-day wages? Why should a peasant spend the whole day working under the scorching heat of the tropical sun but cannot afford a decent living with his or her whole year's earnings? Why should thousands of children die every day of hunger and other poverty-related causes while heads of governments and leaders are keeping millions of dollars in personal accounts in foreign banks?

The issues raised here are but a few of the existential questions with which the church and theology in Africa have to grapple. Church leaders and theologians must fearlessly speak on behalf of the weak, the poor and the exploited. The church that is called by Christ's name cannot find a comfortable home in an oppressive and dehumanizing situation. The church as a liberating community cannot attach itself to the oppressive status quo, resisting and resenting change.

The church of Christ in Africa is facing more tremendous challenges than ever before. But to meet these challenges the church must first exorcise its own demons before it can "learn to do good, seek justice [and] correct oppression" (Isaiah 1:17). For example, the church cannot speak against the discrimination against African women in governments or in the civil service if the church refuses to ordain women or excludes them from its hierarchy.

If political instability is a great contributing factor to Africa's predicament and suffering, then the churches cannot shy away from political issues. They must be in the forefront in the struggle against poverty and injustice in Africa. What makes this struggle obligatory to the Christian churches in Africa is that, by and large, it has been those who profess to be Christians who are responsible for the plight and the pauperization of our people. This is equally true whether one speaks of powerful external forces of exploitation or of internal oppressive forces.

On the one hand, it was Christian (Western) Europe which enslaved, colonized and exploited Africa. North America was to join later. Today, with the exception of Japan, all multinational corporations and other major external exploitative forces are from the so-called Christian West. On the other hand, at the local or national level the overwhelming majority of all civilian and military heads of governments and leaders in responsible positions in most sub-Saharan African countries since independence have been Christian. Even in a country like Nigeria, where the population is predominantly Muslim, there has been a significant number of Christians in leadership positions.

Should the churches in Africa continue sharing the common faith with countries that exploit their people? Should we give a respectful hearing to those who call themselves Christians but whose activities continue to perpetuate the suffering and impoverishment of our people? Or should African Christianity dissociate itself from Western Christianity, which has long been used as an instrument of enslavement, domination and oppression of Africans? If, in essence, Christianity as taught by Jesus of Nazareth and proclaimed by his twelve disciples was not meant to be a tool used to oppress or to exploit but, rather, it was meant to set the captive free, to liberate the poor and the oppressed and to bring meaningful and abundant life (cf. Luke 4:18–19, John 10:10) then the questions raised here should not be considered merely as theological rhetoric but must be taken and examined carefully by the African church. It is only a liberated church that can liberate.

Finally, and perhaps above all, the African struggle for liberation is also a struggle against psychological or mental bondage. No statement has expressed so well the need for our struggle for mental freedom as the one expressed by Steve Biko that the strongest tool in the hands of any oppressor is the mentality of the oppressed. The psychological wounds created by both colonialism and apartheid—whereby the black African considered himself or herself an inferior serving and producing wealth for the colonial or white master—are not yet healed. Even after three decades of political decolonization, the export-import pattern dramatically reflects this mentality. Political independence alone, as Laurenti Magesa has noted, does not bring self-confidence to a people who have been denied human dignity for so long. There is therefore the need for a psychological independence, which will take a cultural evolution or revolution to make people psychologically free.[11]

It is for this very reason that theology in black Africa emphasizes anthropological dignity and not only political and socioeconomic liberation. This aspect of our struggle is indeed essential, for, in most Africans, long after political colonization has been laid to rest, intellectual colonization lingers on still. The good news of liberating Africans from alienation and all forms of oppression is a message of hope which is at the very heart of the gospel of Jesus Christ and of all true prophecy. As a prophetic, pertinent and provocative theology, black African theology is speaking of this glorious hope as the coming of the reign of God, when God's will may be done here on earth.

NOTES

1. Bujo, *African Theology in Its Social Context*, p. 10.

2. Ibid., p. 69.

3. See, for example, Kwame Nkrumah, *I Speak of Freedom*, p. 107, where in his famous midnight pronouncement of independence for Ghana in early 1957, he declared that the independence of Ghana—the first country in black Africa to free itself from colonial oppression—"is meaningless unless it is linked up with the total liberation of the African continent."

4. Cited in Per Frostin, *Liberation Theology in Tanzania and South Africa*, p. 34; cf. Julius Nyerere, "Selected Speeches and Writings by J. K. Nyerere," in *Foreign Policy of Tanzania, 1961-1981: A Reader*, edited by K. Mathews and S. S. Mushi (Dar-es-Salaam: Tanzania Publishing House, 1981), p. 247.

5. Henry L. Bretton, *Power and Politics in Africa* (Chicago: Aldine Publishing Co., 1973), p. 20.

6. Cf. ibid., p. 19.

7. Ibid., p. 3.

8. Leatt, et al., *Contending Ideologies in South Africa*, p. 155.

9. See chapters 1 and 2 for my discussion of Cabral and Nkrumah respectively. See Cabral, *Unity and Struggle*; Nkrumah, *Consciencism*; also his *Neocolonialism* and *Revolutionary Path*.

10. Fenner Brockway, *The Colonial Revolution* (London: Hart-Davis, Mac-Gibbon, 1973), pp. 572-73; cited in Appiah-Kubi and Torres, *African Theology En Route*, pp. 155-56.

11. Laurenti Magesa, "Toward a Theology of Liberation for Tanzania," in *Christianity in Independent Africa*, edited by E. W. Fashole-Luke, et al. (London: Rex Collins, 1978), pp. 506-7.

Bibliography

AACC. *A Compendium of Documents for Sections/Groups* – Report of the Fifth General Assembly of the AACC held in Lome, Togo, 18–25 August 1987.
———. *Africa in Transition: The Challenge and the Christian Response.* Geneva: WCC, 1962.
———. *Consultation Digest: A Summary of Reports and Addresses.* Geneva: WCC, 1965.
———. *Drumbeats from Kampala.* London: Lutterworth, 1963.
———. *Engagement: Abidjan 1969.* Nairobi: AACC, 1970.
———. *The Struggle Continues.* Nairobi: AACC, 1975.
Abble, A., et al. *Des Prêtres noirs s'interrogent.* Paris, 1956.
Abogunrin, S. O. "The Church and Cultural Renewal in Africa." *Indian Missiological Review*, vol. 10, no. 3, July 1988.
Abraham, K. C., ed. *Third World Theologies: Commonalities and Divergences.* Maryknoll, N.Y.: Orbis Books, 1990.
Abraham, William E. *The Mind of Africa.* Chicago: University of Chicago Press, 1962.
Adegbola, Adeolu A. "A Christian Interpretation of the African Revolution." In AACC, *Consultation Digest: A Summary of Reports and Addresses.* Geneva: WCC, 1965. Also in Georg F. Vicedom, ed. *Christ and the Younger Churches.* London: SPCK, 1972.
———. "Christian Responsibility in the Political Economy of Africa." *The Ecumenical Review*, vol. 37, no. 1, January 1985.
Akwue, Francis. "A Growing African Vision of the Church's Mission." *Voices from the Third World,* vol. 8, no. 2, June 1985.
Amirtham, Samuel, ed. *A Vision for Man: Essays On Faith, Theology and Society.* Madras, India: The Christian Literature Society, 1978.
Amoah, Elizabeth, and Mercy Oduyoye. "The Christ for African Women." In Virginia Fabella and Mercy Oduyoye, eds. *With Passion and Compassion: Third World Women Doing Theology.* Maryknoll, N.Y.: Orbis Books, 1988.
Ankrah, Kodwo E. "Church and Politics in Africa." In Kofi Appiah-Kubi and Sergio Torres, eds. *African Theology En Route.* Maryknoll, N.Y.: Orbis Books, 1979.
Appiah-Kubi, Kofi. "The Ecumenical Importance of African Theology." *Voices from the Third World,* July 1986.
———. "Indigenous African Churches: Signs of Authenticity." In Kofi Appiah-Kubi and Sergio Torres, eds. *African Theology En Route.* Maryknoll, N.Y.: Orbis Books, 1979.
———. "Jesus Christ – Some Christological Aspects from African Perspectives." In John Mbiti, ed. *African and Asian Contributions to Contemporary Theology.* Geneva: WCC, 1977.

————. "Who do you Africans say I (Jesus) am?" *Voices from the Third World*, vol. 11, no. 2, December 1988.

Appiah-Kubi, Kofi, and Sergio Torres, eds. *African Theology En Route*. Maryknoll, N.Y.: Orbis Books, 1979.

Arinze, Francis Cardinal. "Pastoral Attention to African Traditional Religion: Letter of the President of the Secretariat for Non-Christians to the Presidents of all Episcopal Conferences in Africa and Madagascar." *Bulletin* 68 XXIII.2, 1988.

Ashcroft, Bill, Gareth Griffiths, and Helen Tiffin. *The Empire Writes Back: Theory and Practice in Post-Colonial Literature*. New York/London: Routledge, 1989.

Ayadike, Obinna. "Toxic Terrorism." *West Africa*, no. 3696 (London) June 20, 1988.

Azikiwe, Nnamdi. "The Future of Pan-Africanism." In J. Ayo Langley, ed. *Ideologies of Liberation in Black Africa, 1856-1970*. London: Rex Collings, 1979.

Baëta, C. G., ed. *Christianity in Tropical Africa*. London: Oxford, 1968.

Balbus, Isaac D. *Marxism and Domination*. Princeton, N.J.: Princeton University Press, 1982.

Banana, C. S. *Theology of Promise: The Dynamics of Self-Reliance*. Harare, Zimbabwe: College Press, 1982.

Bascom, William R., and Melville J. Herskovits, eds. *Continuity and Change in African Culture*. Chicago/London: University of Chicago Press, 1959.

Bates, R. H. "Modernization, Ethnic Competition and the Rationality of Politics in Contemporary Africa." In Donald Rothchild and Victor A. Olorunsola, eds. *State Versus Ethnic Claims: African Policy Dilemmas*. Boulder, Colo.: Westview Press, 1983.

Battlinger, Arnold, ed. *The Church Is Charismatic*. Geneva: WCC, 1981.

Becken, Hans-Jürgen, ed. *Relevant Theology for Africa*. Durban: Lutheran Publishing House, 1973.

Beidelman, T. O. *Colonial Evangelism: A Socio-Historical Study of an East African Mission at the Grassroots*. Bloomington, Ind.: Indiana University Press, 1982.

Bengu, Sibusiso M. "A Social and Political Analysis of Apartheid/Racism from a Black Lutheran Perspective." In A. Pero and A. Moyo, eds. *Theology and the Black Experience*. Minneapolis: Augsburg Publishing House, 1988.

Bennet, Bonita. "A Critique on the Role of Women in the Church." In I. J. Mosala and B. Tlhagale, eds. *The Unquestionable Right to be Free*. Maryknoll, N.Y.: Orbis Books, 1986.

Berg, Robert J., and Jennifer S. Whitaker, eds. *Strategies for African Development*. Berkeley: University of California Press, 1986.

Berger, Peter. *The Social Reality of Religion*. London: Penguin Books, 1973.

Biko, Steve. "Black Consciousness and the Quest for a True Humanity." In Basil Moore, ed. *The Challenge of Black Theology in South Africa*. Atlanta: John Knox Press, 1974.

————. *I Write What I Like: A Selection of His Writings*. Ed. Aelred Stubbs. San Francisco: Harper & Row Publishers, 1986.

Bimwenyi, O. *Discours théologique négro-Africain. Problèmes de fondements*. Paris: Présence Africaine, 1981.

————. "L'Inculturation en Afrique et attitude des agents de l'évangélisation." *Aspects du Catholicisme au Zaïre*. Kinshasa: Faculté Théologie Catholique, 1981.

Blomjous, Joseph. "Development in Mission Thinking and Practices 1959-1980: Inculturation and Interculturation." *AFER*, vol. 22, no. 6, 1980.

Blyden, Edward Wilmot. "Africa for the African." In H. S. Wilson, ed. *Origins of West African Nationalism*. London: MacMillan, 1969.
————. "African Accomplishments and Race Pride." In H. S. Wilson, ed. *Origins of West African Nationalism*. London: MacMillan, 1969.
————. "African Life and Customs." In H. S. Wilson, ed. *Origins of West African Nationalism*. London: MacMillan, 1969.
————. "Africa's Service to the World." In H. S. Wilson, ed. *Origins of West African Nationalism*. London: MacMillan, 1969.
————. *Christianity, Islam and the Negro Race*. New Edition. London: Edinburgh University Press, 1967.
————. "Study and Race." In H. S. Wilson, ed. *Origins of West African Nationalism*. London: MacMillan, 1969.
Boahen, A. Adu, ed. *General History of Africa,* vol. VII: *Africa Under Colonial Domination 1880-1935*. Abridged Edition. Berkeley: University of California Press/ UNESCO, 1990.
Boesak, Allan A. *Black and Reformed: Apartheid, Liberation and the Calvinist Tradition*. Maryknoll, N.Y.: Orbis Books, 1984.
————. "The Black Church and the Future." *EcuNews Bulletin* 24, August 3, 1979.
————. "Civil Religion and the Black Community." *Journal of Theology for Southern Africa*, no. 19, June 1977.
————. "Coming in out of the Wilderness." In Sergio Torres and Virginia Fabella, eds. *The Emergent Gospel: Theology from the Developing World*. Maryknoll, N.Y.: Orbis Books, 1978.
————. *Farewell to Innocence: A Socio-Ethical Study of Black Theology and Power*. Maryknoll, N.Y.: Orbis Books, 1977.
————. *The Finger of God: Sermons on Faith and Responsibility*. Maryknoll, N.Y.: Orbis Books, 1982.
————. *If This Is Treason, I Am Guilty*. Grand Rapids, Mich.: Eerdmans/African World Press, 1987.
————. "Liberation Theology in South Africa." In K. Appiah-Kubi and S. Torres, eds., *African Theology En Route*. Maryknoll, N.Y.: Orbis Books, 1979.
————. "The Relationship Between Text and Situation, Reconciliation and Liberation in Black Theology." *Voices from the Third World,* vol. 2, no. 1, June 1979.
————. "Wholeness Through Liberation." *Church and Society*, May 1981.
Boff, Leonardo, and Virgil Elizondo, eds. *Concilium, 199—Theologies of the Third World: Convergences and Differences*. Edinburgh: T & T Clark, 1988.
Bosch, David J. "Currents and Crosscurrents in South African Black Theology." In Gayraud S. Wilmore and James H. Cone, eds. *Black Theology: A Documentary History, 1966-1979*. Maryknoll, N.Y.: Orbis Books, 1979.
Boulaga, F. Eboussi. *Christianisme sans fétiche. Révélation et domination*. Paris: Présence Africaine, 1981.
————. *Christianity Without Fetishes: An African Critique and Recapture of Christianity*. Maryknoll, N.Y.: Orbis Books, 1984.
————. "Le Bantou Problématique." *Présence Africaine*. 66. 2nd Quarterly, 1968.
Bretton, Henry L. *Power and Politics in Africa*. Chicago: Aldine Publishing Company, 1973.
Brunello, Anthony R. "Liberation Theology and Third World Social Transformation." *TransAfrica Forum*, vol. 4, no. 4, Summer 1987.
Brydon, Lynne, and Sylvia Chant. *Women in the Third World: Gender Issues in Rural*

and Urban Areas. New Brunswick, N.J.: Rutgers University Press, 1989.

Bujo, Bénézet. *African Theology in Its Social Context.* Maryknoll, N.Y.: Orbis Books, 1992.

Burke, Fred. *Africa.* Revised Edition. Boston: Houghton Mifflin, 1970, 1974.

Buthelezi, Manas. "An African Theology or a Black Theology?" In Basil Moore, ed. *The Challenge of Black Theology in South Africa.* Atlanta: John Knox Press, 1974.

————. "Black Theology and the Le Grange-Schlebusch Commission." *Pro Veritate,* October 1975.

————. "Change in the Church." *South African Outlook,* August 1973.

————. "The Christian Institute and Black South Africa." *South African Outlook,* October 1974.

————. "The Relevance of Black Theology." *South African Outlook,* vol. 104, no. 1243, December 1974.

————. "Six Theses: Theological Problems of Evangelism in the South African Context." *Journal of Theology for Southern Africa,* no. 3, June 1973.

————. "Theological Ground for an Ethic of Hope." In Basil Moore, ed. *The Challenge of Black Theology in South Africa.* Atlanta: John Knox Press, 1974.

————. "Theological Meaning of True Humanity." In Basil Moore, ed. *The Challenge of Black Theology in South Africa.* Atlanta: John Knox Press, 1974.

————. "Toward a Biblical Faith in South African Society." *Journal of Theology for Southern Africa,* no. 19, June 1977.

————. "Toward Indigenous Theology in South Africa." In Sergio Torres and Virginia Fabella, eds. *The Emergent Gospel: Theology from the Developing World.* Maryknoll, N.Y.: Orbis Books, 1978.

Cabral, Amilcar. *Unity and Struggle: Speeches and Writings.* New York: Monthly Review Press, 1979.

Calvin, John. *Institutes of the Christian Faith,* vol. 2. Edited by John T. McNeill and translated by Ford Lewis Battles. Philadelphia: Westminster Press, 1960.

Carlston, Kenneth S. *Social Theory and African Tribal Organization: The Development of Socio-Legal Theory.* Chicago: University of Illinois Press, 1968.

Carnes, John R. *Axiomatics and Dogmatics.* New York: Oxford University Press, 1982.

Carr, Burgess. "An African Christian Response." In J. G. W. Ryan, ed. *Christian Faith and the New World Order.* Washington, D.C.: Interreligious Peace Colloquium, 1978.

————. "The Engagement Of Lusaka." *South African Outlook,* vol. 104, no. 1237, June 1974.

————. "The Relation of Union to Mission." In G. H. Anderson and T. F. Stransky, eds. *Mission Trends no. 3 — Third World Theologies.* New York/Grand Rapids, Mich.: Paulist Press/Eerdmans, 1976.

Césaire, Aimé. *Discourse on Colonialism.* New York: Monthly Review Press, 1972.

Chikane, Frank. "Bible Study and Theological Reflection." *South African Outlook,* vol. 115, no. 1367, May 1985.

————. "Doing Theology in a Situation of Conflict." In C. Villa-Vicencio and J. W. de Gruchy, eds. *Resistance and Hope: South African Essays in Honour of Beyers Naudé.* Grand Rapids, Mich.: Eerdmans, 1985.

————. "EATWOT and Third World Theologies: An Evaluation of the Past and

Present." In K. C. Abraham, ed. *Third World Theologies.* Maryknoll, N.Y.: Orbis Books, 1990.

————. *No Life of My Own.* Maryknoll, N.Y.: Orbis Books, 1988.

Chipenda, José B. "Theological Options in Africa Today." In Kofi Appiah-Kubi and Sergio Torres, eds. *African Theology En Route.* Maryknoll, N.Y.: Orbis Books, 1979.

Christensen, Thomas G. *An African Tree of Life.* Maryknoll, N.Y.: Orbis Books, 1990.

Clark, Leon E. *Through African Eyes: Cultures in Change.* New York: Praeger Publishers, 1970.

Cleage, Albert B., Jr. *The Black Messiah.* Trenton, N.J.: African World Press, 1989.

Cone, James H. "A Black American Perspective on the Future of African Theology." In Kofi Appiah-Kubi and Sergio Torres, eds. *African Theology En Route.* Maryknoll, N.Y.: Orbis Books, 1979.

————. "Black Theology: Its Origin, Methodology, and Relationship to Third World Theologies." In Virginia Fabella and Sergio Torres, eds. *Doing Theology in a Divided World.* Maryknoll, N.Y.: Orbis Books, 1985.

————. "Black Theology and Black Liberation." In Basil Moore, ed. *The Challenge of Black Theology in South Africa.* Atlanta: John Knox Press, 1974.

————. *Black Theology and Black Power.* Minneapolis: Seabury Press, 1969.

————. *A Black Theology of Liberation.* 2nd ed. Maryknoll, N.Y.: Orbis Books, 1986.

————. "The Content and Method of Black Theology." *The Journal of Religious Thought,* vol. 32, no. 2, Fall-Winter 1975.

————. *For My People: Black Theology and the Black Church.* Maryknoll, N.Y.: Orbis Books, 1984.

————. "From Geneva to São Paulo: A Dialogue Between Black Theology and Latin American Liberation Theology." In S. Torres and J. Eagleson, eds. *The Challenge of Basic Christian Communities.* Maryknoll, N.Y.: Orbis Books, 1981.

————. *God of the Oppressed.* New York: Seabury Press, 1975.

————. *My Soul Looks Back.* Maryknoll, N.Y.: Orbis Books, 1986.

————. "Reflections from the Perspective of U.S. Blacks: Black Theology and Third World Theology." In Virginia Fabella and Sergio Torres, eds. *Irruption of the Third World: Challenge to Theology.* Maryknoll, N.Y.: Orbis Books, 1983.

Cone, James H., and Gayraud S. Wilmore. "Black Theology and African Theology: Considerations for Dialogue, Critique, and Integration." In Gayraud S. Wilmore and James H. Cone, eds. *Black Theology: A Documentary History, 1966-1979.* Maryknoll, N.Y.: Orbis Books, 1979.

Cutrufelli, Maria Rosa. *Women of Africa: Roots of Oppression.* London: Zed Press, 1983.

Damann, E. *Les Religions d'Afrique noire.* Paris: Payot, 1964.

Danaher, Kevin. "Neo-Apartheid: Reform in South Africa." In David Mermelstein, ed. *The Anti-Apartheid Reader: South Africa and the Struggle Against White Racist Rule.* New York: Grove Press, 1987.

Davidson, Basil. *Modern Africa.* New York/London: Longman, 1983.

De Carvalho, Emilio J. M. "What do the Africans say that Jesus Christ is?" *African Theological Journal* vol. 10, no. 2, 1981.

————. "Who is Jesus Christ for Africa Today?" *African Theological Journal,* vol. 10, no. 1, 1981.

De Gruchy, John. "The Challenge of South African Theology—The Making of

South African Theology: From Colonial Theology to the Kairos Document." A paper delivered at the Hoff Lectures, n.d.

———. *The Church Struggle in South Africa.* Grand Rapids, Mich.: Eerdmans, 1979.

———. "South African Theology Comes of Age." *Religious Studies Review*, vol. 17, no. 3, July 1991.

———. "Theologies in Conflict: The South African Debate." In C. Villa-Vicencio and J. W. de Gruchy, eds. *Resistance and Hope: South African Essays in Honour of Beyers Naudé.* Grand Rapids, Mich.: Eerdmans, 1985.

De Gruchy, John, and Charles Villa-Vicencio, eds. *Apartheid Is a Heresy.* Grand Rapids, Mich.: Eerdmans, 1983.

De Kiewiet, C. W. *A History of South Africa: Social and Economic.* London: Oxford University Press, 1957.

Deschamps, H. *Les Religions de l'Afrique noire.* Paris: Presses Universitaires de France, 1954.

Dickson, Kwesi A. "The African Theological Task." In Sergio Torres and Virginia Fabella, eds. *The Emergent Gospel: Theology from the Developing World.* Maryknoll, N.Y.: Orbis Books, 1978.

———. "African Theology: Origin, Methodology and Content." *The Journal of Religious Thought,* vol. 32, no. 2, Fall-Winter, 1975.

———. *Aspects of Religion and Life in Africa.* Accra: Ghana Academy of Arts and Sciences, 1977.

———. "Continuity and Discontinuity Between the Old Testament and African Life and Thought." In Kofi Appiah-Kubi and Sergio Torres, eds. *African Theology En Route.* Maryknoll, N.Y.: Orbis Books, 1979.

———. "Relation Between Religion and Culture." *The Ghana Bulletin of Theology,* vol. 1, no. 9, Trinity Term 1961.

———. *Theology in Africa.* Maryknoll, N.Y.: Orbis Books, 1984.

———. *Uncompleted Mission: Christianity and Exclusivism.* Maryknoll, N.Y.: Orbis Books, 1991.

Dickson, Kwesi, and Paul Ellingworth, eds. *Biblical Revelation and African Beliefs.* London: Oxford University Press, 1969.

Diop, Cheikh Anta. *Civilization or Barbarism: An Authentic Anthropology.* Westport, Conn.: Lawrence Hill, 1991.

———. *The African Origin of Civilization: Myth or Reality.* Westport, Conn.: Lawrence Hill, 1974.

Dodge, Ralph E. *The Unpopular Missionary.* Westwood, N.J.: Fleming H. Revell, 1964.

Donders, Joseph G. *Non-Bourgeois Theology: An African Experience of Jesus.* Maryknoll, N.Y.: Orbis Books, 1985.

DuBois, W. E. B. *The Souls of Black Folk.* New York: Bantam Books, 1903, 1989.

Ebeling, Gerhard. *Word and Faith.* London: SCM Press, 1963.

Edet, Rosemary N. "Mariology." In Mercy Oduyoye, ed. *The State of Christian Theology in Nigeria 1980-81.* Ibadan, Nigeria: Daystar Press, 1986.

Edet, Rosemary, and Bette Ekeya. "Church Women of Africa: A Theological Community." In V. Fabella and M. Oduyoye, eds. *With Passion and Compassion.* Maryknoll, N.Y.: Orbis Books, 1988.

Ekeya, Bette J. M. "A Christology from the Underside." *Voices from the Third World,* vol. 11, no. 2, December 1988.

Ela, Jean-Marc. *African Cry.* Maryknoll, N.Y.: Orbis Books, 1986.

——. *L'Afrique des villages*. Paris: Karthala, 1982.

——. "La Foi des pauvres en acte." *Telema*, no. 35, July-September 1983.

——. *Le Cri de l'homme africain*. Paris: L'Harmattan, 1980.

——. "Le Role des Églises dans la libération du continent africain." *Bulletin de Théologie Africaine*, vol. 6, julliet-décembre 1984.

——. *Ma foi d'africain*. Paris: Karthala, 1985.

——. *My Faith as an African*. Maryknoll, N.Y.: Orbis Books, 1988.

Elphick, Richard, and Hermann Giliomee, eds. *The Shaping of South African Society, 1652-1840*. Middletown, Conn.: Wesleyan University Press/Maskew Miller Longman, 1979, 1988.

Elwood, Douglas J., ed. *Asian Christian Theology: Emerging Themes*. Philadelphia: Westminster Press, 1980.

Fabella, Virginia, ed. *Asia's Struggle for Full Humanity*. Maryknoll, N.Y.: Orbis Books, 1980.

Fabella, Virginia, and Mercy Oduyoye, eds. *With Passion and Compassion: Third World Women Doing Theology*. Maryknoll, N.Y.: Orbis Books, 1988.

Fabella, Virginia, and Sergio Torres, eds. *Doing Theology in a Divided World*. Maryknoll, N.Y.: Orbis Books, 1985.

——. *Irruption of the Third World: Challenge to Theology*. Maryknoll, N.Y.: Orbis Books, 1983.

Fanon, Frantz. *The Wretched of the Earth*. New York: Grove Weidenfeld, 1963.

Fashole-Luke, E. W. "Footpaths and Signposts to African Christian Theologies." *Scottish Journal of Theology*, vol. 34, no. 5, 1981.

——. "The Quest for African Christian Theologies." *Scottish Journal of Theology*, vol. 29, 1976.

——. "The Quest for African Christian Theology." *The Journal of Religious Thought*, vol. 32, no. 2, Fall-Winter 1975.

Fashole-Luke, E. W., R. Gray, A. Hastings, and G. Tasie, eds. *Christianity in Independent Africa*. London: Rex Collins, 1978.

Ferm, Deane William, ed. *Third World Liberation Theologies: A Reader*. Maryknoll, N.Y.: Orbis Books, 1986.

——. *Third World Liberation Theologies: An Introductory Survey*. Maryknoll, N.Y.: Orbis Books, 1986.

Flannery, Austin, ed. *Vatican Council II: The Conciliar and Post Conciliar Documents*. Revised Edition. Grand Rapids, Mich.: Eerdmans, 1975, 1984.

Ford, David F., ed. *The Modern Theologians: An Introduction to Christian Theology in the Twentieth Century*, vol. 2. New York/London: Basil Blackwell, 1989.

Fortes, M., and E. E. Evans-Pritchard, eds. *African Political Systems*. New York/London: Oxford University Press, 1940.

Fortes, Meyer, and Germaine Dieterlen, eds. *African Systems of Thought*. New York/London: Oxford University Press, 1965.

Frostin, Per. *Liberation Theology in Tanzania and South Africa: A First World Interpretation*. Lund, Sweden: Lund University Press, 1988.

Gallina, Ernesto. *Africa Present: A Catholic Survey of Facts and Figures*. Translated by Dorothy White. London: Geoffrey Chapman, 1969.

Garvey, Amy Jacques, ed. *The Philosophy and Opinions of Marcus Garvey or Africa for the Africans*, vols. 1 and 2. Dover, Mass.: Majority Press, 1986.

Geertz, Clifford. *The Interpretation of Cultures*. New York: Basic Books, 1973.

Gerhart, Gail M. *Black Power in South Africa: The Evolution of an Ideology*. Berkeley: University of California Press, 1978.

Giblin, Marie J. "African Christian Theological Resources." In Regina M. Bechtle and John J. Rathschmidt, eds. *Mission and Mysticism—Evangelization and the Experience of God*. Maryknoll, N.Y.: Maryknoll School of Theology, 1987.

———. "Taking African History Seriously: The Challenge of Liberation Theology." In Marc H. Ellis and Otto Maduro, eds. *The Future of Liberation Theology*. Maryknoll, N.Y.: Orbis Books, 1989.

Gibson, Richard. *African Liberation Movements: Contemporary Struggles Against White Minority Rule*. New York/London: Oxford University Press, 1972.

Gilliland, Dean S. "How 'Christian' Are African Independent Churches?" *Missiology*, vol. 14, no. 3, July 1986.

Goba, Bonganjalo. "An African Christian Theology: Towards a Tentative Methodology from a South African Perspective." *Journal of Theology from Southern Africa*, no. 26, March 1979.

———. *An Agenda for Black Theology: Hermeneutics for Social Change*. Johannesburg: Skotaville Publishers, 1988.

———. "The Black Consciousness Movement: Its Impact on Black Theology." In I. J. Mosala and B. Tlhagale, eds. *The Unquestionable Right to be Free*. Maryknoll, N.Y.: Orbis Books, 1986.

———. "A Black South African Perspective." In V. Fabella and S. Torres, eds. *Doing Theology in a Divided World*. Maryknoll, N.Y.: Orbis Books, 1985.

———. "Corporate Personality: Ancient Israel and Africa." In Basil Moore, ed. *The Challenge of Black Theology in South Africa*. Atlanta: John Knox Press, 1974.

———. "Doing Theology in South Africa: A Black Christian Perspective." *Journal of Theology for Southern Africa*, no. 31, June 1980.

———. "Emerging Theological Perspectives in South Africa." In V. Fabella and S. Torres, eds. *Irruption of the Third World: Challenge to Theology*. Maryknoll, N.Y.: Orbis Books, 1983.

———. "The Interrelatedness of Oppression: A Black South African Perspective." In Virginia Fabella and Sergio Torres, eds. *Doing Theology in a Divided World*. Maryknoll, N.Y.: Orbis Books, 1985.

———. "The Kairos Document and its Implications for Liberation in South Africa." *The Journal of Law and Religion*, vol. 5, no. 2, 1987.

———. "Perspectives on Ethnic and Racial Conflicts in South Africa: A Critical Assessment of the Churches' Response from 1960 to the Present." *Journal of Black Theology in South Africa*, vol. 4, no. 1, May 1990.

———. "The Role of the Black Church in the Process of Healing of Human Brokenness." *Journal of Theology for Southern Africa*, no. 28, September 1979.

———. "The Task of Black Theological Education in South Africa." *Journal of Theology for Southern Africa*, no. 22, March 1978.

———. "Three Christological Models in Third World Theology." *Theologia Evangelica*, vol. 15, no. 2, September 1982.

———. "Toward a Black Ecclesiology: Insights from Sociology of Knowledge." *Missionalia*, vol. 9, no. 2, August 1981.

———. "Toward a Quest for Christian Identity: A Third World Perspective." *Journal of Black Theology*, vol. 2, no. 2, November 1988.

———. "The Urban Church: A Black South African Perspective." *South African Outlook*, vol. 3, no. 13176, March 1981.

————. "The Use of Scripture in the Kairos Document: A Biblical Ethical Perspective." *Journal of Theology for Southern Africa*, no. 56, September 1986.

————. "What Is Faith?" In Susan B. Thistlethwaite and Mary P. Engel, eds. *Lift Every Voice: Constructing Christian Theology from the Underside.* New York/San Francisco: Harper & Row Publishers, 1990.

Gray, Richard. "Christianity." In Andrew Roberts, ed. *The Colonial Moment in Africa: Essays on the Movements of Minds and Materials, 1900-1940.* New York/ Cambridge: Cambridge University Press, 1986.

Greenberg, Joseph H. *The Languages of Africa.* Bloomington, Ind.: Indiana University Press, 1966.

————. *Studies in African Linguistic Classification.* New Haven, Conn.: Compass Publishing, 1955.

Gugelberger, Georg M. *Marxism and African Literature.* Trenton, N.J.: Africa World Press, 1985.

Hafkin, Nancy J., and Edna G. Bay, eds. *Women in Africa: Studies in Social and Economic Change.* Stanford: Stanford University Press, 1976.

Haight, Roger. *Dynamics of Theology.* New York/Mahwah, N.J.: Paulist Press, 1990.

Hastings, Adrian. *African Catholicism: Essays in Discovery.* Philadelphia: Trinity Press International/SCM Press, 1989.

————. *African Christianity.* New York: Seabury Press, 1976.

————. *A History of African Christianity, 1950-1975.* New York/Cambridge, Cambridge University Press, 1979.

————. "On African Theology." *Scottish Journal of Theology*, vol. 37, no. 3, 1984.

Hebga, M., ed. *Personnalité africaine et catholicisme.* Paris: Présence Africain, 1963.

Hertz, Karl. "Tutu and Boesak: Liberation Theology as Praxis." *Mid-stream,* vol. 26, no. 1, January 1987.

Holland, Joe, and Peter Henriot. *Social Analysis: Linking Faith and Justice.* Revised and Enlarged Edition. Maryknoll, N.Y.: Orbis Books/Center of Concern, 1983.

Hood, Robert E. *Must God Remain Greek? Afro Cultures and God-Talk.* Minneapolis: Fortress Press, 1990.

Hope, Marjorie, and James Young. *The South African Churches in a Revolutionary Situation.* Maryknoll, N.Y.: Orbis Books, 1981.

Hopkins, Dwight N. *Black Theology USA and South Africa: Politics, Culture and Liberation.* Maryknoll, N.Y.: Orbis Books, 1989.

Hountondji, P. *African Philosophy: Myth and Reality.* Bloomington, Ind.: Indiana University Press, 1983.

————. *Sur la philosophie africaine.* Paris: Maspero, 1977.

Howe, Russell Warren. *Black Africa: Africa South of the Sahara From Pre-History to Independence,* vol. 2—*From the Colonial Era to Modern Times.* New York: Walker & Company, 1966.

Hyden, Goran. "African Social Structure and Economic Development." In Robert J. Berg and Jennifer S. Whitaker, eds. *Strategies for African Development.* Berkeley: University of California Press, 1986.

Idowu, E. Bolaji. *African Traditional Religion: A Definition.* Maryknoll, N.Y.: Orbis Books, 1975.

————. *Olodumare: God in Yoruba Belief.* London: Longmans, 1962.

————. *The Selfhood of the Church in Africa.* Mushin, Lagos State: Methodist Church Nigeria, n.d..

————. *Towards an Indigenous Church.* London: Oxford University Press, 1965.

Imasogie, Osadolor. *Guidelines for Christian Theology in Africa.* Achimota, Ghana: Africa Christian Press, 1983.

Institute for Contextual Theology. "Contextual Theology for Groups in South Africa." *Women in a Changing World*, no. 27, May 1989.

———. "What Is Contextual Theology?" Part I. *AACC Magazine*, vol. 2, no. 3, December 1984.

———. "What Is Contextual Theology?" Part II. *AACC Magazine*, vol. 3, no. 1, May 1985.

Jackson, Robert H., and Carl G. Rosberg. *Personal Rule in Black Africa: Prince, Autocrat, Prophet, Tyrant.* Berkeley: University of California Press, 1982.

Jahn, Janheinz. *Muntu: An Outline of Neo-African Culture.* New York: Grove Press, 1961.

———. *Neo-African Literature: A History of Black Writing.* New York: Grove Press, 1968.

Johnson, Willard R. "Africanization of Management." In James E. Turner, ed. *The Next Decade.* Ithaca, N.Y.: Cornell University Press, 1984.

July, Robert W. *A History of the African People.* New York: Charles Scribner's Sons, 1970.

Kabasélé, François. "Christ as Ancestor and Elder Brother." In Robert J. Schreiter, ed. *Faces of Jesus in Africa.* Maryknoll, N.Y.: Orbis Books, 1991.

Kagame, Alexis. *La philosophie bantu-rwandaise de l'être.* Brussels: Académie Royale de Sciences Coloniales, 1956.

Kalilombe, Patrick A. "Black Theology." In David F. Ford, ed. *The Modern Theologians: An Introduction to Christian Theology in the Twentieth Century.* New York/London: Basil Blackwell, 1989.

———. "Cross-fertilization in EATWOT." In K. C. Abraham, ed. *Third World Theologies.* Maryknoll, N.Y.: Orbis Books, 1990.

———. "A Malawian Example: The Bible and Non-Literate Communities." In R. S. Sugirtharajah, ed. *Voices from the Margin: Interpreting the Bible in the Third World.* Maryknoll, N.Y.: Orbis Books, 1991.

———. "The Salvific Values of African Religions." *AFER*, vol. 21, no. 3, June 1979.

———. "Self-Reliance of the African Church: A Catholic Perspective." In Kofi Appiah-Kubi and Sergio Torres, eds. *African Theology En Route.* Maryknoll, N.Y.: Orbis Books, 1979.

Kalu, Ogbu, U. "Church Presence in Africa: A Historical Analysis of the Evangelization Process." In Kofi Appia-Kubi and Sergio Torres, eds. *African Theology En Route.* Maryknoll, N.Y.: Orbis Books, 1979.

Karis, Thomas, and Gwendolen M. Carter, eds. *From Protest to Challenge: A Documentary History of African Politics in South Africa 1882-1964,* vol. I. Stanford: Hoover Institution Press, 1972.

Kato, Byang H. *Theological Pitfalls in Africa.* Kisumu, Kenya: Evangel Publishing House, 1975.

Kayitakibga, Mérard. "L'Eglise Catholique en Afrique Face aux Traditions Religieuses Africaines." *Bulletin — Secretariatus Pro Non Christianis*, XXII/3 69, 1989.

Kee, Alistair. *Domination or Liberation: The Place of Religion in Social Conflicts.* London: SCM Press, 1986.

Kenyatta, Jomo. *Facing Mount Kenya: The Tribal Life of the Gikuyu.* London: Secker & Warburg, 1938.

Ki-Zerbo, J., ed. *General History of Africa,* vol. I — *Methodology and African Prehis-*

tory. Berkeley: University of California Press/UNESCO, 1981, 1990.

Klinghoffer, Arthur Jay. *Soviet Perspectives on African Socialism.* Rutherford, N.J.: Fairleigh Dickinson University Press, 1969.

Kretzschmar, Louise. *The Voice of Black Theology in South Africa.* Johannesburg: Ravan Press, 1986.

Kuma, Afua. *Jesus of the Deep Forest.* Accra, Ghana: Asempa Publishers, 1980.

Kurewa, John W. Z. "The Meaning of African Theology." *Journal of Theology for Southern Africa,* no. 11, June 1975.

———. "Who do you say that I am?" *Voices from the Third World,* vol. 8, no. 1, March 1985.

Kwarteng, Charles. "External Influences on Africa's Economic Decolonization." *TransAfrica Forum,* vol. 6, no. 3 and 4, Spring-Summer 1989.

Lacour-Gayet, Robert. *A History of South Africa.* New York: Hastings House, 1978.

Lamola, Malesela J. "The Thought of Steve Biko as the Historico-Philosophical Base of South African Black Theology." *Journal of Black Theology in South Africa,* vol. 3, no. 2, November 1989.

Langley, J. Ayo, ed. *Ideologies of Liberation in Black Africa, 1856-1970: Documents on Modern African Political Thought from Colonial Times to the Present.* London: Rex Collins, 1979.

Lanternari, Vittorio. *The Religions of the Oppressed: A Study of Modern Messianic Cults.* New York: Alfred A. Knopf, 1963.

Leatt, James, Theo Kneifel, and Klaus Nurnberger, eds. *Contending Ideologies in South Africa.* Grand Rapids/Cape Town: Wm. B. Eerdmans/David Philip, 1986.

Lee, Margaret. "SADCC and Post-Apartheid South Africa." *TransAfrica Forum,* vol. 6, no. 3 and 4, Spring-Summer 1989.

Legassick, Martin. "The Northern Frontier to c.1840: The Rise and Decline of the Griqua People." In Richard Elphick and Hermann Giliomee, eds. *The Shaping of South African Society: 1652-1840.* Middletown, Conn.: Wesleyan University Press/Maskew Miller Longman, 1979.

Legum, Colin, ed. *Africa: A Handbook to the Continent.* New York: Frederick A. Praeger, 1962.

Lewis, I. M., ed. *Islam in Tropical Africa.* Second Edition. Bloomington/London: Indiana University Press, 1980.

Lindars, Barnabas, and Stephen S. Smalley, eds. *Christ and Spirit in the New Testament.* New York/London: Cambridge University Press, 1973.

Logan, Willis H., ed. *The Kairos Covenant: Standing with South African Christians.* New York: Meyer-Stone Books/Friendship Press, 1988.

Long, Charles H. "Structural Similarities and Dissimilarities in Black and African Theologies." *The Journal of Religious Thought,* vol. 32, no. 2, Fall-Winter 1975.

Lorde, Audre. *Sister Outsider.* New York: The Crossing Press, 1984.

Lugira, Aloysius M. "African Christian Theology." *African Theological Journal,* vol. 8, no. 1, 1979.

Luthuli, Albert J. "Apartheid: This Terrible Dream." In David Mermelstein, ed. *The Anti-Apartheid Reader: South Africa and the Struggle Against White Racist Rule.* New York: Grove Press, 1987.

Mackey, James P. *Jesus: The Man and the Myth.* London: SCM Press, 1979.

Magesa, Laurenti. *The Church and Liberation in Africa.* Eldoret, Kenya: Gaba Publications, 1976.

———. "The Church and Politics." In *AFER,* vol. 21, no. 1, 1979.

------. "Politics and Theology in Africa." *AFER*, vol. 31, no. 3, June 1989.

------. "Toward a Theology of Liberation for Tanzania." In E. W. Fashole-Luke, et al., eds. *Christianity in Independent Africa*. London: Rex Collins, 1978.

Magubane, Bernard. "The Political Economy of the Black World – Origins of the Present Crisis." In James E. Turner, ed. *The Next Decade*. Ithaca, N.Y.: Cornell University Press, 1984.

Maimela, Simon. "Black Theology." *All Africa Conference of Churches Magazine*, vol. 2, no. 1, May 1984.

------. "Christian Socialism as Precursor of Liberation Theology." *Journal of Black Theology in South Africa*, vol. 3, no. 2, November 1989.

------. "Current Themes and Emphases in Black Theology." In I. J. Mosala and B. Tlhagale, eds. *The Unquestionable Right to be Free*. Maryknoll, N.Y.: Orbis Books, 1986; also in *Voices from the Third World*, vol. 10, no. 3, September 1987.

------. "Jesus Christ: The Liberator and Hope of Oppressed Africa." *Voices from the Third World*, vol. 11, no. 2, December 1988.

------. "The Twofold Kingdom – An African Perspective." In A. Pero and A. Moyo, eds. *Theology and the Black Experience*. Minneapolis: Augsburg Publishing House, 1988.

Maimela, Simon, and Dwight Hopkins, eds. *We Are One Voice: Black Theology in the USA and South Africa*. Johannesburg: Skotaville Publishers, 1989.

Mandela, Nelson. "De Klerk's Referendum Gives Veto Power to Whites." *Los Angeles Times*, February 26, 1992.

Manning, Patrick. *Francophone Sub-Saharan Africa 1880–1985*. New York/Cambridge: Cambridge University Press, 1988.

Martey, Emmanuel. "African Women and Theology in Africa and the Third World." *Voices from the Third World*, vol. 13, no. 2, December 1990.

------. "Church and Marriage in African Society: A Theological Appraisal." *African Theological Journal*, vol. 20, no. 2, 1991.

Marx, Karl, and Frederick Engels. *The Holy Family or Critique of Critical Critique*. Moscow: Foreign Languages, 1956.

------, and Frederick Engel. *The Individual and Society*. Moscow: Progress Publishers, 1984.

Masanja, Patrick. "Neocolonialism and Revolution in Africa." In Sergio Torres and Virginia Fabella, eds. *The Emergent Gospel*. Maryknoll, N.Y.: Orbis Books, 1978.

Massie, Priscilla, ed. *Black Faith and Black Solidarity*. New York: Friendship Press, 1973.

Mazrui, Ali A. *The African Condition*. New York: University of Cambridge, 1980.

------. *The Africans: A Triple Heritage*. Boston/Toronto: Little, Brown & Co., 1986.

------. "Francophone Nations and English-Speaking States: Imperial Ethnicity and African Political Formations." In Donald Rothchild and Victor A. Olorunsola, eds. *State Versus Ethnicity: African Policy Dilemma*. Boulder, Colo.: Westview Press, 1983.

------. *On Heroes and Uhuru-Worship*. London: Longman, 1967.

Mazrui, Ali A., and Michael Tidy. *Nationalism and New States in Africa: From about 1935 to the Present*. London: Heinemann, 1984.

Mbali, Zolile. *The Churches and Racism: A Black South African Perspective*. London: SCM Press, 1987.

Mbefo, Luke. "Theology and Inculturation: Problems and Prospects – The Nigerian Experience." *The Nigerian Journal of Theology*, vol. 1, no. 1, December 1985.

Mbiti, John S. *African Religions and Philosophy*. London: Heinemann, 1969.

――――. "The Biblical Basis for Present Trends in African Theology." In Kofi Appiah-Kubi and Sergio Torres, eds. *African Theology En Route*. Maryknoll, N.Y.: Orbis Books, 1979.

――――. "Christianity and African Culture." *Journal of Theology for Southern Africa*, no. 20, September 1977.

――――. *Concepts of God in Africa*. London: SPCK, 1970.

――――. "Flowers in the Garden: The Role of Women in African Religion." In Jacob K. Olupona, ed. *African Traditional Religions in Contemporary Society*. New York: Paragon House, 1991.

――――. *Indigenous Theology and the Universal Church*. Bossey: Bossey Ecumenical Institute, 1979.

――――. *New Testament Eschatology in an African Background*. Oxford: Oxford University Press, 1971.

――――. "ο σωτηρ ημων as an African Experience." In B. Lindars and S. S. Smalley, eds. *Christ and Spirit in the New Testament*. New York/London: Cambridge University Press, 1973.

――――. "Some African Concepts and Christology." In Georg F. Vicedom, ed. *Christ and The Younger Churches*. London: SPCK, 1972.

――――. "The South African Theology of Liberation: An Appreciation and Evaluation." In Samuel Amirtham, ed. *A Vision For Man: Essays on Faith, Theology and Society*. Madras, India: The Christian Literature Society, 1978.

――――, ed. *African and Asian Contribution to Contemporary Theology*. Geneva: WCC, 1977.

Mboukou, Alexandre. "The Pan-African Movement, 1900-1945: A Study in Leadership Conflicts Among the Disciples of Pan-Africanism." *Journal of Black Studies*, vol. 13, no. 3, March 1973.

Meli, Francis. *A History of the ANC: South Africa Belongs to Us*. Bloomington, Ind.: Indiana University Press, 1988.

Mermelstein, David, ed. *The Anti-Apartheid Reader: South Africa and the Struggle Against White Racist Rule*. New York: Grove Press, 1987.

Mgojo, K. E. M. "Church and Africanization." In Buti Tlhagale and Itumeleng Mosala, eds. *Hammering Swords into Ploughshares: Essays in Honor of Archbishop Mpilo Desmond Tutu*. Grand Rapids, Mich.: Eerdmans/Africa World Press, 1986.

Milingo, E. *The World in Between: Christian Healing and the Struggle for Spiritual Survival*. Maryknoll, N.Y.: Orbis Books, 1984.

Miller, Christopher L. *Theories of Africa: Francophone Literature and Anthropology in Africa*. Chicago: University of Chicago Press, 1990.

Minogue, Martin, and Judith Molloy, eds. *African Aims and Attitudes: Selected Documents*. New York/Cambridge: Cambridge University Press, 1974.

Mofokeng, Takatso A. "The Cross in the Search for True Humanity: Theological Challenges Facing the South African Church." *Voices from the Third World*, vol. 12, no. 1, June 1989.

――――. *The Crucified Among the Crossbearers: Towards a Black Christology*. Kampen: J. H. Kok, 1983.

――――. "The Evolution of the Black Struggle and the Role of Black Theology." In I. J. Mosala and B. Tlhagale, eds. *The Unquestionable Right to be Free*. Maryknoll, N.Y.: Orbis Books, 1986.

Moltmann, Jürgen. *The Crucified God: The Cross of Christ as the Foundation and*

Criticism of Christian Theology. London: SCM Press, 1974.

Moodie, T. Dunbar. *The Rise of Afrikanerdom: Power, Apartheid, and the Afrikaner Civil Religion*. Berkeley: University of California Press, 1975.

Moore, Basil, ed. *The Challenge of Black Theology in South Africa*. Atlanta: John Knox Press, 1974.

Morrison, D. G., R. C. Mitchell, J. N. Paden, and H. M. Stevenson. *Black Africa: A Comparative Handbook*. New York: Free Press, 1972.

Mosala, Bernadette I. "Black Theology and the Struggle of the African Woman in Southern Africa." In I. J. Mosala and B. Tlhagale, eds. *The Challenge of South African Black Theology*. Maryknoll, N.Y.: Orbis Books, 1986.

Mosala, Itumeleng J. "African Traditional Beliefs and Christianity." *Journal of Theology for Southern Africa*, no. 43, June 1983.

———. *Biblical Hermeneutics and Black Theology in South Africa*. Grand Rapids, Mich.: Eerdmans, 1989.

———. "The Relevance of African Traditional Religions and Their Challenge to Black Theology." In I. J. Mosala and B. Tlhagale, eds. *The Unquestionable Right to be Free*. Maryknoll, N.Y.: Orbis Books, 1986.

———. "The Theology of Ideology and the Ideology of Theology in the Black and White Church Struggle in South Africa." Pretoria: HSRC, 1988.

———. "The Use of the Bible in Black Theology." In I. J. Mosala and B. Tlhagale, eds. *The Unquestionable Right to be Free*. Maryknoll, N.Y.: Orbis Books, 1986.

Mosala, Itumeleng J., and Buti Tlhagale, eds. *The Unquestionable Right to be Free: Black Theology from South Africa*. Maryknoll, N.Y.: Orbis Books, 1986.

Motlhabi, Mokgethi. "Black Theology: A Personal Opinion." In Mokgethi Motlhabi, ed. *Essays in Black Theology*. Johannesburg: University Christian Movement, 1972.

———. *Challenge to Apartheid: Toward a Moral National Resistance*. Grand Rapids, Mich.: Eerdmans, 1988.

———. "The Concept of Morality in African Tradition." In Buti Tlhagale and Itumeleng Mosala, eds. *Hammering Swords into Ploughshares*. Grand Rapids, Mich.: Eerdmans/Africa World Press, 1986.

———. "The Historical Origins of Black Theology." In I. J. Mosala and B. Tlhagale, eds. *The Unquestionable Right to be Free*. Maryknoll, N.Y.: Orbis Books, 1986.

———, ed. *Essays in Black Theology*. Johannesburg: University Christian Movement, 1972.

Moyo, Ambrose M. "The Quest for African Christian Theology and Problem of the Relationship Between Faith and Culture – The Hermeneutical Perspective." *African Theological Journal*, vol. 12, no. 2, 1983.

Mpunzi, Ananias. "Black Theology as Liberation Theology." In Basil Moore, ed. *The Challenge of Black Theology in South Africa*. Atlanta: John Knox Press, 1974.

Mshana, Eliewaha, E. "The Challenge of Black Theology and African Theology." *Africa Theological Journal*, vol. 5, December 1972.

———. "Nationalism in Africa as a Challenge and Problem to the Christian Church." *African Theological Journal*, no. 1, February 1968.

Mudimbe, V. Y. *The Invention of Africa: Gnosis, Philosophy and the Order of Knowledge*. Bloomington, Ind.: Indiana University Press, 1988.

Mueller-Vollmer, Kurt. *The Hermeneutics Reader: Texts of the German Tradition from the Enlightment to the Present*. New York: Continuum, 1988.

Mugambi, J. N. K. "A Summary Report" [Ghana Consultation on African and

Black Theology]. *The Journal of Religious Thought*, vol. 32, no. 2, Fall-Winter 1975.

Mugambi, J. N. K., and Laurenti Magesa, eds. *The Church in African Christianity: Innovative Essays in Ecclesiology*. Nairobi, Kenya: Initiatives Publishers, 1990.

———. *Jesus in African Christianity: Experimentation and Diversity in African Christology*. Nairobi, Kenya: Initiatives Publishers, 1989.

Mulago, Vincent. "Evangélisation et Authenticité." *Aspects du catholicisme au Zaïre*. Kinshasa: Faculté de Théologie Catholique, 1981.

———. *Un Visage africain du Christianisme*. Paris: Présence Africaine, 1965.

Munslow, Barry, ed. *Africa: Problems in the Transition to Socialism*. London/Atlantic Highlands, N.J.: Zed Books, 1986.

Mushete, Ngindu. "Authenticité et christianisme en Afrique Noire. Le cas du Zaïre." *Le Monde Moderne*, 12, 1976.

———. "Courants actuels de la théologie en Afrique." *Bulletin de Théologie Africaine*, vol. 6, juillet-décembre 1984.

———. "L'Eglise et le dialogue des cultures." *Bulletin de Théologie Africaine*, vol. II, no. 3, 1980.

———. "The History of Theology in Africa: From Polemics to Critical Irenics." In Kofi Appiah-Kubi and Sergio Torres, eds. *African Theology En Route*. Maryknoll, N.Y.: Orbis Books, 1979.

Muzorewa, Gwinyai H. *An African Theology of Mission*. Lewiston, N.Y.: Edwin Mellen Press, 1991.

———. "A Definition of a Future African Theology." *African Theological Journal*, vol. 19, no. 2, 1990.

———. *The Origins and Development of African Theology*. Maryknoll, N.Y.: Orbis Books, 1985.

Mveng, Engelbert. "African Liberation Theology." In L. Boff and V. Elizondo, eds. *Concilium 199 (5/1988): Theologies of the Third World — Convergences and Differences*. Edinburgh: T & T Clark, 1988.

———. *L'Afrique dans l'Eglise: paroles d'un croyant*. Paris: L'Harmattan, 1985.

———. *L'Art d'Afrique noire. Liturgie et Langage religieux*. Paris: Mame, 1965.

———. "Black African Art as Cosmic Liturgy and Religious Language." In K. Appiah-Kubi and S. Torres, eds. *African Theology En Route*. Maryknoll, N.Y.: Orbis Books, 1979.

———. "Christ, liturgie et culture." *Bulletin de Théologie Africaine*, vol. II, no. 4, 1980.

———. "A Cultural Perspective." In V. Fabella and S. Torres, eds. *Doing Theology in a Divided World*. Maryknoll, N.Y.: Orbis Books, 1985.

———. *Dossier culturel pan-africain*. Paris: Présence Africaine, 1960.

———. "Essai d'anthropologie négro-africaine." *Bulletin de Théologie Africaine*, vol. 1, no. 2, 1979.

———. "Récents developpements de la théologie africaine." *Bulletin de Théologie Africaine*, vol. 5, no. 9, janvier-juin 1983.

———. "Third World Theology — What Theology? What Third World?: Evaluation by an African Delegate." In V. Fabella and S. Torres, eds. *Irruption of the Third World*. Maryknoll, N.Y.: Orbis Books, 1983.

Mveng, Engelbert, and Zwi Werblowsky. *L'Afrique Noire et la Bible*. Jerusalem: Interfaith Committee, 1974.

Nasimiyu-Wasike, Anne. "Christology and an African Woman's Experience." In J.

N. K. Mugambi and Laurenti Magesa, eds. *Jesus in African Christianity*. Nairobi, Kenya: Initiatives Publishers, 1989.

Ndiokwere, Nathaniel I. *Prophecy and Revolution: The Role of Prophets in the Independent African Churches in the Biblical Tradition*. London: SPCK, 1981.

Ndruudjo, N. "Evangelization in French-Speaking Africa: A Historical Survey." *Indian Missiological Review*, vol. 10, no. 3, July 1988.

Nebechukwu, Augustine. "The Dialectics of Liberation Theology and Inculturation: A Critical Evaluation." *The Nigerian Journal of Theology*, May 1991.

Ngugi, James. "National Culture." In M. Minogue and J. Molloy, eds. *African Aims and Attitudes: Selected Documents*. New York/Cambridge: University of Cambridge Press, 1974.

Nkrumah, Kwame. *Africa Must Unite*. New York: International Publishers, 1963.

———. *Axioms of Kwame Nkrumah*. London: Thomas Nelson, 1967.

———. *Class Struggle in Africa*. New York: International Publishers, 1970.

———. *Consciencism: Philosophy and Ideology for Decolonization*. New York: Monthly Review Press, 1970.

———. *Ghana: The Autobiography of Kwame Nkrumah*. New York: Monthly Review Press, 1971.

———. *Handbook of Revolutionary Warfare*. London: Panaf Books, 1968.

———. *I Speak of Freedom: A Statement of African Ideology*. New York: Frederick A. Praeger, 1961.

———. *Neocolonialism: The Last Stage of Imperialism*. New York: International Publishers, 1966.

———. *Revolutionary Path*. New York: International Publishers, 1973.

———. *Towards Colonial Freedom: Africa in the Struggle Against World Imperialism*. London: Panaf Books, 1973.

Nolan, Albert. *God in South Africa: The Challenge of the Gospel*. Grand Rapids, Mich.: Eerdmans/David Philip, 1988.

———. "The Option for the Poor in South Africa." In C. Villa-Vicencio and J. W. de Gruchy, eds. *Resistance and Hope: South African Essays in Honour of Beyers Naudé*. Grand Rapids, Mich.: Eerdmans, 1985.

Nyamiti, Charles. "African Christologies Today." In J. N. K. Mugambi and Laurenti Magesa, eds. *Jesus in African Christianity*. Nairobi, Kenya: Initiatives Publishers, 1989.

———. "The African Sense of God's Motherhood in the Light of Christian Faith." *Voices from the Third World*, vol. 8, no. 3, September 1985.

———. *African Theology: Its Nature, Problems and Methods*. Kampala: Gaba Publications, 1969.

———. *African Tradition and the Christian God*. Eldoret, Kenya: Gaba Publications, n.d.

———. "Approaches to African Theology." In Sergio Torres and Virginia Fabella, eds. *The Emergent Gospel: Theology from the Developing World*. Maryknoll, N.Y.: Orbis Books, 1978.

———. *Christ as Our Ancestor: Christology from an African Perspective*. Gweru, Zimbabwe: Mambo Press, 1984.

———. *The Way to Christian Theology for Africa*. Eldoret, Kenya: Gaba Publications, 1975.

Nyerere, Julius K. "The Dilemma of the Pan-Africanist." In J. Ayo Langley, ed. *Ideologies of Liberation in Black Africa, 1856-1970*. London: Rex Collings, 1979.

————. *Freedom and Socialism: Uhuru na Ujamaa*. London: Oxford University Press, 1968.

————. *Freedom and Unity: Uhuru na Umoja*. London/Dar-es-Salaam: Oxford University Press, 1966.

Obijole, Olubayo. "South African Liberation Theologies of Boesak and Tutu—A Critical Assessment." *Voices from the Third World*, vol. 10, no. 3, September 1987.

Oduyoye, Mercy Amba. "An African Woman's Christ." *Voices from the Third World*, vol. 11, no. 2, December 1988.

————. "Be a Woman, and Africa Will Be Strong." In Letty M. Russell et al., eds. *Inheriting Our Mothers' Gardens: Feminist Theology in Third World Perspective*. Philadelphia: Westminster Press, 1988.

————. "Christian Feminism and African Culture: The 'Hearth' of the Matter." In Marc H. Ellis and Otto Maduro, eds. *The Future of Liberation Theology: Essays in Honor of Gustavo Gutiérrez*. Maryknoll, N.Y.: Orbis Books, 1989.

————. "Commonalities: An African Perspective." In K. C. Abraham, ed. *Third World Theologies*. Maryknoll N.Y.: Orbis Books, 1990.

————. "Feminism: A Pre-Condition for a Christian Anthropology." *African Theological Journal*, vol. 11, no. 3, 1982.

————. *Hearing and Knowing: Theological Reflections on Christianity in Africa*. Maryknoll, N.Y.: Orbis Books, 1986.

————. "Reflections from a Third World Women's Perspective: Women's Experience and Liberation Theologies." In Virginia Fabella and Sergio Torres, eds. *Irruption of the Third World: Challenge to Theology*. Maryknoll, N.Y.: Orbis Books, 1983.

————. "The Values of African Religious Beliefs and Practices for Christian Theology." In K. Appiah-Kubi and S. Torres, eds. *African Theology En Route*. Maryknoll, N.Y.: Orbis Books, 1979.

————. "Who Does Theology? Reflections on the Subject of Theology." In V. Fabella and S. Torres, eds. *Doing Theology in a Divided World*. Maryknoll, N.Y.: Orbis Books, 1985.

————. "Women Theologians and the Early Church: An Examination of Historiography." *Voices from the Third World*, vol. 8, no. 3, September 1985.

————, ed. *The State of Christian Theology in Nigeria 1980-81*. Ibadan, Nigeria: Daystar Press, 1986.

Oduyoye, Mercy, and Musimbi R. A. Kanyoro, eds., *The Will To Arise: Women, Tradition, and the Church in Africa*. Maryknoll, N.Y.: Orbis Books, 1992.

Oduyoye, Modupe. *The Sons of the Gods and the Daughters of Men: An Afro-Asiatic Interpretation of Genesis 1-11*. Maryknoll, N.Y.: Orbis Books, 1984.

Ofoatey-Kodjo, W. "Pan-Africanism, A Contemporary Restatement: Fundamental Goals and Changing Strategies." In James E. Turner, ed. *The Next Decade: Theoretical and Research Issues in Africana Studies*. Ithaca, N.Y.: Cornell University Press, 1984.

Okure, Teresa. "Biblical Perspectives on Women, Eve, The Mother of all Living. Genesis 3:20." *Voices from the Third World*, vol. 8, no. 3, September 1985.

————. "Women in the Bible." In Virginia Fabella and Mercy Oduyoye, eds. *With Passion and Compassion: Third World Women Doing Theology*. Maryknoll, N.Y.: Orbis Books, 1988.

Oliver, Roland, and Brian M. Fagan. *Africa in the Iron Age, c 500 B.C. to A.D. 1400.* Cambridge: Cambridge University Press, 1975.

Oloruntimehin, B. "The Struggle Against Inequality: The Situation of Women and Youth." In Mercy Oduyoye, ed. *The State of Christian Theology in Nigeria 1980-81.* Ibadan, Nigeria: Daystar Press, 1986.

Olupona, Jacob K. *African Traditional Religions in Contemporary Society.* New York: Paragon House, 1991.

Omari, C. K. "Emerging Themes on Rural Development in Nyerere's Thoughts." *African Theological Journal,* vol. 6, no. 2, 1977.

Opoku, Kofi Asare. "Changes Within Christianity: The Case of the Musama Disco Christo Church." In O. U. Kalu, ed. *The History of Christianity in West Africa.* New York/London: Longman Group Ltd., 1980.

———. "Issues in Dialogue Between African Traditional Religion and Christianity." A paper presented at WCC's Sub-Unit on Dialogue with People of Living Faiths Consultation held at Mindolo Ecumenical Foundation, Kitwe, Zambia September 22-25, 1986. See the Report "Towards a Dialogue between Christian and Traditionists in Africa" (Kitwe: WCC, 1986).

———. "The Relevance of African Culture to Christianity." *Mid-stream,* vol. 13, no. 3-4, Spring-Summer 1974.

———. "Religion in Africa During the Colonial Era." In A. Adu Boahen, ed. *General History of Africa,* vol. VII: *Africa Under Colonial Domination.* Berkeley: University of California Press, 1990.

Padmore, George. *Pan-Africanism or Communism?* London: Dobson, 1956.

Parratt, John, ed. *A Reader in African Christian Theology.* London: SPCK, 1987.

Parrinder, Geoffrey. *African Traditional Religion.* London: Hutchinson's University Library, 1954.

———. "The Religion of Africa." In *Africa South of the Sahara 1977-78.* London: Europa Publications Ltd., 1977.

Penner, H. "The Study of Religions." In Keith Crim, et al. *The Perennial Dictionary of World Religions.* San Francisco: Harper and Row, Publishers, 1989.

Pero, Albert, and Ambrose Moyo, eds. *Theology and the Black Experience: The Lutheran Heritage Interpreted by Africans and African-American Theologians.* Minneapolis: Augsburg Publishing House, 1988.

Pheko, Motsoko. *Apartheid: The Story of a Dispossessed People.* London: Marram Books, 1984.

Pieris, Aloysius. *An Asian Theology of Liberation.* Maryknoll, N.Y.: Orbis Books, 1988.

———. "Toward an Asian Theology of Liberation: Some Religio-Cultural Guidelines." In Douglas J. Elwood, ed. *Asian Christian Theology: Emerging Themes.* Philadelphia: Westminster Press, 1980.

———. "The Place of Non-Christian Religions and Cultures in the Evolution of Third World Theology." In V. Fabella and S. Torres, eds. *Irruption of The Third World: Challenge to Theology.* Maryknoll, N.Y.: Orbis Books, 1983.

Pityana, Nyameko. "What Is Black Consciousness?" In Basil Moore, ed. *The Challenge of Black Theology in South Africa.* Atlanta: John Knox Press, 1974.

Pobee, John S. "I Am First an African and Second a Christian?" *Indian Missiological Review,* vol. 10, no. 3, July 1988.

———. *Toward an African Theology.* Nashville: Abingdon, 1979.

———, ed. *Religion in a Pluralistic Society.* Leiden: E. J. Brill, 1976.

Pobee, John S., and B. Wartenberg-Potter, eds. *New Eyes for Reading: Biblical and Theological Reflection by Women from the Third World.* Geneva: WCC, 1986.

Pomeroy, William J. *Apartheid: Imperialism and African Freedom.* New York: International Publishers, 1986.

Ramodibe, Dorothy. "Women and Men Building Together the Church in Africa." In V. Fabella and Mercy Oduyoye, eds. *With Passion and Compassion: Third World Women Doing Theology.* Maryknoll, N.Y.: Orbis Books, 1988.

———. "Women and Men Re-creating Together the Church in Africa." *Voices from the Third World,* vol. 13, no. 2, December 1990.

Ray, Richard. "Christianity." In Andrew Roberts, ed. *The Colonial Moment in Africa: Essays on the Movement of Minds and Materials, 1900-1940.* New York/ Cambridge: Cambridge University Press, 1990.

Ricoeur, Paul. *Freud and Philosophy: An Essay on Interpretation.* Translated by Denis Savage. New Haven, Conn.: Yale University Press, 1970.

Roberts, Andrew, ed. *The Colonial Moments in Africa: Essay on the Movement of Minds and Material, 1900-1940.* New York/Cambridge: Cambridge University Press, 1990.

Rodney, Walter. *How Europe Underdeveloped Africa.* Washington, D.C.: Howard University Press, 1982.

Rogers, Cornish. "Pan-Africanism and the Black Church: A Search for Solidarity." *Christian Century,* November 17, 1971.

Romero, Patricia W. "W. E. B. Du Bois, Pan-African Movement, and Africa." *Journal of Black Studies,* vol. 6, no. 4, 1976.

Rothchild, Donald, and Robert L. Curry. *Scarcity, Choice, and Public Policy in Middle Africa.* Berkeley: University of California Press, 1978.

Rothchild, Donald, and Victor A. Olorunsola, eds. *State Versus Ethnic Claims: African Policy Dilemmas.* Boulder, Colo.: Westminster Press, 1983.

Russell Letty M., Kwok Pui-lan, Ada María Isasi-Díaz, Katie Cannon, eds. *Inheriting Our Mothers' Gardens: Feminist Theology in Third World Perspective.* Philadelphia: Westminster Press, 1988.

Ryan, J. G. W. *Christian Faith and the New World Order.* Washington, D.C.: Interreligious Peace Colloquium, 1978.

Sanneh, Lamin. *Translating the Message: The Missionary Impact on Culture.* Maryknoll, N.Y.: Orbis Books, 1989.

———. *West African Christianity: The Religious Impact.* Maryknoll, N.Y.: Orbis Books, 1983.

Sarpong, Peter K. "Christianity Meets Traditional African Cultures." In G. H. Anderson and T. F. Stransky, eds. *Mission Trends no. 5 — Faith Meets Faith.* New York/Grand Rapids: Paulist Press/Eerdmans, 1981.

———. "Evangelism and Inculturation." *West African Journal of Ecclesial Studies,* vol. 2, no. 1, 1990.

Sawyerr, Harry. *Creative Evangelism: Towards a New Christian Encounter with Africa.* London: Lutterworth Press, 1968.

———. "What Is African Theology?" *African Theological Journal,* vol. 4, August 1971.

Schatzberg, Michael G. *The Dialectics of Oppression in Zaire.* Bloomington/Indianapolis: Indiana University Press, 1988.

Schineller, Peter. *A Handbook on Inculturation.* New York: Paulist Press, 1990.

168 BIBLIOGRAPHY

Schneider, Harold K. *The African: An Ethnological Account.* Engelwood Cliffs, N.J.: Prentice-Hall, Inc., 1981.

Schneider, Louis, ed. *Religion, Culture and Society: A Reader in the Sociology of Religion.* New York: John Wiley, Inc., 1981.

Schoffeleers, Matthew. "Black and African Theology in Southern Africa: A Controversy Re-examined." *Journal of Religion in Africa,* vol. XVIII – Fasc. 2, June 1988.

———. "Folk Christology in Africa: The Dialectics of the Nganga Paradigm." *Journal of Religion in Africa,* vol. XIX – Fasc. 2, June 1989.

Schreiter, Robert J. *Constructing Local Theologies.* Maryknoll, N.Y.: Orbis Books, 1985.

———, ed. *Faces of Jesus in Africa.* Maryknoll: N.Y.: Orbis Books, 1991.

Schroeder, Edward H. "Lessons for Westerners from Setiloane's Christology." *Mission Studies,* vol. 2, 2, 1985.

Scipio. *Emergent Africa.* Foreword by Philip E. Mosely. New York: Simon & Schuster, 1965.

Sebidi, Lebamang. "The Dynamics of the Black Struggle and Its Implication for Black Theology." In I. J. Mosala and B. Tlhagale, eds. *The Unquestionable Right to be Free.* Maryknoll, N.Y.: Orbis Books, 1986.

Segundo, Juan Luis. *The Liberation of Theology.* Maryknoll, N.Y.: Orbis Books, 1976.

Senghor, Léopold S. "African-Style Socialism." In William Frieland and Carl Rosberg, eds. *African Socialism.* Stanford: Stanford University Press, 1964.

———. "Negritude and African Socialism." In M. Minogue and J. Molloy, eds. *African Aims and Attitudes: Selected Documents.* New York/Cambridge: Cambridge University Press, 1974.

Setiloane, Gabriel M. *African Theology: An Introduction.* Johannesburg: Skotaville Publishers, 1986.

———. "Black Theology." *South African Outlook,* vol. 101, no. 1197, February 1971.

———. "I Am An African." *Mission Trends no. 3 – Third World Theologies.* Edited by Gerald H. Anderson and Thomas F. Stransky. New York: Paulist Press/Eerdmans, 1976.

———. *The Image of God Among the Sotho-Tswana.* Rotterdam: A. A. Balkema, 1976.

———. "Theological Trends in Africa." *Missionalia,* vol. 8, 1980.

———. "Where Are We in African Theology?" In Kofi Appiah-Kubi and Sergio Torres, eds. *African Theology En Route.* Maryknoll, N.Y.: Orbis Books, 1979.

Shivji, Issa G. *Class Struggle in Tanzania.* New York/London: Monthly Review Press, 1976.

Shorter, Aylward. *African Christian Theology: Adaptation or Incarnation?* Maryknoll, N.Y.: Orbis Books, 1977.

———. *Toward a Theology of Inculturation.* Maryknoll, N.Y.: Orbis Books, 1988.

Slovo, Joe. "The Working Class and Nation Building." In Maria van Diepen, ed. *The National Question in South Africa.* Atlantic Highlands, N.J./London: Zed Books, 1988.

Smith, David M. *Update: Apartheid in South Africa, 1987 Edition.* New York: Cambridge University Press, 1987.

Smith, Edwin W., ed. *African Ideas of God.* London: Edinburgh House Press, 1950.

Smith, Patrick. "The Slow Progress of Africa's Recovery." *West Africa,* no. 3710 (London) September 19-25, 1988.

Sofola, 'Zulu. "The Theater in the Search for African Authenticity." In Kofi Appiah-Kubi and Sergio Torres, eds. *African Theology En Route*. Maryknoll, N.Y.: Orbis Books, 1979.

Souga, Thérèse. "The Christ-Event from the Viewpoint of African Women: A Catholic Perspective." In V. Fabella and M. Oduyoye, eds. *With Passion and Compassion*. Maryknoll, N.Y.: Orbis Books, 1988.

Soyinka, Wole. *Myth, Literature and the African World*. Cambridge: Cambridge University Press, 1976.

Stockton, Ronald R. "The Dilemma in South Africa." *TransAfrica Forum*, vol. 4, no. 4, Summer 1987.

Sugirtharajah, R. S., ed. *Voices from the Margin: Interpreting the Bible in the Third World*. Maryknoll, N.Y.: Orbis Books, 1991.

Sundkler, Bengt G. M. *Bantu Prophets in South Africa*. London: Oxford University Press, 1948.

————. *Zulu Zion and Some Swazi Zionists*. London: Oxford University Press, 1976.

Tappa, Louise. "The Christ-Event from the Viewpoint of African Women: A Protestant Perspective." In V. Fabella and M. Oduyoye, eds. *With Passion and Compassion*. Maryknoll, N.Y.: Orbis Books, 1988.

————. "God in Man's Image." In John S. Pobee and B. von Wartenberg-Potter, eds. *New Eyes for Reading: Biblical and Theological Reflection by Women from the Third World*. Geneva: WCC, 1986.

Tekere, Ruvimbo. "The Challenge of the Non-Latin Americans: The Africans." In S. Torres and J. Eagleson, eds. *The Challenge of Basic Christian Communities*. Maryknoll, N.Y.: Orbis Books, 1981.

Tempels, Placide. *La Philosophie Bantoue*. Paris: Présence Africaine, 1948.

Thetele, Constance B. "Women in South Africa: The WAAIC." In Kofi Appiah-Kubi and Sergio Torres, eds. *African Theology En Route*. Maryknoll, N.Y.: Orbis Books, 1979.

Thomas, Bert J., ed. *The Struggle for Liberation: From Du Bois to Nyerere*. New York: Theo. Gaus Ltd., 1982.

Tlhagale, Buti. "Towards a Black Theology of Labour." In C. Villa-Vicencio and J. W. de Gruchy, eds. *Resistance and Hope: South African Essays in Honour of Beyers Naudé*. Grand Rapids, Mich.: Eerdmans, 1985.

Tlhagale, Buti, and Itumeleng Mosala, eds. *Hammering Swords into Ploughshares: Essays in Honor of Archbishop Mpilo Desmond Tutu*. Grand Rapids, Mich.: Eerdmans/African World Press, 1986.

Torres, Sergio, and John Eagleson, eds. *The Challenge of Basic Christian Communities*. Maryknoll, N.Y.: Orbis Books, 1981.

Torres, Sergio, and Virginia Fabella, eds. *The Emergent Gospel: Theology from the Developing World*. Maryknoll, N.Y.: Orbis Books, 1978.

Towa, Marcien. *Essai sur la problématique philosophie dans l'Afrique actuelle*. Yaoundé: Clé, 1971.

Tracy, David. *Plurality and Ambiguity: Hermeneutics, Religion, Hope*. San Francisco, Harper & Row, 1987.

Trimingham, J. Spencer. "Islam in Africa." In Colin Legum, ed. *Africa: A Handbook to the Continent*. New York: Frederick A. Praeger, 1962.

Tshibangu, T. *Le propos d'une théologie africaine*. Kinshasa: Presses Universitaires du Zaïre, 1974.

————. "The Task of African Theologians." In Kofi Appiah-Kubi and Sergio Torres, eds. *African Theology En Route*. Maryknoll, N.Y.: Orbis Books, 1979.

―――. *Théologie positive et théologie speculative. Position traditionelle et nouvelle problématique*. Louvain-Paris: Beatrice Nauwelaerts, 1965.

Turner, James E., ed. *The Next Decade: Theoretical and Research Issues in African Studies*. Ithaca, N.Y.: Cornell University Press, 1984.

Tutu, Desmond. "Apartheid: An Evil System." In David Mermelstein, ed. *The Anti-Apartheid Reader: South Africa and the Struggle Against White Racist Rule*. New York: Grove Press, 1987.

―――. "Black Theology." *Frontier* 17, Summer 1974.

―――. "Black Theology/African Theology—Soul Mates or Antagonists?" In Gayraud S. Wilmore and James H. Cone, eds. *Black Theology: A Documentary History 1966-1979*. Maryknoll, N.Y.: Orbis Books, 1979.

―――. *Crying in the Wilderness*. London: Mowbray, 1982.

―――. *Hope and Suffering*. Grand Rapids, Mich.: Eerdmans, 1984.

―――. "Spirituality: Christian and African." In Charles Villa-Vicencio and John W. de Gruchy, eds. *Resistance and Hope: South African Essays in Honour of Beyers Naudé*. Grand Rapids, Mich.: Eerdmans, 1985.

―――. "The Theology of Liberation in Africa." In K. Appiah-Kubi and S. Torres, eds. *African Theology En Route*. Maryknoll, N.Y.: Orbis Books, 1979.

Udofia, D. E. "Imperialism in Africa: A Case of Multinational Corporations." *Journal of Black Studies*, vol. 14, no. 3, March 1984.

Ukpong, Justin S. *African Theologies Now: A Profile*. Eldoret, Kenya: Gaba Publications, 1984.

―――. "Theological Literature From Africa." In Leonardo Boff and Virgilio Elizondo, eds. *Concilium 199— Theologies of the Third World: Convergences and Differences*. Edinburgh: T & T Clark, 1988.

Van Bergen, Jan P. "Initial Reaction to the Research Program on the Church and Rural Development in Tanzania." *African Theological Journal*, vol. 7, no. 1, 1978.

Van den Berghe, Pierre. *South Africa: A Study in Conflict*. Berkeley: University of California Press, 1965.

Van Diepen, Maria, ed. *The National Question in South Africa*. Atlantic Highlands, N.J./London: Zed Books, 1988.

Vicedom, Georg F., ed. *Christ and the Younger Churches*. London: SPCK, 1972.

Villa-Vicencio, Charles. *Trapped in Apartheid: A Socio-Theological History of the English-Speaking Churches*. Maryknoll, N.Y.: Orbis Books, 1988.

―――. "The Use of Scripture in Theology: Toward a Contextual Hermeneutic." *Journal of Theology for Southern Africa*, no. 37, December 1981.

―――, ed. *Theology and Violence: The South African Debate*. Grand Rapids, Mich.: Eerdmans, 1988.

Villa-Vicencio, Charles, and John W. de Gruchy, eds. *Resistance and Hope: South African Essays in Honour of Beyers Naudé*. Grand Rapids, Mich.: Eerdmans, 1985.

Von Sicard, Sigvard. "African Socialism: Communism or Communalism?: A Case Study." *African Theological Journal*, vol. 11, no. 1, 1982.

Wa Ilunga, Baloke. *Paths of Liberation: A Third World Spirituality*. Maryknoll, N.Y.: Orbis Books, 1984.

Wallerstein, Immanuel. *Africa, The Politics of Unity: An Analysis of a Contemporary Social Movement*. New York: Random Press, 1967.

Wambutda, Daniel N. "Hermeneutics and the Search for Theologia Africana." *African Theological Journal*, vol. 9, no. 1, April 1980.

Wan-Tatah, Victor. *Emancipation in African Theology: An Inquiry on the Relevance of Latin American Liberation Theology to Africa.* New York: Peter Lang, 1989.

Weber, Max. "Aspects of Religion as Culture." In Louis Schneider, ed. *Religion, Culture and Society: A Reader in the Sociology of Religion.* New York: John Wiley & Sons, 1964.

————. *The Sociology of Religion.* Boston: Beacon Press, 1963.

West, Cornel. "Black Theology and Marxist Thought." In Gayraud S. Wilmore and James H. Cone, eds. *Black Theology: A Documentary History, 1966-1979.* Maryknoll, N.Y.: Orbis Books, 1979.

————. "The Challenge of the Non-Latin Americans: The North American Blacks." In S. Torres and J. Eagleson, eds. *The Challenge of Basic Christian Communities.* Maryknoll, N.Y.: Orbis Books, 1981.

————. *Prophesy Deliverance! An Afro-American Revolutionary Christianity.* Philadelphia: Westminster Press, 1982.

Williams, M. W. "Nkrumahism and the Ideological Embodiment of Leftist Thought Within the African World." *Journal of Black Studies*, vol. 15, no. 1, September 1984.

Wilmore, Gayraud S. "African and Black Theology—Ghana Consultation: A Summary Report." *The Journal of Religious Thought,* vol. 32, no. 2, Fall-Winter 1975.

————. "The Role of Afro-America in the Rise of Third World Theology: A Historical Reappraisal." In Kofi Appiah-Kubi and Sergio Torres, eds. *African Theology En Route.* Maryknoll, N.Y.: Orbis Books, 1979.

Wilmore, Gayraud S., and James Cone, eds. *Black Theology: A Documentary History, 1966-1979.* Maryknoll, N.Y.: Orbis Books, 1979.

Wilson, Henry S., ed. *Origins of West African Nationalism.* London: MacMillan, 1969.

Wilson, William J. *The Declining Significance of Race: Blacks and Changing American Institutions.* Chicago: University of Chicago Press, 1978.

————. *Power, Racism and Privilege: Race Relations in Theoretical and Sociohistorical Perspective.* New York: Free Press, 1973.

Witvliet, Theo. *A Place in the Sun: An Introduction to Liberation Theology in the Third World.* Maryknoll N.Y.: Orbis Books, 1985.

————. *The Way of the Black Messiah: The Hermeneutical Challenge of Black Theology as a Theology of Liberation.* Oak Park, Ill.: Meyer Stone Books, 1987.

Yansané, Aguibou Y., ed. *Decolonization and Dependency: Problem of Development in African Societies.* Westport, Conn.: Greenwood Press, 1980.

Young, Crawford. *Ideology and Development in Africa.* New Haven/London: Yale University Press, 1982.

Young, Josiah U. "African Theology: From 'Independence' Toward Liberation." *Voices from the Third World*, vol. 10, no. 4, December 1987.

————. *Black and African Theologies: Siblings or Distant Cousins?* Maryknoll, N.Y.: Orbis Books, 1986.

————. *A Pan-African Theology: Providence and the Legacies of the Ancestors.* Trenton, N.J.: Africa World Press, 1992.

Zahan, Dominique. *The Religion, Spirituality, and Thought of Traditional Africa.* Chicago/London: University of Chicago Press, 1979.

Zoé-Obianga, Rose. "Les Femmes Africaines et la Libération de l'Afrique." *Bulletin de Théologie Africaine*, vol. VI, no. 12, juillet-décembre 1984.

————. "From Accra to Wennappuwa: What Is New? What More." In Virginia

Fabella, ed. *Asia's Struggle for Full Humanity.* Maryknoll, N.Y.: Orbis Books, 1980.

————. "Resources in the Tradition of the Renewal of Community." *Voices from the Third World*, vol. 8, no. 3, September 1985.

————. "The Role of Women in Present-Day Africa." In K. Appiah-Kubi and S. Torres, eds. *African Theology En Route.* Maryknoll, N.Y.: Orbis Books, 1979.

Index